The
EVERYTHING®
Alternative Careers Book

Dear Reader:

Do you yearn for adventure, to feel a gentle ocean breeze or the spraying sting of whitewater rapids in your face? Stop daydreaming about it, and make it happen. Do you want to sail the seven seas—as on a real-life Love Boat—or to be of service in developing nations with the Peace Corps? Then just do it. If you want to tell your boss to take this job and shove it and become an entrepreneur or work from home—go for it.

The Everything® Alternative Careers Book tells you about the many ways you can make a living that do not involve the depressing drudgery of office work, with a debilitating commute at either end of the day. Most of these jobs are for people who want to march to the beat of that proverbial different drummer. They are jobs for the independent-minded, the adventurous of spirit. You will learn about what these exciting jobs entail and get the resources and contact information you need to make things happen.

This is not a how-to guide on how to make millions. If you seek peace of mind and the opportunity to "gather ye rosebuds while ye may," if your priorities are the quality of your life and the savoring of the precious, present moment, then this book is for you. Some of the glamorous careers in this book do have the potential to catapult you into a high-income bracket . . . if you have the right stuff. For the most part, however, these careers are for people who want to do what they love and love what they do.

Are you ready? In the words of the poet e. e. cummings, "Listen, there's a hell of a good universe next door: let's go!"

The EVERYTHING® Series

Editorial

Publishing Director	Gary M. Krebs
Managing Editor	Kate McBride
Copy Chief	Laura MacLaughlin
Acquisitions Editor	Bethany Brown
Development Editor	Larry Shea
Production Editor	Jamie Wielgus

Production

Production Director	Susan Beale
Production Manager	Michelle Roy Kelly
Series Designers	Daria Perreault
	Colleen Cunningham
Cover Design	Paul Beatrice
	Frank Rivera
Layout and Graphics	Colleen Cunningham
	Rachael Eiben
	Michelle Roy Kelly
	John Paulhus
	Daria Perreault
	Erin Ring
Series Cover Artist	Barry Littmann

Visit the entire Everything® Series at everything.com

THE
EVERYTHING®
ALTERNATIVE
CAREERS
BOOK

Leave the office behind and embark
on a new adventure!

James Mannion

Adams Media
Avon, Massachusetts

*To my father, Jim Kaeter, who knew that I should work
for myself long before I would admit it.*

An Everything® Series Book.
Everything® and everything.com® are registered trademarks of F+W Publications, Inc.

Published by Adams Media, an F+W Publications Company
57 Littlefield Street, Avon, MA 02322 U.S.A.
www.adamsmedia.com

ISBN: 1-59337-038-5
Printed in the United States of America.

J I H G F E D C B A

Library of Congress Cataloging-in-Publication Data
Mannion, James.
The everything alternative careers book / James Mannion.
  p.   cm.   (An everything series book)
    ISBN 1-59337-038-5
1. Career changes. 2. Vocational guidance. 3. Job hunting.
    I. Title. II. Series: Everything series.

HF5384.M355 2004
331.702—dc22

2003025541

*This book is available at quantity discounts for bulk purchases.
For information, call 1-800-872-5627.*

Contents

Acknowledgments

The author gratefully acknowledges the contributions of Bethany Brown and everyone else at Adams Media, whose editorial expertise has immeasurably enhanced the book you now hold in your hands.

Top Ten
Crazy Careers

1. **Body-double model:** Display your assets for shy celebs in movies and television.

2. **Circus clown:** Bring joy to children of all ages.

3. **Road rat:** Drive oversized vehicles from manufacturers to dealerships.

4. **Greenpeace activist:** Ever wanted to put yourself in between a whale and any harpoons that might be aimed at it?

5. **Craftsmaker:** Turn your creativity into a moneymaking enterprise.

6. **Personal coach:** Get in on the ground floor of this emerging new service.

7. **Private detective:** Take your natural nosiness and make it your career.

8. **Trapeze artist:** Fly through the air with the greatest of ease.

9. **Peace Corps volunteer:** Do some good, see the world, and celebrate diversity.

10. **Ballooning guide:** Go up, up, and away to give brave souls a bird's-eye view of the landscape.

Introduction

▶ WELCOME TO THE BRAVE NEW WORLD WE LIVE IN. This
tumultuous period in history is dramatically different from those
simpler times that our parents faced. The rules have changed, and
we can no longer rely on the things (like a job for life, or
satisfaction from a conventional career) that people have long taken
for granted.

The days are over when people made their job at a single
company into their life's work. Even jobs in civil service and with a
union, both long-time sources of safety and stability for the middle
class, are not so safe and stable anymore. Unions have lost much
of their power, and cash-starved cities and states are laying their
civil servants off. We are pretty much on our own in this cold, cruel
world, and our only options are to sink or swim.

So why not swim in an ocean of our own making? Why not do
something that we enjoy? It is said that eight out of ten people do
not enjoy getting up in the morning and going to work. The plain
and simple truth is that most people hate their jobs. Their work is a
means to an end, and it is increasingly the case that the end in
question is simply to survive—enjoying a comfortable, fulfilled life is
a goal too distant for many people's reach. We work to put food on
the table, keep a roof over our heads, and provide for our near and
dear ones. Too many of us merely exist, leading lives of quiet
desperation. This doesn't have to be the case. You have your destiny
in your hands. Reclaim it today.

There is precious little loyalty in the business world these days. No matter what job you have, you are already basically working for yourself. And since you are working for yourself, you might as well have some fun along the way. You can do work that you love, have plenty of leisure time, and still be able to plan for the future. You can tell "the Man" to "Take this job and shove it," and then go off to greener pastures.

In this book, you'll find an introduction to a wide variety of alternative and creative careers. You will find the information and inspiration you need to follow your bliss and do the kind of work you love. You will discover many things to think about, and you'll be directed to the resources that will help turn your dreams into reality.

This is a book for people who want to shed the shackles of the nine-to-five grind. Even the phrase "nine to five" is now a relic from a more innocent age. Very few white-collar jobs still feature eight-hour days with an hour for lunch. Those workers who do want to go home at a reasonable hour are not regarded as team players, and they are often left behind when it is time for raises and promotions. The business world wants your blood, sweat, toil, and tears—and it no longer offers much in return.

The Everything® Alternative Careers Book will guide you in finding a career that you will find personally satisfying. The goal here is not necessarily to lure you with promises of a new, exciting career that will make you millions. This is a book for people whose first priority is the search for a higher quality of life—not the number of zeroes on their bank balance.

You can make a nice living, find personal and professional fulfillment, and plan for your future. Many folks spend their time struggling to plan for a distant retirement. This book will show you how to live in the here and now, all the while enjoying each present, wonderful moment.

Life's too short to let your dreams wait until tomorrow, or the day after. The time to take control of your life and your career is right now. (E)

Chapter 1

It's Time to Follow Your Dream

The world is a very different place than it was only a few short years ago. Gone is the sense of stability and reliability, whether real or illusory, that we thought would always be there. Though it may seem paradoxical, here in the midst of these uncertain times, now is the best time to switch canoes midstream and do what you really enjoy. Why, you may ask? All things considered . . . why not!

The Times They Are a-Changin'

The days when a man spent his entire career at the same job and his wife was a stay-at-home mom are now the stuff of old sitcom reruns on TV Land and other cable channels. That way of life seems to have worked fine in the world of *Father Knows Best* and *Leave It to Beaver*, but as a status quo that world is long gone. Some people believed that many of these traditional social structures prevented people, particularly women, from following their dreams. They were happy to see the old ways disappear into the historical sunset. Other people, however, believe that all these recent social changes have come at a different price. Now both parents have to work harder just to keep their heads above water, and they now spend less time with their kids. This is a recipe for a social dilemma of a different sort.

It may still be true that many women still enjoy being homemakers and that they enjoy having the luxury of choosing that lifestyle. But for many more it is not an option any more. For a lot of couples, two incomes are necessary if they're going to enjoy the amenities of life. For others, two paychecks are a requirement for them just to scrape by and support their offspring.

FACT

According to the U.S. Census Bureau, most working women are still employed in what are called "pink collar" jobs: secretaries, bookkeepers, sales supervisors, nurses, waitresses, receptionists, and cooks. If you're a woman, and these careers are not to your liking, then go out there and do what it takes to find your dream job.

We are in a new century now. It's a new millennium, in fact. Back in the 1960s, young people sang of the dawning of the Age of Aquarius, but our world today is not shaping up to be the "Peace, baby" idyll they envisioned. Workers will find little sympathy and understanding in the corporate working environments of today. For blue-collar workers, the situation is even worse, as their jobs are being lost to people in other countries for whom a few dollars a day is a lot of money.

Even if you manage to hold on to your job, steady employment is no guarantee of happiness. In the world of civil service and government bureaucracy, it may be next to impossible to get fired. But how many bureaucrats and paper pushers greet the new day with a spring in their step and a song in their hearts? How many workers in any industry can say that they do? Not many, statistics tells us.

Since you are reading this book, it is possible that you, too, dread waking up every day to head off to a job that is uncertain, unprofitable, and unfulfilling. Fear not. You'll soon find that there is a big wide wonderful world out there where you can march to the beat of that fabled different drummer.

Downsized and Out

Many industries have been devastated by the new social and financial climate. A perfect example was the life and death of the notorious "dot-coms," companies whose foundations were not even as sturdy as sand. They were built on nothing more substantial than the ethereal impulses that course through fiber-optic cables between massive Web servers and millions of computers with Internet connections.

The Rise of the Dot-Coms

The story of a typical dot-com is a modern retelling of the ancient fable of the grasshopper and the ant, a "dot-com-edy" of errors starring a bunch of yuppies who fiddled while Rome burned. The companies believed they were hip, cutting-edge, and superior in methodology and ethics to the "old economy" businesses. Hip interior design and furniture was installed at considerable expense while employees enjoyed fat paychecks and stock options that in many cases made them instant millionaires—if only on paper. Conference rooms were supplied with crayons, and the staff was encouraged to write on the walls in an effort to encourage their "inner child" to make a mess, hoping that out of the chaos there might emerge "the next new thing."

There was no dress code—that was simply too Old World. Free lunch was provided, and other delectables were placed in common areas throughout the day. These and many other "quality of working life" policies were enacted to create an environment so satisfying that people could not wait to get to the office and go the extra mile. The message was that they were one big happy family making the workplace a better place through e-commerce.

FACT

The rise and fall of the dot-coms is a perfect example of an industry built on high hopes and great expectations that never materialized. These "new economy" businesses were like the "new math" that they used to teach in schools. Just as two plus two no longer had to equal four, business did not have to equal profit.

The intent was also to create a family atmosphere, necessary because dot-com workers saw each other more than they did their families. They were expected to spend most of their waking hours on the job. Eighteen-hour days were not the exception; they were the norm. Those who managed to complete their tasks within regular business hours and then elected to split the scene at a decent time were told they were not team players, and this might reflect badly at performance review time. Still, as the companies' stock prices kept rising, and the employees' stock options kept skyrocketing in value, it all seemed worth it.

The Inevitable Fall

Unfortunately, a house built on sand will always fall down eventually. The paradise of the dot-coms was lost as the economy began to fail. The layoffs started, and the old corporate extravagance devolved into parsimonious nickel-and-diming. Most employees ended up getting a tap on the shoulder. Turning, they saw their managers, each accompanied by a large security guard, telling them to back away from their workstations, much like a highway patrolman might order you to step away from your vehicle. Their computers were seized. They surrendered their cell phones and Palm Pilots and were politely but firmly thrown out of the building. The personnel department would be in touch with the details of their severance package, if any. The survivors of the purge were told they were safe for the time being, but harder work and longer hours were required.

More and more companies are turning their staff into "independent contractors" in order to save on paying their portion of Social Security cost, employee medical benefits, and other forms of insurance. Do not be surprised if your manager taps you on the shoulder one day to tell you of this change in your professional status.

The prevailing attitude was one of oblivious avarice. People were living one day at a time but in the worst sense of the philosophy. It is nothing better than foolish and arrogant to live "in the now" while ignoring the handwriting on the wall. Pride goeth before a fall, as they say. At one company, the stock price dropped from more than $100 to a mere seventeen cents a share, all in less than a year. When the dot-com world fell apart, thousands of people who were living the high life found themselves pinching pennies, clipping coupons, and (if they were lucky) working at The Gap.

Why an Alternative Career? Why Not!

As we can see, there is no longer much loyalty toward the worker in the cold corporate world. The company demands craven loyalty, but it does not respond in kind. Rather than get stuck in the depressing trap that is the daily grind of most workers, why not take stock of your situation and decide what you really want to do? Do some brainstorming. Make a list, and check it twice. Change your way of thinking. Nowadays, we call this "thinking outside the box." Take the concept a step further: Throw the old box in the recycle bin, and get a bright and shining new one. Expand your horizons. Believe that you can make your dreams come true.

Get Ready to Conquer Your Fears

If you feel overwhelmed by the situation in your workplace, take a step back and realize a few things. Your boss is not your buddy. The corporation does not care about you. You are expendable and replaceable. But you should not let this get you down. These attitudes are not a reflection on your worth as a worker or as a human being. You have a wealth of untapped potential and hidden resources that are just waiting to be exploited. Use them wisely, and use them well.

Don't Wait!

The cranky eighteenth-century philosopher Thomas Hobbes observed that life is "nasty, brutish, and short." And indeed it was in those not-so-good old days. For most of us who are lucky enough to live in the early twenty-first century, life is not particularly nasty and brutish. But it is still short. True, medical advances have been made, and longevity is continually increasing. That does not change the fact that life is precious, fragile, and short—in the sense that time indeed does fly. It seems to fly faster the older we get. Now, more than ever, is a time for reflection and reevaluation. Rather than toiling at an exhausting job simply to pay the bills, it is time to try to do those things that bring you joy and feed your spirit.

QUESTION?

Is living in the now a practical lifestyle?
The saying goes, "Seize the day, and gather ye rosebuds while ye may." And how right that is. There is no time like the present to pursue your dreams. Of course planning for the future is necessary, but we should not live there. All we have is the present moment, so enjoy it.

"Time for a Change" Quiz

Take a look at the following questions. Your answers will tell you whether you might be due for a career change sometime in the near future.

1. Do you dread the sound of the alarm in the morning?
2. Do you always feel tired, even if your job is not especially strenuous?
3. Do you take the stress and strain of the job home with you, making it difficult for you to enjoy your leisure time?
4. Does your job, and the cast of characters you interact with during the day, invade your dreams by night? This is a sure sign that it is time for a change. (Dreams about an attractive coworker do not apply.)

If you answered "Yes" to any or all of these questions, it is definitely time for you to take the first steps toward considering an alternate career.

Turn a Crisis into an Opportunity

The Chinese written language is composed of characters. The Chinese character for the English word "crisis" is a combination of two other characters that represent the concepts "danger" and "opportunity."

This is an excellent way to think about a situation that may be causing you to be hesitant and anxious. In view of the danger, however, it is often easy to overlook the opportunity. Changing careers and embarking on a brand-new exciting adventure would certainly give anyone pause. We all, to some extent, fear the unknown. There is an old Irish expression that goes, "The devil you know is better than the devil you don't." Maybe this describes the way that you feel about the unfulfilling, but relatively safe and familiar, job you find yourself in.

Don't Let Fear Stop You

Do not approach newness with fear. Face it with enthusiasm and a sense of adventure. If you are discontented enough to make a major life change, then you probably already know the change is necessary for your physical and mental health. So take the leap of faith into an exciting future. If you are truly ready for a major life change, you have everything to gain by overcoming your fear of the new and unproven. You will make yourself sick if you sit and stew in the winter of your discontent. Make it a glorious summer of striving and success.

Follow Your Bliss

In the popular public television series *The Power of Myth*, Joseph Campbell, noted scholar of world mythology, introduced the phrase "follow your bliss" into the collective consciousness. What exactly does this mean?

Campbell explained it this way: "If you follow your bliss, you put yourself on a kind of track, which has been there all the while waiting for you, and the life that you ought to be living is the one you are living."

Many a self-help guru has expressed the same sentiment in seminars and best-selling books. There's *Feel the Fear and Do It Anyway*, *Do What You Love and the Money Will Follow,* and probably hundreds of others. The basic premise is a simple one. If you do what you love you will be happier. If you stay on the path to fulfilling your dreams, you will find that opportunities and situations will present themselves.

FACT

The truly successful people in life have not been afraid of change. They have embraced it and made new conditions work to their advantage. They turned the lemons into lemonade and not only survived, but thrived.

Baseball executive Branch Rickey once said, "Luck is the residue of design." If you look at the life story of many an "overnight" star, you will find that they worked for years, sometimes decades, to achieve that sudden fame. For most successful people, the seedlings of their success started early. They always had an interest in and passion for the field or subject that ultimately brought them acclaim. That's true even if they toiled at many other tasks before their dreams came true. And they are not all *wunderkind*—boy and girl geniuses who sprang full-bloom into their own. There are plenty of late bloomers who achieved and succeeded in their middle and even their golden years. It is never too late to make a change.

The First Day of the Rest of Your Life

Once you have decided on the different direction you would like to take on the road to personal and professional happiness, you may feel a combination of anxiety and relief. When you have made the decision and are ready to go, you are, as the cliché states, beginning the first day of the rest of your life. Just don't expect miracles to happen overnight.

Sometimes that's exactly how miracles do happen, but these events are all too rare. That is why we call them miracles. You had to go through a series of events in your life to get where you are. Naturally, you will have to jump through a succession of hoops to get where you want to be. If you walk ten miles into the middle of a huge, dense forest, you are going to have to walk ten miles to get out of it. Don't count on divine intervention to immediately take you to your destination.

The rest of this book is full of ideas, inspiration, and resources that you can use to make your dreams come true and find a more rewarding work life. You have already taken the first step, simply by reading this far. Now, you just have to put one foot in front of the other. You will find that the journey gets easier, not more difficult. Certainly there will be occasional obstacles and bumps along the way, but they are nothing you can't handle. Enjoy the adventure! E

Chapter 2

A View from Abroad

Tired of the daily grind in your little corner of the world? Why not try leaving the country? Working abroad can be a rewarding and educational experience. It can expand your horizons and broaden your mind. In this chapter, we explore several opportunities for working in other countries.

Celebrating Diversity

Celebrating diversity has become something of a cliché these days. The phrase carries a political meaning that has become a rallying cry for many and a source of disdain to as many other. But if we distill these words to their purest form—or, perhaps, use a comparable French phrase, *vive le différence*—then being open to the diversity the world has to offer becomes an unequivocally positive notion.

It is natural to be proud of your heritage. Your ancestry is part of what makes you who you are. However, a belief that yours is clearly the superior heritage can easily transcend pride and become prejudice. No doubt, some aspects of other cultures are worthy of criticism. But the same is true of your own heritage and culture, whatever it may be. To exist in a state of xenophobia, with a dislike for anything outside your narrow view, is no way to live your life. Exposure to other traditions and lifestyles is a positive thing.

A great way to broaden your outlook on life is to experience other countries and cultures. There are plenty of them out there. The expression "It takes all kinds" applies not just to the people you meet, but to the global community as well. Even if you are not a lady or gentleman of leisure, and you cannot afford the luxury of going around the world in eighty days, you can still find plenty of opportunities to be paid to see the world.

Before you step off your native soil and embark on this great adventure, you have to ask yourself some questions:

1. Where would you like to go?
2. What would you like to do?
3. How can you make these two desires compatible?

Discovering your desires requires research, but you probably already have some ideas. For example, if you want to be a ski instructor, you would go to Switzerland and not the Sudan. Or perhaps you have a location in mind, while the work is secondary. Take the time to do the research, and decide what is best for you. It's a big world out there with possibilities that are literally endless. The rest of this chapter offers some suggestions and provides sources you can use to turn your daydreams into reality.

Tourism is a major industry in many of the countries abroad where you might be considering working. Johnson & Wales University is a hospitality college that specializes in subjects like food service management, travel and tourism, and hotel management. You can learn about career and learning opportunities in these fields at their Web site (✍ *www.jwu.edu*).

Finding Jobs Abroad

The Internet is the quickest and most efficient tool you can use in your hunt for positions abroad. Web sites that will help you in your quest may focus on particular countries or industries, or they may be associated with particular work-abroad programs. You'll find an eclectic collection of assignments that are long and short term, full and part time. Some are geared for students, while others are for anyone.

Jobs in Tourism

You can see that there are all sorts of opportunities for working overseas. One way of getting paid to work in an appealing locale is to seek employment in the tourist industry. Tourism is the world's biggest business, and plenty of opportunities are available for anyone who is not afraid of hard work and long hours. The bad news is that the work is not glamorous, nor is the pay great. On the other hand, the good news is that room and board are often included with the position. And best of all, you can spend your free time wandering some of the most beautiful locales in the world.

Most tourist jobs are seasonal, often only lasting through the summertime. Summertime occurs at different times in the world, depending on which hemisphere you're in. From May to October, for instance, you could work at a summer resort in Europe, and then move on to one in Australia from November through April. If traveling "down under" to follow the sun is too difficult, you could spend the winter working at a European ski resort. (Working in the skiing industry will be covered in Chapter 4.)

FACT

Club Med (✍ *www.clubmedjobs.com*) calls its interview process an "audition." Club Med auditions last three hours and are not unlike the audition process for a theatrical production. This makes sense, since working in one of these self-contained resort villages would require that one always be "on."

In this case, the location is probably more important than the work. (You know ahead of time that the job will probably be less than stimulating.) Therefore, you should pick the place first. Unlike a person seeking a career in the Peace Corps, you will likely find work in the more wealthy and developed nations, though some less-than-wealthy nations have concentrations of self-contained tourist sites, such as Club Med and Hedonism.

Cruising for a Living

Did you grow up watching *The Love Boat?* You can sail the seven seas working on a cruise ship. One of the prerequisites for this work is the ability to deal with the general public, which is often a difficult and trying task. You have to be a people person—or at least be able to successfully fake it. Tour guides have to deal with the public intimately, while other jobs, such as those in the kitchen, for instance, have minimal interpersonal contact. You have to decide your tolerance level and choose accordingly.

Qualifications vary for working on cruise ships, but the bottom-end age requirement is usually between eighteen and twenty-one. Depending on where you would like to work, a working knowledge of the native language is helpful. Despite the low pay and the long hours, you will find the competition for jobs to be intense. Once you've picked the part of the world you might like to visit, check out the big cruise lines in the region and contact them. Most will have a presence on the Internet, and the Web site will most likely have job listings posted. For example, the job listings page on the Cunard cruise line's Web site (✍ *www.cunard.com*) recently posted positions that included the following:

- Sound technician for onboard entertainment
- Waiter/waitress
- "Chef de partie" (requiring a chef's diploma and five years of experience working in at least two different five-star establishments)

Beautiful Balloon

An offbeat and growing alternative career is being a member of the ground crew for a hot-air balloon business. This industry is rising in Europe as more and more tourists and locals fancy the romance of a scenic balloon flight. The season runs from May to October, with a brief winter season in January and February. Your mission, should you decide to accept it, will involve working in the takeoff and landing team, inflating and deflating the balloons, refueling, and assisting customers in and out of the balloon basket. A ground crew member should weigh at least 150 pounds and have a valid European Union working permit. You also have to know how to drive. Remember that in most European countries you drive on the right side of the road, while the steering wheel is sometimes on the right side of the car. This is disorienting to many Americans and takes some getting used to.

FACT

As a kid, were you into playing Dungeons & Dragons and collecting medieval memorabilia? There are many fixed and traveling Renaissance festivals where you could turn your passion for the past into a paying job.

Most Europeans have a working knowledge of English, but it would be helpful to have some facility in French, German, or Italian. Balloon ground crews receive a small salary, but room and board (and most likely the occasional balloon flight) are included. You will get to see

Europe from the ground and from the air. For more information on the ground crew and other positions at one European balloon touring company, visit Bombard's Web site at ✍ *www.bombardsociety.com/jobs.*

Fruit Picking

If you are going on a backpacking tour of Europe, one way to make some money along the way and get a place to flop for the night is to work as a migrant fruit picker. For some this may sound demeaning, but for many young Americans it can be a good way to experience life in another country from a completely different perspective. It also may also turn out to be a good first experience in rolling up the old sleeves and doing a little hard work.

FACT

The British online publication *Tramp News* (at ✍ *www.payaway.co.uk*) is a good source for information on transitory employment, including the various harvest seasons in different nations and when the farmers will need people to work in their fields.

You can work your way across Europe during the spring and summer. This kind of work is as far away from punching a clock as it gets. For everything there is a season, as the good book says, and your work as a fruit picker depends on the crop, its season and harvest time. European countries that hire seasonal workers include France, Germany, Denmark, Holland, Switzerland, Italy, Spain, Portugal, Greece, Norway, and the United Kingdom; some countries outside Europe—such as Canada, Australia, and New Zealand—do as well. Australian farmers rely heavily on foreign labor, but in some European countries the work is become more and more mechanized. If you want to sample the nightlife of Amsterdam, you can investigate being a seasonal bulb packer in Holland. Tulips, like Heineken, are a main export of Holland.

The main requirement is a willingness and ability to put in a hard day's work. Climbing up and down ladders and lots of bending are part of the daily grind. It is physically demanding work. If you have never done it before you will ache at night, but by the end of your stay you will be in better shape and perhaps even enriched spiritually through working with the land. And you will have money in your pocket to enable you to move on to the next stop on your journey. In agricultural work, you are paid based on how much work you do, which is determined by how many bushels you present the foreman at day's end. It is truly a results-oriented job.

Au Pair

If you are a young woman under twenty-seven years of age (though this age varies from country to country) and like working with children, you might consider going abroad as an au pair. Many women come to the United States to fill these positions for American families, but the reverse cultural exchange is also common. Jobs are available all year round. Positions are available in areas such Western Europe, Canada, Israel, and Turkey. A typical day involves child care and light housework. The au pair might be asked to babysit on some evenings and is guaranteed one day off a week, plus study time if she is a student. An au pair should be single. Nonsmokers are preferred, and a driver's license is sometimes required. Most jobs last six months to a year. The pay is not great, but you'll have a place to stay, and your meals are provided. You will also receive other fringe benefits that may include airfare, the work visa fee, and money toward schooling.

FACT

"Au pair" is a French phrase that can be translated in English as "on par" or "on equal terms." This is meant to imply that the au pair is not merely domestic help, but rather that she is regarded as something more akin to a member, albeit temporarily, of the family.

An Internet search will deliver many au pair placement sites. Shop around to find the best one for your needs. You can also attempt to hook up with a family on your own by either placing or responding to an ad in a magazine.

Teaching Abroad

Teaching is a rewarding career on one's native soil. It can be equally and maybe even more satisfying in a foreign land. The public school system in most major cities is, quite frankly, a mess. Teachers must double as security guards and referees and are occasionally the victims of physical violence. Even in the better suburban schools, teachers have to deal with the many requirements imposed by out-of-touch educational bureaucrats, and students are often an unmotivated and unruly lot.

American teachers who work abroad have an entirely different experience. By and large, these expatriate educators meet with respectful students who are eager to learn. For the first time in years for the veterans, and the first time ever for many, they fully experience what it means to be a teacher. They do not have to butt heads with administrators and annoying parents, and the classroom sizes are often significantly smaller.

The international section of the Internet job search site ✍*www.monster.com* has information on how to get a permit to work in the countries of the European Union, as well as other European job-seeking resources.

For the enthusiastic and dedicated teacher, the opportunity to teach abroad opens the door to a brave new world. It can renew their faith and give their flagging spirits a welcome and needed boost. As a teacher in a different country, you will go where you have never gone before.

You have to have the right personality for the journey ahead. As an expatriate teacher—especially if you undertake your teaching adventure alone—you will find yourself feeling homesick. You will often feel like the ultimate outsider, yet you will also bond with student and colleagues and possibly form friendships that will last the rest of your life. Remember that the whole point of the journey was to expose yourself to a different culture with different customs. Leave your preconceptions at home. Each day is likely to bring new experiences and new problems to solve. You will need to be flexible and adaptable with a penchant for improvisation.

You may be in an area with sporadic electricity, or none at all. You may be in front of a group of students with no textbooks. You will often have to wing it.

ALERT!

The Web site ✍ *www.teachabroad.com* offers all kinds of information about teaching and studying abroad. You'll find sources for internships, language schools, "eco-adventures," travel arrangements, and other critical information that anyone thinking about leaving the country needs to know.

Another thing to keep in mind as you leave the United States to teach abroad is that we take many things for granted in this country that are luxuries in most parts of the world. Living conditions, for instance, may not be what you are used to. You can expect to find the greatest differences in plumbing—citizens of many countries enjoy hot water only at specified times of day, for instance. Depending on where you choose to go, there is a chance you will encounter poverty and human misery on a scale that was previously unimaginable to you. You must be mentally prepared for this discovery, which can be overwhelming.

English as a Second Language

One of the teaching skills that is most in demand is the ability to teach English. Teaching English as a second language (ESL) is a valuable tool to have. If you can read these words aloud and understand what they mean, then you have the basic qualifications to teach English as a second language to students in other countries. There is a little more that you will need to do, as you'll see below.

The Benefits of Speaking English

In earlier centuries, French was considered the "universal language" that people of culture sought to learn. At one time, members of the Russian royal family spoke French almost exclusively, believing their native tongue to be coarse and worthy only of the peasants. Today, English can be fairly called the universal language. Most Europeans have a working knowledge of English. All air traffic controllers and commercial airline pilots around the world communicate in the English language. The United States is the leader in business and commerce. It is the only political superpower left standing, which has led other nations and other peoples to adopt a "when in Rome" attitude toward learning English. They want to play with the big boys in business, attend America's universities, visit, and maybe even move here.

Alliances Abroad (✉ *www.alliancesabroad.com*) lists many alternative career opportunities, both abroad and in the United States. Listings cover a wide range, from working in English pubs to ranching in the Australian outback to teaching English in China, Ecuador, and other countries. Alliances Abroad also offers information about volunteer programs in countries such as South Africa, Costa Rica, and Venezuela.

One of the advantages of teaching ESL is that you do not have to know the language of the people you are teaching. However, just because you speak English does not mean that you can effectively convey your understanding of the language to others. There is an art and a craft to teaching anything, let alone something as complicated as a foreign language. By the end of this section you will know whether you have both the desire and the inclination to take the plunge.

There are many programs that send ESL teachers abroad. You need to do the research to find the right one for you. You must be prepared to make at least a one-year commitment to your job. This makes sense—most teachers you have had in your time were with you from September to June, were they not?

You can choose to send yourself anywhere, to classrooms ranging from a grass-and-mud hut in a rain forest to a fancy private school in a cultured European capital. You have to decide where you want to go and what you want to get out of the experience. Examine yourself to find your "dedication factor." Do you want to teach kids in the south of France, or are you itching to roll up your sleeves and work hard in Somalia? Nations both rich and poor are in need of ESL teachers. The salaries vary from country to country. You can expect, for instance, that an oil-rich Arab nation will pay well, while an underdeveloped third world nation will often pay virtually nothing. Benefits also vary, ranging from health coverage and other financial benefits to the simple and spiritual rewards that come from making a difference. Presumably, big bucks are not your driving force; if they were, you would be looking into other job opportunities.

ALERT!

EFLWEB (*www.eflweb.com*) is a site that includes job oportunities for teaching English. It also has a section called the TravelZone with useful information on the culture and customs of the many countries where ESL teachers are in demand.

The best place for Americans to look for jobs teaching ESL is in Asia and Latin America. In Western Europe, there are plenty of British and Irish citizens who can teach English to their European neighbors. In the time since the European countries, including those of the United Kingdom, banded together to became the European Union (EU), it has become easier for the British and Irish to get these European teaching positions. Naturally enough, is harder for an American to get an EU work permit and visa. You also may face some anti-American bias in Western Europe these days. Eastern Europe, which until the early 1990s suffered in many way under the control of the former Soviet Union, is friendlier to Americans. You may have a better chance teaching ESL in Eastern Bloc nations such as Russia, Poland, or the Czech Republic.

The world is yours for the taking. You can see wonders you have never before beheld. You can teach English in a tropical paradise or the mountains of Tibet, in a big city or in the middle of nowhere. You can provide a valuable service to eager and willing students and present a positive image of the average, typical American citizen—often a misunderstood and disliked breed these days.

Certified Versus Noncertified

You may already have your ESL teaching credentials. In that case, you have an advantage, though it is possible to get an ESL job without one. It also helps—but, as we mentioned before, is not necessary—to speak the native language. If you have made the decision to try to be an ESL teacher abroad, you have to decide if you want to go for the certification or attempt to work without one.

There are various levels of ESL certification. Each level is signified by a different acronym; to earn the right to put such letters after your name will require 100 to 120 hours of study in ESL training. You can try for an ESL position without such training, but chances are that the places interested in hiring you will be less desirable or reputable than those that prefer candidates who are certified. Depending on your timetable, you can take a one-month, highly concentrated course, or you can spread it out over a period of several months. The cost of an ESL certification course ranges from $1,000 to $4,000.

FACT

The University of Michigan's International Center (on the university's Web site at ✎ www.umich.edu/~icenter) includes information and many links about working and teaching abroad. If you are in college or a college graduate, see if your school has a similar international center.

When investigating schools, make sure that the one you choose has placement programs for graduates. The school should have international contacts and connections at major headhunting firms. Some will even spring for the plane fare to your destination. The schools with no connections and that offer no assistance will be cheaper, but you may end up spending the difference on a placement firm's finder's fee.

Once you are certified, you can decide whether you want to look for work from the comfort of home or travel to the country you have decided on and pound the pavement there. Obviously, the wise thing to do is to find a job and make the arrangements before leaving the country. But it's also true that teaching positions can pay more if you apply and are hired in person. Another downside to finding a job before traveling abroad is that you cannot thoroughly investigate the foreign school from across the sea, unless a reliable agency is acting as middleman. If you are going it alone, you may be in for quite a surprise when you get to the location. People have been known to travel thousands of miles and discover that the school is a hole in the wall or is no longer open for business.

Some schools will hire uncertified teachers, but the truth is that without a certificate, you are less likely to get a job. There are teaching opportunities in the Peace Corps and missionary work (detailed in Chapter 16). These programs are ideal for the recent college graduate and offer excellent on-the-job training. Some governments sponsor exchange programs. The Japanese government offers the Japanese Exchange and Teaching Program. In this program, Westerners help Japanese teachers with English instruction in the classroom at the junior high and high school levels. (You can call ✆ 1-800-INFOJET for more information.) Investigate the country you are interested in, and see if they have a similar program.

If you are not interested in working with children, there are many people other than school-age kids who want to learn English. You could teach businessmen who want to be able to better communicate with their American counterparts. The work is not as steady, but the hourly rate is higher. You can also find night schools where you can teach adults. Ⓔ

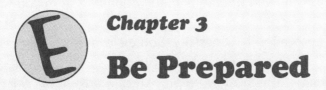

Chapter 3

Be Prepared

Once you've given some thought to where you would like to go and what you might like to do in foreign lands, you'll now need to take the concrete steps to get over there. In particular, you need to know the cultural differences and possible problems you may encounter.

See the World

Okay, you are ready to leave the country and see the world. Excited as you are about this great adventure, you need to do certain things and contemplate certain realities before you take your sojourn abroad. You'll need to get the appropriate documentation, take health precautions, and be aware of the customs and traditions of the country where you will be working.

Some of this preparation is necessary. Some steps are highly recommended but not mission critical. As with any student who has a final exam approaching, it is best to be prepared in advance—do not wait until the last minute and scramble to get things done! Going to work for an extended period in a foreign country is a major life change. The better you prepare, the more smoothly your transition and adjustment period will go.

The passport services section of the U.S. State Department's Web site (at ✍ *www.travel.state.gov*) will direct you to the places that are nearest to your neck of the woods where you can apply for a passport. You'll also find lots of other pertinent information on this site that anyone traveling abroad needs to know.

Passport to Adventure

You might already have a passport. If not, you definitely need one. That is, of course, a passport. You can apply for a passport at more than 5,000 locations across the country—most post offices, state and federal courthouses, many county and municipal facilities, and even some libraries. There is probably a convenient location near your home or office. You should apply in person. A parent should apply on behalf of children under thirteen years of age.

If you are impatient and hate waiting in line—who doesn't?—you can beat the lines by downloading and filling out the forms in advance. To get started, the main form you need is the DSP-11; you can find it at the

Web site ✎ *www.travel.state.gov.* If you do not have a computer, you can call the National Passport Information Center at ☎ 1-900-225-5674 and have the forms mailed to you. As of this writing, the total cost for a new passport is $85 ($70 for those under sixteen years old). This includes a $30 execution fee, which you won't have to pay if you are simply renewing a valid passport.

FACT

The whole point of a passport photo, as with any official form of photo identification, is that it gives the authorities evidence they can use to verify your identity. They must be able to tell that you are the same person whose name is given in the passport. A woman recently sued the state, claiming that her religious beliefs required her to keep her face covered, even for her driver's license photo. She lost her suit.

Picture Perfect

To apply for your passport, you will also need to provide a form of identification. Your birth certificate, driver's license, or other kind of government-issued picture ID will do. Speaking of pictures, you need to have two passport photographs taken. The picture may be taken either in color or in black and white. Many camera shops offer this service, as do businesses such as Sears, Kinko's, The UPS Store, American Automobile Association (AAA), and many others.

There are specific requirements for your passport photograph. The two pictures must meet the following criteria:

- Measure 2 x 2 inches.
- Display an image of you that measures between 1 inch and $1\frac{3}{8}$ inches from the bottom of your chin to the top of your head.
- Be the same picture, not different shots from the same photo session.
- Be less than six months old—it must be recognizable as you.
- Be a full-face shot. (You may be enamored of your profile, but the passport authorities won't be.)

- Show you in normal street attire—no fancy costumes or other accessories.
- Not show you in a uniform. If you wear a head covering for religious reasons, you must include a written explanation of why.
- Show prescription glasses, a hearing aid, or any other accessory that you wear on your head or face.
- Not show sunglasses or tinted glasses, unless they are necessary for medical reasons. If so, you may have to provide the appropriate documentation.

Planning Ahead

While it is possible to get a passport in a hurry, it is advisable to plan ahead and get it a few months in advance of your departure. It will take five to six weeks from the day you apply to the day your passport arrives in the mail. During that time—ideally, at least—you will be giving your alternative career a lot of thought and be making a detailed "to do" list. An extended stay in another country is not something you should jump into with reckless abandon, and careful planning will help you to avoid potential problems.

QUESTION?

Can you get a passport in a hurry?
Yes, exceptions can be made to speed up the process. The U.S. State Department's Web site (✎ *www.travel.state.gov*) will tell you how you need to proceed. There will be extra fees for the expedited services (at present, $60), but it is worth it if you absolutely, positively have to leave the country ASAP.

If you have a passport and need to renew it, this procedure can be done by mail. You can download or send for form DSP-82. Return your current passport with the renewal fee (as of this writing, $55).

By the way, if your passport is ever lost or stolen while you're still in the United States, you should call ☎ 202-955-0430 immediately. If your passport is lost or stolen while you are in a foreign country, you should contact the nearest American embassy. They will be able to help.

The same applies if you let your passport expire while in another country. This is something you should not let happen, as it will create major headaches and trap you in a tangle of bureaucratic and diplomatic red tape. If there is any possible chance your passport will expire before you return to the United States, renew it before you leave.

Are you in a *really* big hurry to get your passport? Several businesses not affiliated with the government can—for an additional fee—expedite your passport application and get you a passport within twenty-four hours. One such agency is American Passport Express, on the Web at *www.americanpassport.com*.

The U.S. State Department urges citizens to make copies of all their identification and documentation and keep them in a separate place from the originals when you travel. With this method, you have backup paperwork in case something happens to some of your possessions. This will make it much easier to clear up the situation should problems arise.

Only Irish Need Apply

In addition to your American passport, you may find that you are also eligible for a passport from a different country. Many Irish Americans apply for, and receive, an Irish passport. If one of your parents hails from the Emerald Isle, you are eligible for dual citizenship. The advantage of this is that you can travel abroad with an Irish passport. This can be helpful—sometimes it's even essential—in becoming eligible to work in countries such as those in the European Union. And at a time when Americans may meet with an unpleasant welcome (or much worse) abroad, having a passport from another country can be a very good idea. If your parents, or even your grandparents, were not born in the United States, check out your eligibility to have a passport from their birthplace.

A Shot in the Arm

Another thing you must look into before traveling overseas is what, if any, vaccinations you may need for different countries. Local populations build up immunities to the microbes and other microscopic menaces that may be present in the water, food, and even the air. For you, however, as a newcomer to the area, there are plenty of pesky pestilences out there that can make you very sick. Your system may have difficulty handling these unfamiliar microscopic assaults, and the results could be anything from embarrassing gastric distress to something downright deadly. On the extreme end of things, there is still the occasional plague that sweeps through a region. This happens mostly in underdeveloped countries, where sanitary conditions are often less than satisfactory, and health care is not on par with what you are used to.

You have to do a little research about the country you plan to visit. You should address these factors:

- Health history of the country or region
- The length of time you plan to stay there
- What sort of work you will be doing there
- What environmental conditions you will be exposed to
- Accommodations—whether you stay in a five-star hotel or a tent in a rain forest
- Food and hygiene conditions

If you are going to a modern, industrial country, you probably will not have to worry about contracting malaria. On the other hand, if you are heading to a more remote locale, you will need to be prepared. If you are going to what is nowadays called a "developing nation," you should make a visit before you leave to a doctor or clinic that caters to travelers and is aware of what inoculations you will need. Of course, this should not be done on a Friday when your flight is on Monday. You should see the doctor at least four to six weeks before you travel so any vaccinations will have time to become effective.

It is also advisable that you get a dental checkup, if possible, since the local dentistry might be not up to your usual standards. You do not want to have a toothache in a foreign land and have the local dentist produce a pair of pliers and ask you to open wide.

ALERT!

Before traveling, visit the State Department's travel warning page on their Web site, at ✍ *www.travel.state.gov*. You can click on the first letter of any country's name to check for any current travel warnings. This information lets travelers and other Americans abroad know where the danger zones are and what they can do to protect themselves.

Necessities

When you pack for your trek abroad, there are certain items that you must bring, particularly if you are going to an "out of the way" part of the world. One essential is a first-aid kit. This kit should include not only the obvious items, like bandages and aspirin. If you are taking any prescription medication, keep it there along with a doctor's note. This will come in handy if the local customs officials and other authorities ever rummage through your stuff. You do not want your antidiarrhea pills to be mistaken for contraband by some suspicious civil servant. Make sure you carry your first-aid kit in your purse or another handheld carrying case. You do not want them to get lost in transit. If possible, it would be wise to carry a duplicate set in your larger luggage.

Make sure your insurance covers any illnesses or injury you suffer while abroad. Not all policies do, so it is wise to verify this and switch carriers if necessary. You do not want to be left without coverage if something unpleasant should happen while you are outside the United States.

Don't Drink the Water

Vaccinations are necessary, but they are not 100 percent foolproof when it comes to preventing disease. There are also diseases for which there are no effective vaccines, such as malaria and AIDS. The risk you run, as we've already stressed, depends on where you are going, how long you will be there, and what you will be doing there. An awareness of how diseases are transmitted will help you make decisions and take precautions to ensure that your sojourn is a healthy one.

Some diseases are carried through food and water. Those who have ever suffered a bout of Montezuma's revenge know this only too well. The cliché "Don't drink the water" resonates uncomfortably with those who have toured parts of Mexico and other lands where the drinking water is not as clean as American water. It is a good idea to drink bottled water, and it's also smart to be careful about where and what you eat. Diseases that are transmitted by food and water include cholera, typhoid fever, and hepatitis A.

Diseases from Animals

Another way you can catch a disease is from insects. These are known as vector-borne diseases, the most infamous of which is malaria. Others include yellow fever and encephalitis. Research the locale you are going to. If necessary, bring plenty of insect repellent, and plan to sleep under a mosquito net.

Native wildlife can also transmit diseases to humans. These types of communicable diseases are called zoonoses (pronounced "zoe-oh-nos-es"). You can be exposed to them through several unpleasant avenues, including animal bites or contact with animal blood or waste products. You can also contract zoonoses by eating or drinking locally produced meat or milk. The major zoonoses include rabies, leptospirosis, and hemorrhagic fever— very nasty stuff indeed. Unless your job requires it, avoid contact with the local animals, no matter how cute and cuddly they may appear.

Transmitted Diseases

You have no doubt have had the flu and the common cold more than once in your life. These are examples of airborne diseases. They are transmitted by infected people who breathe, cough, or sneeze in your general direction. Flu and cold bugs can also be transmitted by physical contact—it's a good idea to wash your hands frequently, especially in places where quarters are cramped. In general, when abroad you should be more concerned about protecting your health, not less.

Although a bad case of the flu is no laughing matter, some transmitted diseases are far more serious. AIDS is rampant in certain parts of the world, especially Africa. Contrary to old stereotypes, the victims of this incurable disease are not limited to homosexual men and drug users. It is, however, primarily contracted through sexual contact. There are also many other sexually transmitted diseases, including syphilis and hepatitis B. At this point, medical science offers remedies to these diseases that make it possible to lead a relatively normal life after infection. However, you should realize that contracting any serious sexually transmitted disease will almost certainly have very negative consequences on your general health. Take the practice of safe sex very seriously when abroad.

Malaria

Malaria is a life-threatening fever that is commonplace in more than 100 countries across the globe. It is caused by a microscopic parasite that is transmitted by the bite of a mosquito. Its early symptoms are those of a bad case of the flu, including headache, chills, weakness, and other symptoms. In severe cases it can cause kidney failure, coma, and death. It is estimated that 1 percent of people who contract malaria die from the disease. As with most diseases, early diagnosis and treatment can save your life.

You may love sushi, but do not eat any raw food when traveling abroad. The rule of thumb is to "Boil it, cook it, peel it, or forget it." Make sure any dairy products you consume have been pasteurized.

Malaria is among the most common diseases that Americans contract abroad. Statistics tell us that more than 125 million travelers contract malaria each year. The disease is common in Latin America, the Caribbean, Asia, Africa, and India. It is less common, but not entirely absent, in major urban centers. The more remote the area you visit, the higher the risk. The bad news, as we've mentioned, is that there is no vaccine to keep you from contracting malaria. You should plan to take all necessary precautions and to seek immediate treatment should symptoms arise.

Some people feel the onset of malaria symptoms while they are still in the foreign country; others have a delayed reaction, coming down with the fever long after they have returned home. If you feel feverish within three months after a trip or extended stay overseas, particularly if you have been in a tropical climate, consult a doctor immediately. Keep in mind that pregnant women and their unborn children are at high risk should they be bitten by a malaria-carrying mosquito.

ALERT!

For a detailed look at what you need to know and to do in terms of vaccinations, visit the Web sites of the World Health Organization and the Center for Disease Control. You can find them at *www.who.int* and *www.cdc.gov*.

Other Diseases

More diseases? By now, you might be too scared to leave your house, let alone travel to a seemingly dangerous foreign country. As always, education is the essential first step to prevention. Becoming aware of every bad thing that's out there can help keep you from falling victim to any of them. Here are a few more diseases to be considered before you make your trip abroad:

- **Yellow fever.** It is highly recommended—and in some cases mandatory—that you get a shot for this disease if you plan to travel to an area where it flourishes. You may also need to produce documentation that you have had the inoculation when visiting some countries.
- **Cholera.** You will not be required to get a cholera vaccination to visit any country, but check out the place you are going to see if the shot is recommended.
- **Smallpox.** In 1980, the World Health Organization certified that

smallpox had been completely purged from the planet. The fear of smallpox now comes from its possible use in a terrorist attack. The vaccine for smallpox can have major side effects, including serious illness and death, so you would need to give very serious thought about its risks before getting one.

- **Hepatitis A.** This is a common disease in many parts of the world, and a shot is recommended.

Different Strokes

These days the world is a slightly smaller place. Even if you do not live in an ethnically diverse community, anyone with a television is exposed to different cultures and traditions. Of course, there is nothing like firsthand experience. You can watch a Discovery Channel documentary on the North Pole while sitting in your Florida living room, but you will never feel the bracing cold (except from your central air-conditioning). Similarly, you can learn about a foreign land from a book without getting any real idea of what it is really like to live and work there day in and day out. Most other countries have a language and form of government that are different from yours. Religion may play more of an integral role than it does in American society. You may find that citizens of those countries enjoy more limited freedom, or you may find a social structure that you consider akin to anarchy. Even in the smaller world of today, you will still find plenty of opportunities for a fair amount of culture shock. Like the people in Mark Twain's travelogue, many Americans may feel like "innocents abroad."

FACT

For decades, American women tourists have found themselves being pinched on the bottom by the male residents of Rome and other Italian cities. This tradition, fortunately, is going the way of the dodo as more and more Italian women are suing the men with the wandering hands.

Avoiding Preconceptions and Stereotypes

It is always best to keep an open mind in all your affairs, though a certain amount of prejudice is natural. Not prejudice in a discriminatory or hostile sense, but prejudice in the spirit of its original meaning—to judge ahead of time (prejudge).

Americans do not corner the market on prejudice. According to Princeton University's Study Abroad Program, Americans are usually perceived as any or some combination of the following:

- Outgoing and friendly
- Informal
- Loud, rude, and boastful
- Immature
- Hard-working
- Wealthy
- Generous
- Extravagant and wasteful
- Sure that they have all the answers
- Disrespectful of authority
- Racially prejudiced
- Ignorant of other countries
- Always in a hurry
- Promiscuous

Do you recognize your own traits, or those of any family members or friends, in the above list? You probably do. Stereotypes often have a basis in fact. Negative stereotypes may embody certain aspects of a certain percentage of a culture or ethnic group, which are then amplified and unfairly applied to everyone in that category. When you spend an extended period of time abroad, you will find some examples of popular stereotypes. In many other instances, however, you will find them shattered.

Living in another country is certainly a great adventure. You will experience the thrill of learning about the previously undiscovered country, but being a stranger in a strange land can also be a frustrating and lonely time. There is nothing more isolating than the feeling of being the outsider. Unless you are surrounded by some of your fellow countrymen and women, your early days there may be fraught with anxiety and depression.

Don't let it get you down. Loneliness and homesickness are natural feelings. But as they say, "This too shall pass." And indeed it shall.

Going Native

Obviously you should learn as much as you can about the country in advance of your visit in an effort to prevent a severe culture shock. Talk to people who have been there and any natives you may know. Once you are there, you can take steps to make sure you fit in.

Do not perpetuate the negative stereotype of the ugly American. Do not expect the culture to accommodate your needs. Remember, when you are working in another country, you are not there as a tourist. You won't be afforded all the luxuries and courtesies given to paying customers. Be receptive and adaptable in the society where you are a guest.

Be polite. In many cultures, particularly Asian societies, courtesy is such an important part of life that polite behavior is a choreographed dance of rituals. Learn whether it is customary to greet another person with a bow rather than a hearty handshake. Address people with formality, and use their country's titles, whatever the equivalent of "Mr." and "Ms." may be, at least until someone addresses you in a more informal manner first. No matter how well intentioned, a greeting like "Yo! Wassup!" may not be especially well received.

Language Issues

It is wise to have a working knowledge of the local language. Listen to some instructional tapes before you arrive, and bring them with you. Take the ubiquitous phrasebook as well. Do not be afraid of looking like a tourist. Though many citizens of the world take the time to learn English, do not assume that everyone speaks it or that they will be inclined to address you accordingly. Most people will like to see that you are making the effort to speak to them in their native tongue.

The French are the exception to this rule. As Professor Henry Higgins says in *My Fair Lady,* "The French don't care what they do actually, as long as they pronounce it properly." If you try to speak French with an American accent in Paris, don't be surprised if the waiter responds to you in English. Whether you take this as an insult to your fractured French or an attempt to be helpful to you in your native language is up to you.

If you have a sardonic sense of humor, keep it in check. Not everyone appreciates the singularly American wit. Do not be a blustering, backslapping good old boy with people you have just met. Many cultures find this immediate intimacy uncomfortable and even offensive.

You cannot rely on being able to retrieve your high school French or Spanish courses from your memory banks if you want to spend any time abroad. In any event, you definitely need to know how to say more than "Where is the bathroom?" Before visiting the foreign land you have chosen, find an intensive crash course, either in a classroom or on tape, that immerses you in the native language.

Certain no-brainers need to be observed. If you like your schnapps, do not overindulge in certain foreign lands. Getting drunk and carrying on in a Muslim country will not be well received. Also, avoid talking politics with people you don't know well, as you don't know how your views will be received. At a time where a number of countries may have rising anti-American feeling, this is very sound advice indeed.

Women Abroad

American women may find it particularly difficult to adjust to certain cultures. In many countries of the world, women are still second-class citizens—and sometimes worse. Whereas American men can get in a lot of trouble for an unwelcome compliment, let alone an uninvited touch, there are still places where women are verbally accosted and even pinched on public thoroughfares.

Women should know what to expect in advance of that first incident. Brush up on the male chauvinist factor of the country you are visiting. There is no need for you to stand for any outrageous advance. At the same time, however, you should be aware of what other people consider acceptable—or at least when they're willing to look the other way—in the country and culture you are visiting.

Alternative Lifestyles

In some cultures, particularly in Europe, homosexuality may be as accepted as it is in the United States or even more so. In others, gay men and women still face social ostracization or worse. There are laws on the books in many lands against certain conduct, and those found guilty as charged face harsh penalties. Many parts of the world are not as tolerant as they should be. No one is asking you to deny your true self, but common sense and discretion may be required in many places, particularly in Muslim nations.

ALERT!

If you are concerned about the cultural mores regarding homosexuality of a country you are considering living in, visit the Web site of the International Gay and Lesbian Human Rights Commission (*www.iglhrc.org*) to learn more. There are some places you will simply want to avoid.

Let's Be Careful over There

On a very practical and realistic note, you need to remember that, considering the current international situation, there is a war on. It is not your grandparents' war. This war is of an entirely different nature. And like it or not, there are a lot of people in the world who will hate you simply because you are an American. You need to be aware of this when in a foreign country. Treatment could be anything from just plain rude to conduct more malevolent.

The bottom line is that it's important to put a great deal of thought into your travel plans during these troubled times. Know the risks before you go. If you are aware of the risks and remain determined to spend time in a hot spot where Yankees are not held in high esteem, be careful and good luck. If you are a missionary Christian and are planning to do good work in a region that is not religiously tolerant, rethink that decision. The good Lord wants you alive and well to continue doing good deeds.

Keep in contact with friends and relatives back home. Let people know where you can be reached. They will feel better, and you will have some solace knowing that your loved ones will call the authorities if they do not hear from you for a while.

If you take the proper precautions and do your homework, your extended stay abroad can be an educational and rewarding experience. You will make new friends, have many adventures, and learn a lot of things about the world that you could never get from a classroom or from television. You will enrich your understanding of the human condition, open your mind, and maybe even open your heart. You will learn to appreciate the differences among diverse cultures, and you will marvel at the commonalities that we human beings share. At our basic core, people are alike all over. We are not one big happy family, but we are all members of the human family. Diverse, often dysfunctional, occasionally touching the divine, we are, as Hamlet observed, quite a piece of work. Ⓔ

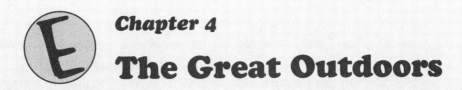

Chapter 4

The Great Outdoors

Is your cubicle giving you cabin fever? Is it festooned with images of purple mountain majesty above some fruited plains? Perhaps you ought to consider a career in the great outdoors. This chapter offers several examples of careers that give you the opportunity to make a living under the sun—or, if you're on the night shift, under the stars.

Back to Nature

There is something deeply spiritual about spending much of your day out in the elements, far from urban centers and their attendant chaos. Unlike the celebrated loafer Henry David Thoreau, however, you will have to keep yourself busy if you want to get a paycheck. You will, however, be spared the proverbial life of quiet desperation.

If you are looking for a position in the great outdoors, we can assume that you have a passion for nature and a disdain for the office milieu. There are of course advantages and disadvantages to the outdoor life. On the positive side, you will be doing something you love free from the glare of fluorescent lights. The downside is a familiar one—you will not become a millionaire. But who wants to be a millionaire when you can romp in the forest primeval and inhale deep draughts of fresh air?

If you already have some outdoor experience and would like to lead others on outdoor adventures, one place to begin your search is the Mountain Workshop. At their Web site (✐ *www.mountain workshop.com*), you can learn about their available jobs as guides and program leaders.

Be All You Can Be—Be a Park Ranger

A park ranger is not the amiable dunce commonly depicted on the Cartoon Network, constantly thwarted by a smarter-than-average bear. Park rangers patrol and manage state and national parks, historical sites, and other recreational facilities. They do a little bit of everything, functioning as law enforcement officers, conservationists, tour guides, and much more. They can tell you the history of that giant redwood, and they can also give you a ticket if you leave a messy campsite behind. You can be a park ranger in Yellowstone National Park or in Manhattan's Central Park. In both places, you will have to contend with the local wildlife.

What It Takes

There are many skill levels for a park ranger. Entry-level positions with no requirements are available, along with an entry-level salary. You can start at a higher level if you have a high school diploma, and higher still with a college degree. Education or life experience in natural or earth sciences, law enforcement, business or public administration, and other related fields will also be helpful. You will be doing a little of all these functions and more as a park ranger. It is a job that is nothing if not eclectic, and the knowledge you will need crosses many disciplines. Of course, your people skills should be above average. Though you will be in the wide-open spaces, you will not be alone amid the flora and fauna. Tourists visit parks. You may find that you would rather deal with a cranky Kodiak bear than a group of obnoxious campers.

When you are finally in the woods, you will get much of your training on the job. The experience you accumulate will help you rise within the ranks. You may also be required (or inspired) to upgrade your skills through career-related courses. These are offered at training centers in Arizona (at the Grand Canyon), West Virginia, and Georgia.

FACT

Potential park rangers who are also armchair detectives should check out Nevada Barr's mystery novels. Her detective is a park ranger, and each novel is set in a different national park.

Working Your Way Up

As a park ranger, you will initially start at a certain level based on your experience and how well you score on your entrance examination. (Entrance examinations will vary depending on which state or agency you are applying to work for, but they commonly contain written sections of multiple-choice and essay questions as well as a physical-ability test.) You will naturally need to take on more responsibility the higher you rise within the system. If you choose to advance within this system, you will certainly need good managerial skills. Your domain of responsibility may or may not cover an extensive physical area, but it will definitely include a wide assortment of personalities, all of which will report to you.

The Paycheck

As is often the case with these alternative careers, a park ranger's job is rewarding in many ways—just not necessarily financially. Starting salaries are low, and even higher-level paychecks will not reach the requirements for a pampered city dweller. You should know this going in, and your decision should be based on the perks and the other satisfactions that life as a park ranger provides.

Where to Apply

The first resource you should check out is USAJOBS, "the Federal Government's Official Job Site" (at *www.usajobs.opm.gov*). This site gives you access to the U.S. Office of Personnel Management, or OPM, which has a comprehensive listing on available positions in hundreds of fields, including park ranger postings. Through the OPM, you can receive information about the examination required. Like any civil service position, you will need to take a test. The federal government is, of course, an equal opportunity employer, but candidates must be United States citizens.

Up the River

If you love the feel of stinging yet invigorating spray of water in your face, you would probably enjoy the thrill of whitewater rafting. If you are interesting in making a living on the rapids but have no paddling experience, there is a lot you have to learn. This is a job where your life and the lives of those in the boat with you may depend on it.

Back to School

There are many schools that will teach you what you need to know and where you will earn the certifications needed to become a professional rafter or river guide. Enter the keywords "raft school" or "river guide training" into any Internet search engine, and you will get dozens of options. You can pick the school that has what you want in the region where you would like to work.

Any accredited rafting school will teach you the following necessary skills:

- How to read water
- How to execute steering strokes
- Strategies for guiding a raft through Class III rapids
- Rafting safety procedures
- How to rescue swimmers
- How to right a flipped raft
- How to "unwrap" a boat
- Strategies for self-rescue
- How to swim rapids
- Wilderness camping skills, with an emphasis on "Leave no trace" ethics
- How to cook meals for many people in a wilderness setting
- How to use and care for rafting equipment

It is advisable that you attend a school in the region where you would like to work. By doing this you will be practicing on the rivers and rapids where you will hopefully soon be shepherding clients. Every river is different. In this job, you will need, in essence, to "be one" with the river. You need to know its currents and its moods, as it were. It is a very Zen way to tune into nature. Of course, as your skills increase, you will be able to brave any river.

Most states require rafting guides to know basic first aid and cardiopulmonary resuscitation (CPR). But not all schools offer this as part of their package, so the cost of any additional training is something you may have to factor into your educational budget.

People Skills

Another important thing to remember is that as a professional rafter, you will be dealing with the general public. This is not always an easy or pleasant task. You will need to have public speaking skills and an ability to communicate concisely and effectively. You will also have to cultivate patience and learn to keep your cool—not to mention resisting the occasional temptation to throw an obnoxious customer overboard.

A Typical Itinerary

Most rafting schools follow a similar program to indoctrinate and acclimate you to a career navigating the wild rivers. You will learn to navigate the different levels of intensity of whitewater rapids. River speeds are rated on a class scale, from Class I through Class VI. The Web site for California River Rafting (⌨ *www.california-river-rafting.com*) describes this standard rating system as follows:

- **Class I: Easy.** Waves are small; passages clear. No serious obstacles. Fun for everyone.
- **Class II: Medium.** Rapids of moderate difficulty with passages clear. Fun for everyone.
- **Class III: Difficult.** Waves are numerous, high, irregular; rocks; eddies; rapids with passages clear though narrow, requiring expertise in maneuvering. Challenging.
- **Class IV: Very difficult.** Long rapids; waves powerful and irregular; dangerous rocks, boiling eddies; powerful and precise maneuvering required. Thrill-seekers.
- **Class V: Extremely difficult.** Long and violent rapids following each other almost without interruption; riverbed extremely obstructed; big drops; violent current; very steep gradient. Experienced thrill-seekers.

You might as well forget about Class VI. It is considered unrunnable, even by seasoned professionals. With a professional guide, most amateurs can handle Class III, but they should not try it alone or with a group of inexperienced buddies.

Like any course of study, the instructor is likely to start off slow, taking you out on a relatively calm stretch of the river. Gradually you will be taken out into rougher waters. Make sure that you get plenty of hands-on experience. This is a job where a theoretical knowledge will only take you so far. The curriculum should also include safety tips and techniques and other essentials. There should be simulated trips, with staff members role-playing as customers and exposing you to the many situations you may encounter when you are piloting a raft on your own. Most courses offer about a week of intensive training and cost under $1,000, usually including meals and equipment.

The Outdoor Network (*www.outdoornetwork.com*) is another great resource for jobs under the sun and the stars. In addition to viewing jobs and learning about the latest news in the many outdoor industries, you can post your resume for employers to see.

Remember that being a rafting guide is seasonal work. It is probably not something you will be doing year round, unless you become a true journeyman who travels to other parts of the country and the world to ride the rapids. When it is winter in the United States, it is summertime in Australia and New Zealand, and there is a brisk whitewater rafting business down under. Or you might be interested in working for the rafting business full time and performing other duties during the off-season. Most rafting guides have other jobs in the off-season that represent a true cross-section of the American public—teachers, law enforcement officials, homemakers, and more.

Hit the Slopes

Like rafting guides, ski and snowboard instructors often work seasonally, though some manage to extend their work into year-round employment. It only snows for part of the year, but it is always snowing somewhere. And nowadays when it doesn't snow, they simply manufacture the fluffy white stuff.

Certification

Approximately 23,000 certified ski instructors, both full- and part-time workers, belong to the Professional Ski Instructors of America (PSIA). The PSIA, founded in 1961, has developed a standardized system for instruction known as the Official American Ski Technique, and they have created a certification of accredited instructors. The different certifications include Alpine, Nordic-track (or cross-country) skiing, Nordic downhill, and the newer addition of snowboarding. You can also get a special certification to teach children, known as the Junior Education Team (JETS).

PSIA is divided into nine geographic regions that conduct training courses. There are three levels of certification. Level III is considered full certification. This level could take years to achieve, but you can be a working ski instructor while striving for this goal. In fact, you don't need to get a certification from PSIA to get a job as a ski instructor, but in this highly competitive time, it is very helpful. As they say, it looks good on your resume.

In this day and age, ski instructors may also be needed to help with other aspects of ski-resort management. Do not bristle if you are asked to do other kinds of work during downtime. As in any seasonal business, you need to be prepared for slow seasons and accompanying layoffs.

The average ski instructor who takes and passes the Level III exam, which involves both a written test and extensive time on the slopes, has been working in the business for four to five years. Certification is based on more than just how well you can ski. You are tested not only on skiing ability but also on your technical knowledge and teaching ability. You have to have a facility for working with people, including children, and you need to able to convey your expertise in a way that the layperson can easily understand and imitate. You also need to be an authority on the slopes in your neck of the woods.

Beating Out the Competition

As mentioned earlier, you do not need a certification to become a ski instructor, but it is recommended. More and more people are seeking not only greener pastures, but whiter slopes as well. Many resorts now require their staff to have some kind of certification or at least to be working toward that goal while gathering on-the-job training. As in all jobs, there is no better teacher than hands-on experience. Hopefully, you will also find a mentor or two among the more veteran ski instructors, who will answer your questions and from whose experience and expertise you can benefit.

There is not a lot of stability or security in the working life of a ski instructor. Many factors, including the economy and the weather, determine the hiring practices of the major ski resorts. Once you have your foot in the door—meaning you have worked at a resort and done well—you will find it easier to return to that resort or find work at another.

Beside the lack of job security, another theme that recurs throughout this book bears repetition—the pay is not that great to start. But if you love what you are doing and the environment where you work, and if you gain satisfaction from passing on your skills to enthusiastic students, the positive effects on your quality of life and peace of mind can outweigh the lack of big bucks.

Private Lessons

One way to make a little extra dough is to establish a reputation as a top-notch instructor. Students will then seek you out for private lessons. "Privates," as they are called, are more prestigious and profitable than group lessons. If you become a good enough instructor that people will wait in line for an appointment with you, then you are at the top of your game in the industry. A little more in the way of financial rewards will come your way.

On the Patrol

If you like to ski and you have an interest on law enforcement, you might consider becoming a member of the National Ski Patrol (or NSP). These approximately 28,500 men and women are essentially the police force and emergency services for skiers and snowboarders in jeopardy. The NSP rescues people who find themselves in danger on the slopes, either by accident, avalanche, or any number of other crises that may arise. They have to have knowledge of first aid and combine a dedication to public service with a love of winter sports.

The NSP is the largest winter rescue organization. It provides education and assistance to other countries interested in establishing ski patrol organizations. Emergency services are of course a primary part of their mission, but they also promote safety through education in many topics important to those in the winter sports industry—search and rescue, avalanche control, mountaineering, ski lift evacuation, and more. The NSP also publishes *Ski Patrol* magazine.

Possible Positions

The categories of positions in the National Ski Patrol include the following:

- **Patroller:** Provides emergency care to skiers on the slopes. He or she patrols on skis or a snowboard and responds to emergencies.
- **Nordic patroller:** Same as a regular patrol, but his or her patrol beat is a cross-country ski area.
- **Auxiliary patroller:** Assists the patroller, but lacks the authority of a patroller. Skiing skills are not mandatory. People in this position also lead training sessions and other educational seminars.
- **Medical associate:** Doctor who volunteers to train patrollers and auxiliary patrollers.
- **Associate member:** A person who has joined the NSP and is in the process of taking courses with the intent of becoming any of the above.

Membership

Both volunteer and paid members of the National Ski Patrol are expected to be working or plan to seek work as a patroller, Nordic patroller, or auxiliary patroller. Members must complete credentialed courses and annual training and refresher courses to keep their skills sharpened at all them. In order to be a member, you must know cardiopulmonary resuscitation and basic life support (CPR-BLS).

When applying for a position, you will be asked to show what you can do on skis. If you pass the test, you become what is known as a patrol candidate. Next, you'll be subjected to more physical and written tests. If you pass, you will be officially invited to become a patroller. If your skiing is not yet up to NSP standards you can begin as an auxiliary.

Camp Counselors

Another way to make your living in the great outdoors is by working as a camp counselor. This is usually seasonal work, and many counselors are college students working in the summertime.

A great place to begin your search is the Web site *www.camp channel.com*. It includes a comprehensive listing of summer camps not only in the United States, but also around the world. Like other seasonal jobs, it is always sunny somewhere. If you really wanted to, you could probably travel to different camps in exotic locales over the course of a year.

Remember that for summer camp positions, you must apply early. Don't wait until the snow melts in April to look for a position. Many camps begin in early spring, so it would be wise to begin your inquiries during the winter.

A recent search on the *www.campchannel.com* job board listed openings in summer camps throughout the United States and even Europe. You can do a detailed search to narrow the results if you have a particular location in mind. It's also possible to post your resume on this site, a service they offer free of charge.

Applications

As with any job search, you need to be proactive in your approach and aggressive in your follow-up. Camps receive many applications, and you have to make yours stand out. The ability to schmooze is a prerequisite for any job interview these days.

References are always important in a job search, but this is especially true when you're applying for a position as camp counselor. You should include a minimum of three references, all with current contact information. Ideally, one or more of the references will have seen you interact with young children and/or teenagers. It is an unfortunate reality that people who will be working with kids need to be checked out thoroughly. Try not to take it personally if you feel like you are being interrogated. The safety of children is of prime importance, and camp staffers and the parents who send their kids to camp deserve to know that the counselors are of good character.

Necessary Skills

If you are a couch potato by nature, then the job of camp counselor is not for you. You have to be in pretty good shape and have the stamina to engage in a variety of physical activities, not to mention the ability and desire to keep up with a bunch of energetic children. You also have to be patient with the (sometimes rowdy) youngsters, and you need to have the ability to motivate those around you. If you are inclined toward the occasional dark mood, hide them well, because you have got to be always "on" when you are a counselor

Each camp has its own structure, but there is a basic organization structure that is usually followed:

- **Counselor:** Usually high school graduates. They are in charge of approximately ten to fifteen campers during a typical session.

- **Junior counselor:** Often high school students on summer vacation. He or she reports to the counselor and assists in daily activities.
- **Intern:** Has the responsibilities of a counselor and is also in training for additional responsibilities. This is not a paying position.
- **Volunteer:** Again, this position has all of the responsibilities and none of the financial benefits of being a counselor, but a volunteer's motives are altruistic and do not involve drawing a paycheck.
- **Support staff:** Every camp needs someone for office support and other clerical tasks. Though not particularly glamorous, these positions keep the camp running smoothly.

In Demand

Opportunities for recreation workers are increasing. This is one of the few careers in which the demand for workers has remained constant, despite the hot-and-cold economic climate. There will always be yuppies who want to unload their puppies for a few weeks every summer, and this means camp counselors will always have opportunities to commune with nature and enrich the lives of their charges.

Out to Sea

There are many aspects to the "great outdoors." People may immediately think of the mountains and the forests, but considering that 70 percent of the planet is covered with water, most of the great outdoors is on the world's oceans.

FACT

Herman Melville wrote that whenever it was a "damp, drizzly November" in the soul, many men looked to the sea. In this modern and mechanized era, a lot of people harbor a romantic notion of the age of the tall ships. This nostalgia and fanciful longing for a bygone era keeps the enrollment of sailing schools full and provides opportunities for those who would like to make their alternative career on the high seas.

If you have no commitments or attachments on land that would prevent you from being offshore for extended periods of time, going to sea is a great chance to get away from it all. This is not the Love Boat, however. You work hard when you are a seaman/woman, and you have to garner a little experience in advance of setting sail. The pay is not great—what else is new?—and you may have to volunteer at first. This is the classic Catch-22 common to so many alternative careers. No one will hire you without experience, but you need to work in the business in order to get experience. So what do you do? When in doubt—volunteer.

Sailing Instructor

One place to gain sailing skills is to become a sailing class instructor. Check out yacht clubs and other sailing clubs that offer classes in your area. If you are not currently living on either coast, that's all right. There are often sailing clubs on the shores of large lakes, though sailing on a placid lake is entirely different from navigating the open sea. If you are a resident of Death Valley, of course, you will have to travel or relocate if you want to take sailing courses.

Like a camp counselor, you will have to have patience dealing with the young ones, since after you learn what you need to know you may be coaching kids in the art and craft of seamanship. You also should not have claustrophobia since you will be in close quarters on a small craft for several days or more at a time.

Any port city is likely to have a sail training ship that you can volunteer to work on. You will not be doing anything glamorous or even seaworthy at first. You may have to be an errand boy (or girl) for the seasoned sailors. But if you work hard and demonstrate a willingness and facility to learn, you will gain their confidence and be given more responsibilities.

What Is a Z-Card?

You need to have a license to be a professional sailor. This license is officially known as a merchant mariner's document (MMD), usually called a Z-card. To obtain one, you must be a U.S. citizen and over eighteen years old. You can find the form to apply for your Z-card at the U.S. Coast Guard Web site, at *www.uscg.mil.*

If you are volunteering on a ship, you must accurately log your time. This recordkeeping is necessary because you need to earn "seatime" to get a license, which is sometimes called your "able seaman's papers." The time you accrue as a volunteer brings you closer to earning your sea legs, so to speak, and to becoming eligible for paying jobs at sea.

You do not need a Z-card to sail on smaller ships, but if you are going to sea on ships that weight over 100 tons, you will need one. Check out the coast guard's site to see the various licenses you may need and what you must do to get one.

Of course, it is an extremely good idea to acquire first aid and lifeguard certifications, both of which cover skills that are definitely necessary if you are going to sea. Your friendly neighborhood YMCA usually offers courses to get these certifications, as does the Red Cross.

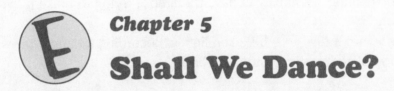

Chapter 5

Shall We Dance?

So you want to be a dancer? If you haven't been cutting the rug much lately, achieving this goal will be challenging, but it's not impossible. If you are realistic in your goals and driven by a desire to express yourself through movement, you can work in the dancing world no matter where you are right now in your career.

Dance Fever

Expressions made through body movement are as eloquent as any spoken language. Sometimes they are more so. There are many forms of dancing, from folk dance, to the old soft shoe, to the infamous Macarena. If you have never been shy about getting up at a social occasion to shake your groove thing, perhaps you have thought of trying to make a living as a dancer.

This is not a desire to be taken lightly. Becoming a dancer takes dedication, determination, and discipline.

FACT

The art of dance probably began in prehistoric times as part of spiritual rites and rituals. There is evidence that before humans could speak, they made music and danced. The predecessors of Britney Spears and Beyonce were most likely tribal shamans who whirled in a spiritual frenzy, seeking to cure an ill tribesman or make a little rain during the dry season.

Only you can ask yourself if you have what it takes. Do you have the determination and devotion, the perseverance and the discipline? Are you willing to put your body through a grueling workout every day for years? Do you have the grit to face the inevitable rejection that even the best must expect, especially in the beginning? The song "What I Did for Love" from *A Chorus Line* is a bittersweet study of what a dancer sacrifices for the love of the dance.

A Competitive World

We have all heard the saying, "There's a broken heart for every light on Broadway." Like most clichés, there is a deep truth hidden within the bromide. A career in dance is extremely competitive, more so than most other callings. The jobs are limited, and the applicants are legion. This is not meant to be a discouraging, but you really must be aware of the rules going in to the game. The gritty and realistic movie *Saturday Night Fever* was followed several years later by a thoroughly ridiculous sequel called

Staying Alive, in which John Travolta's character Tony Manero goes from dancing in a Brooklyn disco to starring in a Broadway show. It is a nice Hollywood fantasy, one that unfortunately does not happen very often in real life. There are notable exceptions to every rule, of course, and you could be one of them. Even if you are not, you can still practice your craft and be paid to do so. (Maybe not paid as much as Britney Spears, but you can make a living.)

If you want to learn more about a dancer's life, two great movies are *The Turning Point,* starring Shirley MacLaine, and Bob Fosse's autobiographical masterpiece, *All That Jazz.* They show the realities of what it takes to be a dancer, the former in the world of ballet and the latter on Broadway. Both movies do a good job of seeing past the glamour of a dancer's life and showing you the real deal.

Getting in Shape

When your body is your livelihood, you have to keep it in shape. As is true for any athlete, an injury for a dancer can stall or even end a career. Most dancers call it quits by their late thirties. Some go on to teaching, choreography, or something else altogether. Bob Fosse was one of the more successful to make such a transition. After moderate success as a working dancer, he realized that, gifted as he was, he lacked that elusive element called "star quality" that other men like Fred Astaire and Gene Kelly had in abundance. When Fosse turned to choreography and directing, his genius found full expression.

If you have been dancing for awhile, you have hopefully had eclectic training. If that's not the case, you must start now and work all the harder. It's daunting, but if you want it badly enough the sweat and muscle aches can be a joy. Unless you are driven to be a ballet dancer and that is the only form that interests you, it is good if those feet of yours can move to the rhythms of jazz, tap, folk, and other styles. This increases your chances of getting work. If you can carry a tune, you might also want to develop your singing voice. Not all dancers are singers, but if you can do both you will be more attractive to all kinds of productions, including opera, musical theater, commercials, and other opportunities.

Rehearsal, for hours a day, goes with the territory. You body is your instrument, and you must keep it finely tuned. Training never stops, no matter how successful you become. It would be ideal for a dancer to begin as a child, as young as five years old. Little girls are usually drawn to dance at an earlier age, especially those who early on show the sure sign of talent, while many boys have to be dragged to dance school.

Auditions

It is not uncommon for dancers who are older and more experienced to spend an eight-hour day in the studio and then venture out into the cruel world of auditions. Auditions are another training ground that will either strengthen a dancer's will or break the spirit entirely. It is in this crucible, upon leaving the classroom and entering the real world, that a dancer sees the extent of the competition. A dancer may have been the superstar of the local dance studio, only to meet the many other local superstars who have converged by train, plane, and automobile to seek fame and fortune in the theater. It is a humbling experience that sends many back home.

The Web site of the theatrical newspaper *Variety* (published in both weekly and daily editions) is ✑*www.variety.com*. You have to be a paying subscriber to make full use of what it offers, but two-week free trial subscriptions are available. It is so widely read and studied in this industry that it has earned the name "the show-business Bible." It is worth your while to study it chapter and verse.

It is not necessary to have a college degree in dance, but a degree can be helpful. In college, a dancer will learn about the history and theory of dance in addition to skill in actual dancing. There is nothing like doing, however, and dancing in school is a good opportunity to perform, both in the classroom and in front of an audience. You may also want to consider dance school if you have any interest in teaching dance. Many successful dancers turn to teaching when their professional careers wind down, as do others who did not have the career that they hoped they would. It is not mandatory to have a college degree in dance to open and run a private dance school or conservatory. Life experience in the school of hard knocks is all you need for that.

Where the Jobs Are

Like most jobs in the entertainment business, you will most likely have to trek to either coast—specifically, to New York or Los Angeles—to make it in the big time. There are also dance companies and ballet troupes in every major city. Many dance companies tour for at least part of the year, so you must be prepared to spend a lot of time on the road. This is one of the reasons that professional dancers often call themselves gypsies. They must travel a lot, their jobs are fleeting, and their lives don't have a whole lot of stability.

Other venues where work can be found include television, music videos, nightclubs, theme parks, dinner theaters, opera companies, and cruise ships. Many dancers who began by studying ballet end up working in these situations, but they are probably not complaining. As working dancers, they are in the minority and happy to be doing what they love.

How Hungry Are You?

Okay, we have suggested that it is difficult, but we do not want to convey that it is impossible. If you did not study dance from the time you learned to walk, and you are considering giving it a shot as an alternative career, the path is not without bumps and roadblocks. At the same time, it is certainly navigable.

Fitness

As described earlier, there are some things that are written in stone about dancing. You just have to be physically fit. Dancing is a strenuous workout, and if you are lucky enough to be a working dancer you will be doing it every day. So first things first—get in shape. If you are in pretty good shape, get in better shape. Go to the gym, swim, or cycle. Build up your stamina and endurance. Watch *Flashdance*. Break out the leg warmers, pop "Maniac" into the CD player, and gyrate into a sweaty frenzy. There is no way around this requirement.

Back to School

You will need to take lessons to learn the different styles of dance. Although we have stressed that the big time is Broadway and Hollywood, there are dancing schools everywhere and working dancers in every corner of the country. You have to get the basic technical skills, and the only way to do this is to take lessons from a professional. The philosophy you must adopt is that the dancing is its own reward. Dance is what you do because you love it and because the hunger burns deep in your spirit. Professionals say that you must be in training for two years before you can call yourself a professional dancer. After that, you can expect that the training, practicing, and studying will never stop.

ALERT!

Despite the realities of the dancer's life, which certainly appear daunting, it is not out of your reach if you have the will. Nevertheless, there are still realities with which to contend. If you are starting in your thirties, you may never dance for a major ballet company. At the same time, you can still dance for a living. There are opportunities on cruise ships and at resorts for entertainers of all kinds, including dancers.

Teaching Dance

Another opportunity for the late bloomer is to become a dance teacher. There are academic programs in most liberal arts college that offer a master of fine arts (MFA) degree in dance. If you want to teach in an academic setting, you are going to have to get teaching credentials as well. The rules vary state by state, so you will need to check with your local board of education to see what you need to do to become a dance teacher at a high school or college.

Schools for Teachers

There are also hundreds of private dance studios across the country that, in addition to offering dance classes for amateurs, also have training programs and certifications for dancing instructors. It appears that there are almost as many types of certifications as there are dancing schools. There is no licensing requirement to become a dance instructor as there is for other careers, like plumbers and electricians. The many certifications out there are all optional. If you are serious about being a dance instructor, then you will need to have something to hang on the wall of your studio for potential clients to see. People are swayed by official documents like diplomas and degrees, and it is simply good business sense to become certified in one or more styles of dance. This will increase your confidence and prove that you are worth the fee you are asking from prospective students.

No state or local government agency requires that you have certification. The fact is that going through a training program will make you a better dancer and give you the tools to teach. Having the skill is one thing, but the ability to effectively convey your knowledge and expertise to others in another skill altogether. Not everyone can do that. In baseball, for example, an all-star player might become manager but not be successful. Sometimes a second-tier player becomes a manager and enjoys great success.

Types of Certification

Choose a certification in a style of dance that appeals to you. Ballroom dancing is perennially popular. The tango is in vogue. Latin, swing, and jazz dancing are other options. You can even become a certified belly dancer. Your best bet is to find a dancing school with a good reputation that teaches many modes of dance. A certificate from a reputable school will help you find work and make you a credible commodity as an instructor.

The following list includes certifications and resources for you to explore if you want to learn more about certification in dance teaching. This is a good starting place to find the right certification for you.

- **United States Imperial Society of Teachers of Dance** (✎ *www.usistd.org*): Both written and practical examinations are required before certification is granted.
- **Arthur Murray** (✎ *www.arthurmurray.com*): You have to be an employee and work for one of the Arthur Murray franchises to receive their certification.
- **Dance Vision** (✎ *www.dancevision.com*): Dance Vision offers practical and written examination–based certifications in international- and American-style ballroom dancing.
- **Fred Astaire** (✎ *www.fredastaire.com*): You have to be an employee and work for one of the Fred Astaire franchises to receive their certification.
- **National Dance Teachers Association** (✎ *www.nationaldanceteachers.org*): Members must have one year of dance instruction experience and pass a written exam.
- **National Dance Council of America** (✎ *www.ndca.org*): This coalition of dance organizations recognizes certifications from all areas of dance.

Walk on the Wild Side

There are many ways to work as a dancer. Some are highbrow, like the life of a prima ballerina, some as less exalted but nevertheless valid and noble livelihoods. If you are a tall woman with a more robust physique than some of the dancers you see on the so-called legitimate stage, perhaps you might look into auditioning to become a Las Vegas showgirl.

Showgirl Life

First of all, like all jobs in the entertainment industry, being a showgirl is not as glamorous as it sounds. Certainly the costumes that showgirls wear are glamorous, and they may cavort on stage with big stars in lavish production numbers, but the work itself is quite demanding. The typical showgirl is up at around 11 A.M., and they usually attend a two-hour dance class in the afternoon. They arrive at the theater at approximately 7 P.M. and dance the night away until the wee small hours of the morning. The career of the average showgirl is over by the time they are forty, and many go find work as dance instructors and teachers. Others fall back on the career they had before dancing, and many more are married with children.

Politically incorrect as it sounds, showgirls are considered to be artwork or human sculpture by the producers and impresarios who run Las Vegas spectacles. The dancing is not fast and furious. They parade across the stage in production numbers and as background ornamentation for the stars, while wearing costumes that sometimes weigh as much as fifty pounds, often with enormous headdresses and three-inch heels. Showgirls back in the day used to call themselves the pack horses of the dancing world.

Many uninformed tourists incorrectly assume that, as prostitution is legal in the state of Nevada, showgirls are part of a similar industry. Not true—being a showgirl is as legitimate as being a member of the Ballet Russe. And more people see a showgirl perform in the course of a year than attend the Russian ballet.

Not Interested in Vegas?

A woman interested in being a showgirl need not limit herself to Las Vegas. There are many other venues across the country, in places like Atlantic City, New Jersey, and other cities and towns, where there are casino and entertainment complexes. As more and more Native American tribes take advantage of the federal regulations that allow them to open casinos on tribal territories, even in states where gambling is illegal, there will be more and more splashy, glitzy pleasure palaces where a woman can find work as a showgirl. There are also nightly performances on cruise ships and at resorts. The procedure for finding this kind of work is the same as that described in the section for actors in Chapter 6. Read *Variety* and *Backstage*. Create a portfolio/resume, try to find a talent agent, and make the rounds at open casting calls.

Chippendales

Let's not forget the men. There is an opportunity for guys who want to dance but have not made it to Broadway. Have you ever wanted to be adored by a frenzied throng of women? Then you might want to trying out to be a Chippendales dancer. There are many touring companies of these few good men. They traverse the continent, bringing joy to thousands of delighted ladies.

There are some requirements. They are not overtly stated but they are implicit. Anyone will understand who recalls the *Saturday Night Live* skit in which the rotund Chris Farley performed as a Chippendale alongside the buff Patrick Swayze. Chippendales dancers must have a certain look, and it is not the Chris Farley physique. For information on how you can become a Chippendales dancer, you can visit their Web site at ✑ *www.chippendales.com.* Ⓔ

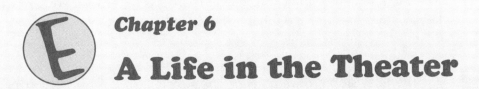

Chapter 6

A Life in the Theater

Every actor would like to make it right away in Hollywood or on Broadway, where they would then earn the chance to deliver their long-rehearsed Oscar or Tony acceptance speech. Alas, that is not always to be. However, you can still find many opportunities for making a living in "the biz."

An Actor's Life

This is meant to be an encouraging book, but it won't help anyone if we use this space to paint an unrealistic picture of the way the world works. The bottom line is that it is very hard to make a living as a working actor. It is difficult, but—and this must be emphasized—it is not impossible to make a decent living (and maybe more) as an actor if you are willing to pay your dues and do what it takes.

The television program *Inside the Actor's Studio*—taped at the fabled acting school that spawned Brando, De Niro, and other giants—gives you an insider's look at what it takes to be a working actor. The story is told in person, by the actors James Lipton interviews before an audience of acting students.

"Whatever it takes" may include many things the serious actor may find demeaning. Check your ego at the door. F. Murray Abraham, the Oscar-winning actor (for *Amadeus*) was once one of the fruits in a Fruit of the Loom underwear commercial. The dedicated actor does not sniff at any assignment in his or her salad days. Anything and everything is good experience, whether you are playing Hamlet in a local theater or Foghorn Leghorn at a Warner Brothers theme park. Though there are theaters and schools all over the country, most people who have the acting bug head for New York or Los Angeles where most of the stage, film, and television work is concentrated.

Many actors worked "straight jobs" for years before being able to work in the business full-time. Comic actor Bob Newhart was an accountant; quirky character actor Steve Buscemi was a New York City fireman.

The Educated Actor

You do not have to go to acting school in order to become a working actor, but it cannot hurt. If you are a full-time student, consider finding a school where you can major in drama; if you are so inclined, you might want to achieve a master of fine arts (M.F.A. degree). Many have gone that route (such as Meryl Streep, a graduate of the Yale School of Drama). On the other hand, however, some of the biggest stars basically stumbled into acting as a profession. In a school setting, you will be exposed to different acting styles and be mentored by professors who have had experience in the theater. You will learn about all avenues of acting. Performing on the stage is an entirely different style than acting in front of a camera for movies and television. In school, you will have the opportunity to study voice and movement, character development, directing, and writing.

FACT

The Herbert Berghof Studio (at Web site ✍ *www.hbstudio.org*) is a famous New York City acting school. Many famous names have passed through the Herbert Berghof Studio and taught there over the decades. Its eclectic curriculum gives drama students a well-rounded foundation in everything from drama to voice lessons to improvisational comedy.

You can decide if you want to take individual courses or a full curriculum of study. If you are a working stiff, investigate a school that offers the occasional course. If you have the time and money on your hands, you might want to go to school full-time.

Audition after Audition

Regardless of whether you attend a school or not, you will have to go on auditions. As we learned in Chapter 5 from our discussion of dancing as a career, auditions can be discouraging and humiliating experiences. When you are turned down for a part, it will not always be in a gentle manner. We have all seen the scenes of a nervous actor or actress taking the stage while shadowy figures in the audience (the director and/or producer) ask a few curt questions, only to deliver an even more abrupt "Thank you!" or "Next!" before the performer has gotten very far into their audition material.

Physical Considerations

Whether you are in school or pounding the pavement, there are things an actor, aspiring or otherwise, must do. Stage acting every night is a workout, both physically and vocally. Exercise of the body and the vocal cords is essential. You never know what the demands of a role might be. Usually a part will require full use of your body and voice, so they have to be kept in optimum condition. You should have some regimen of exercise. Chart one out, and stick with it. Remember, the role of Hamlet has thousands of lines that force the actor to convey a wide range of emotions. This is draining enough, but an actor portraying him also has to end the evening with a vigorous swordfight. You don't want to be an out-of-breath Hamlet, unless your interpretation calls for the melancholy Dane to have a stress-induced asthma condition.

FACT

According to legend, the first actor was a fellow named Thespis who began doing impersonations of other people in Athens, Greece, circa 560 B.C. It is from this ancient version of Rich Little that we get the word "thespian," the highbrow term that simply means "actor." By the way, it's a good idea to beware of actors who call themselves thespians. They tend to be even more full of themselves than the garden-variety ham.

Other Acting Venues

You do not have to work in movies, television, or theater to be a working actor. There is plenty of other work available, including radio voice-over and commercial work, jobs in theme parks, independent films, and many other vehicles for practicing the craft of acting. Commercial work pays very well, and it is difficult for the habitually out-of-work actor to resist the temptation to do them. (Actors who are more successful demand—and receive—a lot of money for commercials, in part because they know it may hurt them professionally.) Sometimes an actor can become a cult figure through advertising. An actor who played the part of the villain on the series finale of the show *Little House on the Prairie* also made a nice living doing commercials for a supermarket chain called Pathmark. His appearance prompted angry calls and letters to the Pathmark corporate office. People were outraged that the company could have such a terrible person as their spokesman.

Working with an Agent

It is very rare for a fledgling actor to make it without hooking up with an agent. It's the agent's job to set the actor up with possible roles, look out for the actor's interests in contract negotiations, and otherwise represent them. Working without an agent is possible but not recommended in New York, and it is basically impossible in Los Angeles. It is easier to represent yourself in most other cities—what is condescendingly called "flyover country" by the elitists on either coast. The reality, however, is that there is a "big time," like it or not, and it's in New York and Los Angeles.

What Agents Can Do for You

In New York you can go on auditions and even begin working without having an agent or joining the union, but you will be obliged to do the latter eventually. Casting directors and agents attend lots of off- and off-off-Broadway plays. As a result, if you have the right stuff, you may experience the thrill of having an agent approach you. The greater likelihood is that you will have to seek one out. You will need an agent right away if you want to work in commercials and industrial films on either coast.

In addition to being necessary, finding an agent is also advisable. Do you think you will be able to decipher the legalese of contracts and negotiate the best deals with savvy and heartless producers? Probably not. It is best to have a businessperson handle the business end of the performing arts business. You may bristle at having to pay the agent's fee, but the deal you get is likely to be better than anything you could get on your own. Having an agent you can trust also frees you from excess worry and enables you to concentrate on your art.

Types of Agents

There are several specialties among agents. Here are the types of agents and the performers that they represent:

- **Commercial agents:** Television commercials
- **Theatrical agents:** Movies and television
- **Legitimate agents:** The theater
- **Voice-over agents:** Radio and other off-camera work
- **Modeling agents:** Models in all media
- **Variety agents:** Nightclub and personal appearance work
- **Full-service agents:** A little bit of everything

The Internet edition of the trade journal *Backstage* can be found at ✍ *www.backstage.com*. Like *Variety* and ✍ *www.variety.com*, it is required reading for anyone pursuing a career in the theater. Also like the *Variety* site, ✍ *www.backstage.com*, it is not free. A monthly online subscription costs $9.95, which is well worth it if you are serious about making a living as a performer.

Unless you are determined to follow one single path in the performing arts, your best bet is to try to get a full-service agent. If you are working in Los Angeles, you are only allowed to sign up with one agent per category. In New York, you can register with as many agents in as many categories as you want.

There are also franchised and unfranchised agents. A franchised agent is licensed to represent union actors. You will get more opportunities and better pay through a franchised agent. There is plenty of nonunion theater out there, but it is frowned upon. To professionally advance, you will need to become a union member at some point.

Getting an Agent

You need to be prepared when approaching an agent or casting director. The fact that you may have been the star of every high school and college production you participated in will not matter much in the real world. The best bet is to get as much working experience as possible under your belt before you begin your hunt.

Research the agents in your area. This can be done on the always-helpful Internet and through trade journals like *Daily Variety* and *Backstage*. You can also check out the Web sites of the main performing arts unions that will be discussed a little later. Another resource for finding agents in NY and LA is the publication *Ross Reports*. This is not as well known outside the industry as the above periodicals, but this monthly publication is worth subscribing to if your acting career is more than a mere dalliance.

Presenting Yourself

You need to get some professional photos taken. These are known as head shots. Your future agent will need these to send to casting directors and producers who are looking for a certain type. Head shots should be taken by a professional photographer in a studio, not by your friend with a Polaroid or digital camera. If you take several "looks," you should put them all together in one composite photograph. The more streamlined the photo/resume, the better. You should basically look as you currently do in the head shots. If they are old, and you have had a makeover, then you need to get new ones.

Finding a Photographer

You will find lots of photographers listed in the yellow pages and the trade papers. If you have been doing this for awhile, you probably know a few actors from cooling your heels in waiting rooms at auditions. You can ask some of your fellow actors whose head shots you admire for the name of the photographer who took their pictures. If they are professionally courteous and not too competitive, they will gladly refer you to their photographer. The local unions will also have lists of reputable photographers.

It is going to cost you a few hundred dollars to get a set of quality head shots, so doing the research is well worth it. You do not want to get stuck with an inferior product. Look at the photographer's portfolio, and talk about the type of look you want to convey. Find out what all the costs will be before you settle the deal. You should get one set of 8 x 10s and another of 5 x 7s.

Your Resume

You must compose a good-looking professional resume. A theatrical resume is similar to any other resume you would send out seeking employment. It lists your training and experience. It should be brief yet informative. Keep it to one page only. Put your talents at the top of the page along with any union affiliations. Unlike a resume for an office job, you should include your physical attributes: height, weight, hair and eye color, and measurements. You need not mention your age.

Do not lie about your credits. They can be easily verified. If you are new to the business, include any drama schools or courses you attended and school and amateur productions in which you appeared. These are usually listed in this order—show title, character you played, director (if he or she has any name recognition), and the name of the theatrical company if it is well known.

You should prepare your resume on a computer so you can easily finesse and tweak it according to the acting job. You will want to highlight certain aspects of your resume if you are interested in a singing part and mention your singing ability lower on the page if you are auditioning for *Macbeth.*

At the bottom of the page, list any other skills that may be applicable. Proficiency in a particular computer application need not be mentioned, but experience in something physical—like fencing or horseback riding—is worth noting. You never know what other parts the casting director may be looking for on his list of upcoming roles.

Prepare a resume for stage performances and one for films. Continually update your resume. As your experience grows, delete your older amateur experience in favor of more current roles. Always keep the resume to one page, even if it requires little tricks like reducing the font size and widening the margins. Include a specific cover letter for each individual situation. Keep it short, no more than a few paragraphs on one page. Make it ingratiating but not obsequious. Stress your qualifications without being too boastful.

Audition Material

You have to have audition material prepared and ready to be performed. You might have to bring a buddy along if it is a two-character scene and not a monologue. When you audition for a part, the producer and casting director will want to see what you can do. So will an agent. You may have to demonstrate your thespian skills to the agent.

You can find a number of anthologies of theatrical monologues in your local bookstore. Specific collections are published for men, women, and kids, as well as some that are just drama or comedy or Shakespeare.

Generally, it is a good idea to be ready to perform something dramatic, something comic, and maybe something from Shakespeare. If you are a singer, be able to belt out a several tunes from memory. Make them popular standards so an accompanying pianist will know them, or buy the sheet music to bring with you to auditions.

Pick monologues that highlight your strengths and that are delivered by characters that resonate with you and that you would love to play one day. Try not to pick parts that are very common or too obscure. The agent or casting director should be familiar with the play, but it will not help if it is something they hear dozens of times each week. Women may want to avoid the Blanche DuBois "kindness of strangers" monologue from *A Streetcar Named Desire,* and men should pass on the "roast beef sandwich" rant from David Mamet's *American Buffalo.* And, of course, pick something other than "To be or not to be" from *Hamlet* as your Shakespeare monologue.

Who Can You Trust?

Be careful: There are many unscrupulous predators who exploit other people's dreams for their own financial gain. Plenty of shady and dishonest agents—or people who *claim* to be agents—take advantage of naïve and ambitious performers.

As mentioned above, if you are able to get a franchised agent, you will avoid the possibility of encountering one of these con artists. You can get a list of franchised agents from the actors' unions, detailed on page 77. Certain things that you should be wary of may seem like no-brainers. Nevertheless, people have fallen for these scams in the past. Most just lost some money, but others have lost a lot more.

Do not agree to meet an agent in any suspicious location, such as a motel room. A reputable agent has an office. Do not tolerate any inappropriate personal questions or someone who wants to "inspect the merchandise" under the pretense that they want to see if you are physically fit. Many people, mostly young women, have been molested and assaulted by criminals masquerading as talent scouts.

ALERT!

Never let yourself be pressured to sign on the dotted line without taking the document home to read closely or to show to people whose opinion you trust. Until you establish a relationship of trust with your agent, it is not a bad idea to have an entertainment lawyer look over your potential contracts.

Never work with an agent who asks for money up front. An agent is paid a percentage of what you make from acting jobs. In the standup comedy world, it is common for an agent to get your bookings for a fee or with the proviso that you fill the venue with friends who will pay a cover and two-drink minimum. The agents are getting a kickback from the clubs that run the comedy nights. If you catch a whiff of anything similar from an agent you are meeting with, do not work with them.

Keep Private Info Private

Given the number of unsavory opportunists out there, it is advisable not to circulate a resume that includes your personal contact information. It is a good idea to use a pager or an answering service as your contact number and a post office box if you have one. At the risk of sounding like a sexist, this is especially advisable for young women. There really are some bad guys out there who will try to take advantage of women with their false promises of auditions and acting jobs.

Be Persistent

If you do not hear back from the agents you have contacted, do not give up. Try and try again. If you are calling them on the phone, call every four to six weeks. If you are sending out mass mailings, send a follow-up mailing as a reminder. Don't resend the same package. Instead, drop a line by means of a postcard-size photo and short note reminding the agent that he or she should have your more complete data on file. Agents are very busy people and will take their time getting back to you.

Do not just sit there and wait for people to return your calls. Be proactive. Find out the names of casting directors, and call them directly. Go on as many open auditions and casting calls as you can. The trade journals list these auditions. Independent films are often in production in big cities. While nonunion work is frowned upon, if you are a newbie without a union or an agent you should take the work you can get. It will not be held against you when you later join a union. (It is only a problem if you do nonunion work as a union member.) Local film schools are always shooting something. Contact them, and see if they are looking for performers. You are not going to get paid for your efforts, but every little bit will help fill out your resume.

Joining the Unions

No matter what your feeling is about unions, to have a successful career as an actor you need to belong to one or both of two unions: the Screen Actor's Guild (SAG) and Actor's Equity. As the name suggests, SAG is for those in the movie business, while Actor's Equity is primarily for stage and television performers. Another union, the American Federation of Television and Radio Artists (AFTRA) is, as of this writing, in talks to merge with SAG and become a larger and more powerful union.

The Screen Actor's Guild

SAG was founded in Hollywood in 1933 to protect the rights of actors working in the movies. You may think that movie people back then lived the proverbial life of Riley, but their lot was not so shiny in the so-called Golden Age. Just as in any business then or now, those men in suits tried to give the working stiffs the business. The actors fought back to secure certain rights like reasonable work hours and a minimum wage, called "scale" in Hollywood lingo.

The minimum wage in SAG is certainly a little better than the kids working behind the counter earn at the local McDonald's. Currently, movie and television actors with speaking parts are paid $636 a day or $2,206 a week. They also have health benefits and a pension plan, and they receive what are called "residuals." This is payment for reruns. If you are on a hit show that goes into syndication, you can do quite nicely with residual payments.

If you begin to work on a mainstream movie, you will have the opportunity to join SAG. Their Web site (✍ *www.sag.org*) says, "Performers may join SAG upon proof of employment or prospective employment within two weeks or less by a SAG signatory company. Employment must be in a principal or speaking role in a SAG film, videotape, television program or commercial." Membership in SAG does not guarantee you work. But if you put in the legwork and never give in to despair, some dreams do come true.

Paying Your Dues

Joining SAG is not cheap. As of this writing, actors must pay an initiation fee of $1,310, plus annual dues of $100. In addition, members pay percentage dues of 1.85 percent of all earnings under SAG contracts up through $200,000, and 0.5 percent on earnings from $200,001 through

$500,000. This may seem a little steep when you consider that 80 percent of SAG members make less than $5,000 a year from acting jobs, and fewer than 5 percent of members earn more than $35,000 a year. This places the likes of Jack Nicholson and Harrison Ford in the extreme minority of SAG wage earners.

Actor's Equity

Actor's Equity (✑ *www.actorsequity.org*) is the union for stage actors and stage managers. Founded in 1913, its more than 400,000 members are entitled to minimum salaries, pension and health benefits, and guaranteed safe working conditions.

Like SAG, you are eligible to join if you have been hired for an acting job. In fact, you are more or less required to join. The initiation fee is also high—$1,100—but you have two years to pay it in full.

The minimum weekly salary for actors in Broadway productions is currently $1,252. Off-Broadway performers get a minimum wage of $440 to $551 a week. Regional theaters across the country are obliged to pay their actors $500 to $728 per week. The union for dancers in opera, ballet, and other dance troupes is the American Guild of Musical Artists, Inc., while dancers in musical theater also join Actor's Equity.

Community theaters are a great way to get started in acting and to have a lot of fun at the same time. For a list of local community theaters, check out the community theatre listing at ✑*http://dmoz.org*.

Acting Around the Country

What if you are not able or willing to head for the big city and face the fierce competition to follow your acting dreams? Though we have mostly been talking about what it takes to make it in the big time, there are many working actors making a living wage, following their bliss, and finding creative satisfaction in areas outside of New York and Los Angeles. There are thousands of local theaters across the country. They perform everything from the classics to new works by unknown writers to old Broadway shows. Local theaters are sometimes made up of volunteers and others hire actors.

Snooty people may sniff at the tradition of dinner theater, but these venues employ thousands of actors and musicians. There are dinner theaters all over the country. For a fixed price, patrons can have a nice meal and see a play. These performances are chosen for universal appeal and high entertainment value and are usually musicals or comedies. It is unlikely, for example, that Eugene O'Neill's brilliant but downbeat and very lengthy *The Iceman Cometh* would be performed at a dinner theater in Akron.

Dinner theater is a great opportunity for fledgling actors to get experience, and it is also a last refuge for many a star whose career is on the decline. Many people who are on television today will be doing dinner theater later in life, just as the actors you grew up watching on the tube are currently toiling in the circuit. A couple of years ago, Cindy Williams and Eddie Mekka ("the Big Ragu") of *Laverne and Shirley* appeared in a Tennessee dinner theater in the musical *Grease*. They were not playing the romantic leads, but the principal and the gym teacher. (You know you're getting old when . . .)

The same rules apply for local community theater and for dinner theater. You have to go on auditions, and it is better to have an agent. Community theater tends to recruit from the neighborhood, while dinner theaters bring in actors from all over. Though still competitive, they tend to be much less cutthroat than New York or Los Angeles.

Another popular form of theater way off Broadway is the interactive play. A popular play called *Tony and Tina's Wedding* recruits audience members to act as guests at a wacky wedding reception. Another popular format is the interactive murder mystery theater, in which the audience interacts with the performers and helps solve a mystery. There are also plenty of theatrically themed summer camps, where professional actors work with kids to put on a show.

With perseverance and drive, you can find work as an actor. It may not be on the Broadway stage or on the silver screen, but it can nevertheless be a source of satisfaction and a fulfillment of a lifelong dream. Ⓔ

Chapter 7

Writing for Fun and Profit

The human desire to tell a story in our own words existed long before the invention of pen and paper. Humanity's penchant for storytelling goes back to the mists of prehistoric times. For many it is merely a rewarding leisure pursuit, but plenty of people have transformed their literary proclivities into full-time careers. This chapter offers advice on how to turn your avocation into a paying gig.

The Writing Life

You have no doubt heard many a friend and acquaintance say, "I could write a book," or "I've got a great idea for a movie." How many of them actually come to you a few months later with a novel or screenplay? Very few, if any. You have to jump through a lot of hoops and navigate a difficult obstacle course if you wish to live the writing life. Many of the barriers and discouragements come from external forces (such as editors or agents) when you have a completed project—on disk and hard copy—that you are attempting to sell. However, your toughest opponent will usually begin to fight with you before you even get started. This is, of course, the enemy within—your own counterproductive impulses. The writing life involves wrestling all manners of demons.

FACT

To improve your writing and advance your career, it is generally believed that every day, you should spend a minimum of four hours writing. Despite your many other obligations, you really must make this effort. You may end discarding much of your writing and saving only a small percentage, but, like an exercise program, you must work out every day to achieve the desired results.

Have You Got the Write Stuff?

The above is a lame and overused pun to be sure, definitely something to avoid in your own writing, but it remains a valid question to ask yourself. It takes a great deal of self-discipline to be a writer. Even if your ambitions are to write a bodice-ripper or science fiction novel that, on the surface, does not seem derived from your life experiences or hit especially close to home, writing is a deeply personal activity. Ernest Hemingway offered the typically curt credo, "Write the truest sentence you know." This applies to everything from investigative journalism to a poem. The writer must strive to, as the philosophers teach, "Know thyself."

Another element required is the ability to start a regimen and stick with it. If you are serious about living the writing life you should write every day without fail. Like a gymnast, you must put your writing skills through their paces lest they atrophy.

Thicken Thy Skin

Another thing a writer must develop is the proverbial "thick skin." Whether pitching a magazine article or your "great American novel" to an editor or agent, you are immediately faced with potential conflict—you think you have created a fine piece of writing, and those you submit it to do not. Editors and agents receive so many manuscripts, articles, and queries that some may not even get back to you at all. Those who are not interested will most likely send a form letter. You must not despair but instead just keep plugging away. If you are ready to take an internal journey and bare your soul for the world to see, you have taken the first step into the writing life.

Start the Presses: Working in Journalism

Have you wanted to be a reporter, mild-mannered or otherwise, for a major metropolitan newspaper ever since you first read a Superman comic book? The life of the journalist has had a romantic aura for decades, perpetuated by movies, television, and the more flamboyant practitioners of the profession.

But—and you knew this was coming—the life of a journalist is also one of high pressure and hard work. At the same time, journalism has its rewards. Before you start working on your first Pulitzer Prize, however, there are, as there always are, some basics that must be addressed.

Brush Up Your English

If you are a student (and even if you are not), it would behoove you to master the elements of English grammar and composition. Do not rely on your word processor's spell checker. It has the capacity to suggest some pretty bizarre options when you run it on a document. It is best to acquaint yourself with that golden oldie, Strunk and White's *The Elements of Style*. Eventually, you will have to familiarize with yourself with some of the other style manuals out there. Different journalistic entities use different style manuals. Some of the more commonly used include the following:

- *The Chicago Manual of Style*
- *Oxford Fowler's Modern English Usage Dictionary*
- *Words into Type*
- *The MLA Style Manual*
- *The Associated Press Stylebook and Briefing on Media Law*
- *Merriam-Webster's Manual for Writers and Editors*
- *The Microsoft Manual of Style for Technical Publications*
- *American Heritage Dictionary*

If you are a student, you should definitely be on the school paper or the college radio station if your school has one. If you are out of school, you might consider submitting articles to your local or community newspapers. You might be doing this for nothing for a while, but you'll be gaining experience, making connections, and padding your portfolio. You will definitely also need computer skills and a familiarity with the Internet. It is also good to be a "people watcher" and an excellent listener. A true reporter is also a student of human nature.

ALERT!

The Web site *www.journalismjobs.com* is an invaluable resource for aspiring and working journalists. It contains news, resources, and job listings for freelance and full-time positions at newspapers, magazines, and television and radio stations.

Internships

If you are able to work for nothing for a little while, an internship is a valuable entry point into the journalism milieu. As an intern, you will most likely be exposed to all aspects of the business, even if it means being a gofer for the hotshot reporter or the local Ted Baxter (of *Mary Tyler Moore* fame) if you intern at a television or radio station. Whatever you are doing as an intern, you are gaining experience that will look good on your resume and serve you well in your job search. You'll also make valuable contacts and perhaps find a mentor who will take a liking to you and help you at some point down the line.

By doing a little bit of everything, you can decide what you're most interested in. You might be better off interning at a small station or newspaper; there, you will be more in demand and have more to do. However, if you sense that you are being used as a beast of burden without getting the chance to learn anything that will help your career, do not stand for it. Move on.

Professional Associations

There are many professional associations for journalists and broadcasters. You can learn more about the business, make valuable contacts, attend conferences and seminars, and network with men and women who are making a living as journalists. Some of the professional associations include the following:

Society of Professional Journalists
3909 N. Meridian Street
Indianapolis, IN 46208
317-920-4789
www.spj.org

Society for Technical Communication
901 N. Stuart Street, Suite 904
Arlington, VA 22203-1854
703-522-4114
www.stc.org

National Association of Broadcasters
1771 N Street NW
Washington, DC 20036
202-429-5300
www.nab.org

Association of American Publishers
71 Fifth Avenue, 2nd Floor
New York, NY 10003-3004
212-255-0200
www.publishers.org

American Academy of Advertising
http://advertising.utexas.edu/AAA

Public Relations Society of America
www.prsa.org

Radio and Television Correspondents Association
U.S. Capitol, Room S-325
Washington, DC 20510
202-224-6421
www.senate.gov/galleries/radiotv

Always on the Job

In 1983, a college student majoring in journalism was interning at a local, family-run weekly newspaper in the Bronx, New York. At 5 P.M. on a Friday, a hot-air balloon landed in the park across the street, certainly an unusual and newsworthy occurrence in the Bronx. The youth was stunned to see the rest of the staff leaving the office and the owner/publisher locking the door. He asked if anyone was going to cover the story and the owner pointed to the sign on the front door: "Business Hours—Monday to Friday, 9 to 5."

Novelists, Inc. (at *www.ninc.com*) maintains a reference site devoted to keeping its members "connected, communicating, and well informed while striving to better the status of fiction writers." It is a membership site, so check out the free preview before you decide to join.

The above story is no tall tale, and rest assured: It is the exception. If you are fortunate to get an entry-level position in journalism, you may find it an extension of an internship, except that you get paid. But your pay won't be much, sad to say. In all the so-called "glamour industries," entry-level salaries are absurdly low. The reason is simple—people are clamoring to get their feet in the door. If you wither under pressure or have a nine-to-five mentality, then the journalism game is not for you. The pressure to meet deadlines can be nerve wracking, and as Citizen Charles Foster Kane said, the news goes on twenty-four hours a day. Expect to work long hours, to sometimes pull all-nighters, and to work weekends if necessary.

The Art of the Novel

The novel is one of the most flexible forms of written expression. It does not have to be formatted like a play or script and does not need actors to give it voice. Like the story and the poem, it is as long or short or straightforward or experimental as you want it to be. An added plus is that you do not have to deal with collaborators or tinkerers. It is all yours. Until, of course, you plan to unveil it to the world and garner all the accolades you are certain it will receive. It is at this point that the fun stops and the stress of getting it ready for anyone to read begins.

What to Write?

Hardboiled mystery writer Mickey Spillane, when asked why he churned out tough-guy yarns featuring the gumshoe Mike Hammer, responded, "I write the kind of books I like to read." This is a good rule of thumb for any writer. Spillane was lucky that his personal taste was in genre fiction, traditionally an easier style for the newcomer to break into. Genre fiction means a certain type of novel—mystery, romance, science fiction, western, and so on. In the good old days there were more opportunities for the genre writer. Still, it is slightly easier to get your genre novel seriously considered for publication than a so-called mainstream or "literary" piece of fiction.

You can crank out a potboiler in the hope of simply being a published author, but if your heart is not in it, agents and publishers will probably sense this. On the chance that you do get through that formidable barrier to publication, there is the reading public to consider. If you do not woo them, your tenure in the literary limelight will be fleeting.

So Mickey Spillane and Ernest Hemingway are both right—write the truest sentences you can in the kind of book you like to read. If to thine own self you are true, thou canst be false to the dear reader. On a related note, you should read a lot of novels if you want to write one. Read everything from the classics to the "trash." Do not be too snooty toward the trash. Mark Twain was right when he said "a classic is a book that people praise but don't read," and Jackie Collins is a millionaire many times over.

Protect Yourself

Once the novel (or short story or screenplay) is ready to be shown to the world, every writer should copyright his or her idea, lest some unscrupulous agent or publisher purloin the plot without your consent. Always employ the Russian adage, "Trust, but verify" when dealing with publishers.

There is one school of thought that all you need to do is seal your manuscript in an envelope and mail it to yourself. The dated postmark on your package is evidence that you came up with the idea on such-and-such a date. If somebody steals your idea and you sue, the envelope would be opened in the courtroom and you would be vindicated. However, there is an easier, safer, and less melodramatic way to copyright your work.

The Writers Guild of America (WGA) and the Writers Guild of America, East (WGAE), are two branches of the same guild for professional writers. They offer an easy alternative to copyrighting your work. This method gives you the means to prove the date of your authorship, in case you ever need to sue for (or defend yourself against) copyright infringement. It does not, however, give you actual ownership over your intellectual property, such as characters, the way a copyright does. The WGAE Web site, at ✎*www.wgae.org*, describes the simple registration process, which will give you peace of mind.

You can register any work of fiction, nonfiction, novel, or screenplay online with the guild for $22. Send in a copy, and the guild will register the date received and keep it for ten years. It can be renewed after that. If you choose not to renew it, the WGAE will destroy it lest it fall into the wrong hands.

Writing for the Big (and Small) Screen

Do you spend more time perusing the shelves at your local Blockbuster than you do at your neighborhood Borders or the public library? In this age of the ever-decreasing attention span, perhaps you are wise to be thinking of a writing a screenplay. In *The Return of the Native*, the great British novelist and poet Thomas Hardy spent several pages describing the landscape where the novel took place. As a reader, would you quickly tire of this geographical narrative? Would you prefer to scan the more succinct "FADE IN: A WINDSWEPT BRITISH HEATH"? If so, screenwriting may be the best mode of expression for you.

FACT

One of the most popular screenwriting software programs on the market is called Final Draft. As you type, it automatically formats your work into the accepted screenplay style, making it easier for you to concentrate on the creative aspects of screenwriting.

The Rules

Selling a screenplay is even more competitive than getting a novel published. More people watch movies and television than read books, and being recognized in Beverly Hills is more desirable to most than being hunted down in a Barnes & Noble. Hence, there are more people pitching scripts than novels to agents and studios.

Since there are so many screenplays crossing the desks of power brokers, you have to observe certain rules. Most important to know is that screenplays are written in a special format. If yours is not, it will be summarily discarded. It is worth your while to invest on a screenwriting software program than automatically formats your work into the accepted industry standard.

You should also be aware that if you are the one of the fortunate writers whose script is turned into a film or television show, the final results on the screen may bear little resemblance to your original screenplay. Everyone from the director and producer to the actors will fiddle and fool around with your work. And unless you are one of the very few powerful screenwriters in the business, you will have nothing to say about it.

When you ask any Hollywood actor or director what the most important thing is to a film's success, they invariably say "the script." Yet writers remain the lowest paid and most ill-used toilers in Tinseltown. Steve Martin said it best when he hosted the 2003 Academy Awards, "Writers, directors, actors . . . if we're stuck here tonight, and we run out of food, that's the order of whom we eat."

Spacey to the Rescue

Actor Kevin Spacey has launched a Web site for aspiring screenwriters. Called *www.triggerstreet.com*, this is a vehicle for unknown writers to get their work seen and critiqued by industry insiders and by fellow writers. Registration is free, and members can upload their script or short digital movie and view other members' work. In fact, the only requirement for membership is to be an active participant. Before you can submit your own script, you have to read and review at least two others.

Be forewarned—you really should copyright your work before sending it out into cyberspace.

The Freelance Adventure

Got a high tolerance for making cold calls and not having them returned? For pitching ideas that are ignored, rejected, and possibly even stolen? Do you have enough in the bank to weather the wait when you are told that "The check is in the mail," and it seems that it must be literally transported on the back of a snail? Welcome to the world of the freelance writer.

FACT

The word "freelance" has medieval origins. A knight who was not in the service of a lord was known as a knight errant, and his weapon, a lance, was his own to use, rather than at his master's beck and call. Like a gunfighter in the Old West, he was free to hire out his weapon to the highest bidder.

Familiarity Breeds Success

Most freelancers make their living in the newspaper and magazine businesses. These industries will be the focus of this section. This may be a no-brainer, but if you want to write for newspapers and magazines, you have to read a lot of newspapers and magazines. You need to familiarize yourself with their various styles and see what stories they tend to cover. At the risk of oversimplifying, you would not send an article about the latest celebrity weight-loss technique to *Popular Mechanics*. On a related note, it is important to know the "voice" of the periodical. *Vogue* has a different voice than *BusinessWeek*, and *Mad Magazine* is far removed from the *National Review*.

When you have an idea that you think is ideal for a particular magazine, you can either pitch the idea as a query in a letter or e-mail or, if you have the time and inclination, write the piece and try to sell it on spec. Many a writer has submitted a query and had it rejected only to see a piece about the same subject appear in the same magazine . . . written by someone else. A coincidence? Maybe, maybe not. This goes with the territory. While there are intellectual copyright laws, you cannot copyright an idea sent in an e-mail or left on a voicemail.

Whom to Contact?

When you're planning to pitch an idea in a cold call, you need to get a contact name. Look at the masthead of the magazine and see who the editors are. It is advisable to direct your call to someone at the associate level. They are still young and (usually) still nice. They are more inclined to be kind and hear you out.

If nobody is picking up the phone, you can also try sending an e-mail. You can "crack the code" of e-mail addresses fairly easily. It is safe to say that almost all magazines and publishers have a presence on the Internet these days. On their Web sites, there will inevitably be a "Contact Us" section. You will often see that the second half of the e-mail address is "@magazinename.com." You can then go to the masthead and find a contact name and experiment with the format. It could be the person's whole name with no space, the whole name with a dot between the first and last name, or the commonly used first name initial/last name in lower caps with no space. Through trial and error, you will get through to an editor.

ALERT!

The Web site ✍ *www.freelancewriting.com* is, as the name suggests, an online resource for freelance writers. It has many resources and job listings for those struggling and succeeding in the freelance world. The About.com site's freelance section (✍*http://freelancewrite. about.com*) also has numerous links covering a variety of topics that the freelance writer needs to be aware of.

In order to be a freelance writer, you must strike the balance between being aggressive and coming off as downright obnoxious. As in so many of these alternative career hunts, do not take rejection personally, difficult though that is.

In order to have a stress-free freelance life, you have to have multiple projects going on. At the same time, you must always be pitching new ideas to a large network of contacts you have built over time. When you're just starting out, this will be difficult—discouragingly, painfully so. If you really want it, however, a freelance writing career can be had if you are willing to take the knocks and the disappointments that come down the pike—and if you never give up.

Finding an Agent

One place that a writer never wants to end up is the dreaded "slush pile." This is where unsolicited manuscripts are consigned. The science fiction/fantasy publisher Baen Books makes no bones about how it treats unsolicited books. They are to be sent to *slush@baenbooks.com*, and the response time in getting back to you is *one year!* In this day and age, the way to avoid being tossed on the slush pile is to get an agent.

Elements of Style

Formatting is very important when submitting a proposal. In fact, it is mission critical. It sometimes seems as if agents are using any excuse not to accept your idea. In fairness to them, they are deluged with manuscripts and proposals, most of which are none too stellar. When they ask for a particular format, they are endeavoring to—excuse the cliché—separate the wheat from the chaff. Follow directions carefully and you're headed in the right direction.

Where the Agents Are

So where do you look? Type "literary agents" into the Amazon.com search field, and you get approximately 100 results. With so many to choose from, where is the best place to begin? The easiest and often best place to start is the Internet. Before you plunk down your hard-earned money for a book that may already include outdated data, you should check out a few Web sites that can help you in your quest for literary representation.

WritersMarket.com is the online presence of a popular publishing resource. It has up-to-date contact information about publishers, agents, and editors for all areas of publishing. You have to register with them to use its services. The good thing is that it is reasonably priced. You can join for $29.95 per year or $2.95 per month. The monthly fee is ideal for those who want to check out the site with no great expenditure or obligation. It is a good way to explore the literary landscape and there are hundreds, if not thousands, of listings of literary agents and publishers.

The *Literary Market Place* (known in the publishing world as the LMP) is a mammoth volume. It is considered the Bible of resources on publishing. Most writers refer to it when visiting the reference section of their local library. Weighty in more ways than one, it is 2,200 pages long and costs $299 if you want to purchase your own copy.

Nor is it cheap to use the LMP Web site, ✍ *www.literarymarket place.com*. A yearly subscription costs $399. You should visit the library and thoroughly peruse the hard copy before you elect to shell out the money for membership to this site. However, you get what you pay for, as they say, and it is a fact that the LMP is a one-stop resource for everything you need to know about publishing. When your writing career is in full swing, it is definitely a worthwhile expense. You can probably include the expense in your deductibles at tax time—but it's always a good idea to consult your accountant first!

ALERT!

The Web site ✍ *www.agentresearch.com* offers free verification that an agent is legitimate and credentialed. There are fees for more detailed searches. Remember—avoid agents who charge an upfront fee to evaluate your query, proposal, or manuscript.

Caveat Scribbler—Let the Writer Beware

Just as there is good and bad in every person, there are reputable and unsavory people in every profession. When you are looking for an agent, it is a good rule of thumb to avoid any agent who charges a fee to read and evaluate your proposal of manuscript. The reputable agent will review your material at no charge. You may get a curt and stinging "Not interested," but at least you will not have paid for the terse dismissal.

Just as there are vanity presses, that is, publishers that publish your book at your expense, there are agents who will charge you for the privilege of their alleged expertise. They are the literary equivalent of ambulance-chasing lawyers, and they should immediately be scratched off your list of prospective agents.

Other Writing Opportunities

There are many ways to make a living in and around the writing trade. When you have been at it for awhile, you could seek out assignments as a ghostwriter. If you are a person of few words, maybe greeting cards are for you. If you have an orderly and analytical mind, you could try your hand at proofreading. Many writers who are capable of paying good attention to detail can supplement their incomes nicely with proofreading assignments.

Working with an agent can be a frustrating experience. You have worked long and hard on your book, and you don't want to be sitting by the phone or constantly checking your e-mail to hear back from those to whom you have sent query letters and sample chapters. Unfortunately, this may be the case until you hook up with an agent who wants to work with you. It is part of the great game of getting published, so hang in there.

Ghostwriting

Ghostwriting is one of the more lucrative categories within the writing life. The downside is something that many writers do not like: anonymity. If you do not seek fame and acclaim for your talents, and a large paycheck is sufficient reward for your work, then ghostwriting may be for you.

Ghostwriting is something to consider as your career advances and you establish credentials, as they are what will get you ghostwriting assignments. You might be surprised how many ghostwriters are lurking in the shadows of the writing world. Any celebrity who writes a book usually has "help." President John F. Kennedy won a Pulitzer Prize for a book he did not write, *Profiles in Courage.* The star of perhaps the most popular science fiction television series of all time seems to crank out a book a month these days. He comes up with the general idea, but after that the well-paid and well-hidden ghosts take over. Even in corporate America, everything from training manuals and stockholder meeting speeches are usually scripted by a ghostwriter.

As you carve out a niche for yourself as a writer, you will develop interests and specialties. You should compile these into a portfolio to present when you are looking for ghostwriting work. If your specialty is business, you will probably not be hired to ghost for a baseball player or rock star. The rest is the footwork, using resources like the LMP and others to find agents and publishers looking for ghostwriters. Sometimes you will see ads in the trade journals and the classified section of mainstream papers place by individuals looking to hook up with the right writer.

Another skill to pick up along the way is the ability to write in a variety of voices. This will widen your opportunities and earning potential. You will be in essence pretending to be another person. The rest of the world must believe that the man or woman whose name and/or picture are on the book has really written it.

Contracts

In any business collaboration, it is wise to get things in writing before you start. When negotiating a contract as a ghostwriter, you need to keep these things in mind:

- Detailed particulars about the work (number of words, etc.)
- Who owns the copyright (usually the person hiring you)
- Expected time frame between start and completion
- How much you are to be paid, and in what manner (lump sum, installments)
- A termination clause, in case either or both parties are not satisfied during the process

If a project doesn't work out, make sure you receive what is known as a kill fee. You deserve to be paid for your time and effort, even if the project never makes it to the bookstores.

Proofreading

Proofreaders can make a good hourly rate and are always in demand. Some even work in different shifts and not during traditional business hours. Many companies and law firms have proofreaders working through the night to have documents letter-perfect first thing in the morning.

Proofreading is different from editing. Editors read a manuscript for style, content, and clarity. They do catch errors in grammar and style, but they are also looking at the bigger picture. A proofreader has to have the ability to pay methodical and meticulous attention to detail. Most writers are not good proofreaders, and writers should never rely on themselves to proofread their own work. A writer can read something he or she has written dozens of times and never catch something that another pair of eyes will easily see. Similarly, publishers have many people go over a manuscript during the development process to see that no errors slip through. One person who has to reread the same material repeatedly will almost certainly lose his or her fine focus. The mind eventually sees what it thinks is there, not the cold type on the screen or on the page.

FACT

If you want to work as a proofreader, you have to familiarize yourself with standard proofreading symbols. These are the notations that the proofreader makes so the next person in the editorial pipeline can make the changes. Examples of the proofreading symbols can be found in most dictionaries or through a Web search.

Many proofreaders read aloud, and all read slowly. They are versed in grammar, spelling, and punctuation in a way many writers are not. The proofreader's approach to a document is more mathematical and clinical than artistic. They cannot afford to be distracted by beauty. They read for different reasons than the casual reader or even the average editor.

Chapter 8
The Artist's Way

If you are an artist by avocation and have thought about turning your passion into a profit-making enterprise, there's no reason to feel guilty about "selling out." While it is true that many artists did not achieve success until after they were dead, there is no reason for you to wait that long.

You Gotta Have Art

Art and artistic expression are the things that make human beings unique. The desire, and for some the overpowering impulse, to express oneself creatively is something the birds and the bees do not have—at least as far as we know. We know that birdsong, beautiful as it is, has a practical purpose. But does a bird ever sing simply to make music?

People make art for reasons other than merely a means of survival. It is a force that burns within them and demands to be manifested in a physical form. Some people make their art privately and never show it to another soul. Others create and place their creations on display for the world to see. Very few artists make a living through their creativity. If this is what you want to do, though, there are ways to go about it.

If you have been creating art for some time, this chapter offers suggestions on how to turn an avocation into a vocation. If you are an artist by nature who has never painted a canvas or sculpted a hunk of clay, then get to work! Express yourself, as Madonna suggested way back in the 1980s. If you know what kind of art you would like to explore, go get the supplies, make a space for yourself in your home, and just do it. If you have a nebulous notion that you want to be an artist but have never tried any particular form, work with a variety of modes until you find the one that resonates deep within your spirit. Either way, it would not hurt to enroll in some adult education art classes. There are certainly some in your area, either in the local college or community center. It is an excellent opportunity to learn about art, find your voice, and meet like-minded men and women.

The Art of Successful Self-Promotion

Maybe you are an artist and you've been working on your craft for years, or perhaps you have always had an interest in art but never explored it. Either way, if you want to make your art an alternative career, this by its very definition entails putting your creative efforts on display for other people to peruse and hopefully to purchase.

The main way to avoid the starving artist syndrome, other than take a job that brings you no joy and merely pays the bills, is to learn how to market yourself. It is an unavoidable fact that you must incorporate the dreaded "B" word—business—into your repertoire if you are to make a living through your artistic endeavors.

A Business Plan

Like any small-businessperson, you need a plan. Throwing yourself into the artistic scene with reckless abandon almost never works. The occasional exception is very lucky indeed or has a muse who is working overtime. If you do not want to wait until your *oeuvre* is posthumously discovered after your death, bringing you a kind of immortality that you will not be able to enjoy, then you have to get noticed right now.

Do not be afraid of "going commercial," as many of your artistic associates may condescendingly call it. There is no shame in making money from your talent. Van Gogh died broke, and now his paintings sell for millions. It is a safe bet he would have preferred to have made that money during his lifetime. He might not have been as inclined to cut off his ear.

If you are an artist who wants to blend your creativity and your career, then you must think of ways and means to get your art displayed and sold. Grit your teeth if you must, but you must take your product to the marketplace and hope some consumers will pay you for the privilege of hanging your wares on their walls. The product you're selling is more than your work itself—you yourself also are also part of the package. People are interested in artists because deep down we all wish we could express ourselves creatively. At galleries and other venues you are going to be the front man or woman for your work. Businessperson and sales rep—these are not words you think of as you struggle to breathe life to a blank canvas, but you must be both.

The Marketplace

Let's assume that you have a body of work in your artistic field. You are now ready, although undoubtedly more than a little anxious, for the world to take a look at what you have created.

Like an actor or model, you will need to make a portfolio. This can be a traditional collection of reprints of your work that you carry around with you in a valise and present to interested parties. Nowadays, however, many artists burn scans or photos of their work onto CDs and personally deliver or send them out to galleries, agents, and others. Leonardo da Vinci did not have this luxury, but you do. With a computer with all the bells and whistles, you can do this yourself. Otherwise, you must find copy shops in your community that can do it for you. If you are serious about this process, it will be worth your while to have a state-of-the-art computer. You will save money in the long run doing this yourself. You will also need a computer if you want to get the other high-tech tool that artists use today—a personal Web site.

Any Internet provider can give you a certain amount of space on their servers for a personal page. You need to have enough space to upload graphics of your work. You might want to consider, if you have the money, securing your own domain name and having a professional build a quality site for you. If you have a graphic-designer friend, or at least a friend who's more computer literate than you, he or she can help you. Make sure you also get business cards printed that include your e-mail and Web site addresses. Other tools of the trade include letterhead stationery; postcards that have one or more samples of your work on one side and contact information on the other; and press releases for the local media. Initially these press releases will be just to publicize the fact that you exist. Many small papers carry regular feature stories on local artists. Future press releases will announce gallery showings and other places where your work will be exhibited.

Learning the Market

Despite the many modern conveniences available to you these days, there is still nothing like a little old-fashioned footwork. You need to do market research. The best place to start is right in your own back yard. Find the local galleries and other places where artwork is displayed. Contact them, try to schedule appointments, and conduct yourself just like you are going on an interview. Bring your portfolio and something to leave with them, whether it is a CD or your business card. If they like you and your work, they may offer to display you in their gallery. Keep in mind that this is a business arrangement, and as such it benefits both parties. The gallery owner makes money from your sales, either in the form of a fee you pay to exhibit or from a percentage of the money you make. This is really no different from the percentage artists in other fields would pay a theatrical or literary agent.

Your Own Studio

Depending on your means and where you live, you may want to get your own artist's studio. Check the classified ads in your area to see what spaces are for rent. Many factories that have gone out of business are converted into loft space for commercial use, residences, and artists' studios. This is the case in the neighborhood in Manhattan known as SoHo. It is extraordinarily expensive to rent there, but in other parts of the country the cost of living is a lot more reasonable. You could also convert part of your home into a studio if you have enough space.

ALERT!

Information about housing and studio space for artists can be found by visiting the Web site ✍ *www.artisthelpnetwork.com.* Here you will get an idea about the availability and expense of finding your own art studio to display your work on your terms and at your convenience.

With your own studio, you eliminate any middlemen and their fees. You set the date, time, and all the minutiae of your showing. It is also your obligation to alert the media and the community that your works are open for inspection. You have to send out the press releases and post the fliers around town.

During the reception, which many studios have following the opening of an exhibit, you should provide some light refreshment. The cliché choice for such affairs is wine and cheese, but make sure you have some nonalcoholic beverages as well. Last but not least, you must play the affable and engaging host or hostess.

Other Venues for Your Work

In addition to local galleries that will charge a commission or a percentage of the gate, there are other places that you can contact that may display your work. You should research nonprofit galleries whose whole reason for being is to support local artists. Space can also be had in museums and university galleries. Beyond that, the Internet is not only a source for your research. There you will also find online galleries that will exhibit your work digitally. Some charge fees, others take a commission, and still others sponsor contests where you will be judged by a panel of experts. The Internet has also made the world your oyster in that you can be seen worldwide and not just by the lucky few who wander into your studio or local gallery. The Web will also guide you to the many artist-in-residence programs, grants, and fellowships that are out there.

National Endowment for the Arts

The National Endowment for the Arts (NEA) is a federal program whose mandate is to enrich "our Nation and its diverse cultural heritage by supporting works of artistic excellence, advancing learning in the arts, and strengthening the arts in communities throughout the country."

ALERT!

The Artist Help Network (✐ *www.artisthelpnetwork.com*) is a wonderful resource for anyone interested in pursuing a career in the arts. It has a wealth of information on all the practical aspects you need to know to make your segue into a career as a full-time working artist as painless and pressure-free as possible.

The intent of the NEA is to preserve art, teach about art, and make the arts more accessible to students and others who might never be exposed to this form of creative expression. For your purposes, it also provides grants and funding for artists. The rules have changed a little since its inception. They have become more rigid, but you can still check out their Web site and see if you are eligible for a government grant or endowment to fund your efforts. Warning—if your passion is in the "clowns on velvet" or "bulldogs playing poker" motif, you will probably not be awarded a NEA grant. Their Web site is *www.nea.gov.*

The Art of the Craft Business

Maybe your artistic impulses aren't to create possibly beautiful, but not very useful objects that one can hang on a wall. On the more practical side, the craft business covers a wide variety of products: toys, furniture, jewelry, ceramics, woodworking, works of gold and silver, and many more kind of trinkets, ornaments, and bric-a-brac. Many people make the rounds at arts-and-crafts fairs, others sell to shops, and many are now taking advantage of the Internet to sell products on their own Web sites.

Selecting and Learning Your Craft

If you have an interest in a particular craft, you are probably already exploring it. As with artists—for a craftsperson *is* an artist—if you do not already have an expertise in a particular craft, you should take some crafting courses offered in your community. Take more than one class until you find the kind of craft you would like to work with. Do not pick the one that you think will make you a lot of money. You will probably not make a lot of money in the beginning. This is something that will happen over time. You have heard it before and you will hear it again: Do what you love, and the money will follow.

The Money Issue

An alternative career like crafting should be entered into because it is something you love to do. Starting and running a crafting business, like any small business, takes dedication and effort if you are to succeed. You could probably make more money working for someone else in a so-called traditional job. If you are reading these words, however, that is something you do not want to do or continue doing. It is a struggle to start a business from scratch, so you might as well be working in a crafting field that gives you pleasure. If you do not love what you are doing, you will be more inclined to give up when the going gets tough.

By starting small, you can avoid spending a lot of money before you have learned about the nature of the business. The early stages will be hit-and-miss, trial-and-error time, so you might as well not spend, and probably lose, large sums of hard-earned cash during your period of growing pains. The main reason so many small businesses fail is that they drown in a sea of debt caused by startup costs that they cannot get out from under. You should being by selling to family and friends and at small, local flea markets and fairs. There you will also meet other craftspeople, and most of them will be happy to offer the benefit of their experience, unless of course you are selling the same kind of product. Even in the kinder, gentler world of handmade crafts, business is business.

Sunshine Artist (at ✍ *www.sunshineartist.com*) is a trade magazine for the professional exhibitor of handmade items. It is a subscription magazine, but you can visit the Web site to see a sampling of typical articles and a listing of craft shows and fairs across the country.

Craft Shows

Local craft shows are a good place to start. There you can learn the ins and outs of selling your wares to the general public in a forum that will teach you much but not cost you a lot. The bigger, national arts and crafts extravaganzas are more costly for exhibitors and you will also incur travel and hotel expenses. So it is better to start at the little show around the corner.

Selling at a local show will allow you to see what sells and what does not among your product line. You can use the results as a litmus test to determine what you need to bring to a larger show. If a George W. Bush bobblehead sells more than a Hillary Clinton nodder, then you know to produce more of the former and less of the latter.

You can search for local craft shows in your area via the ever-reliable Internet. You can also contact your local chamber of commerce as well as the charitable institutions and churches in your neck of the woods. These organizations regularly sponsor flea markets, at which you can rent a table for a nominal sum and sell your crafts. If you live in a part of the country where there are craft and hobby stores like Hobby Lobby, Ben Franklin's, or Christmas Tree Shops, you can contact them to inquire about any shows in the neighborhood.

Arts & Crafts Online Business Resources at the address (✐*www.artcraftmarketing.com*) is a Web site designed to help fellow arts and crafts businesspeople learn how to get a craft-themed Web site up and running.

Other Marketing Techniques

Your craft may be something that a local retail store might be interested in selling. Drop by local merchants with some samples of your work. See if they will either purchase your product wholesale or if you can display a sample with some business cards if you mention their store on your Web site. This is called cross-promotion and often generates sales. As described before, it is wise and easy for an artist, craftsperson, or any small-businessperson to have an Internet presence. You should also donate some crafts to charities with a business card attached to each item, put inexpensive classified ads in the local papers, and use the other methods described throughout this book for new entrepreneurs to get free or cheap publicity.

What to Charge?

It is hard to put a price on a work of art or a handmade item. They are labors of love, of value to the creator and the collector. There is a formula that some craftspeople use to put a price tag on their work.

You can determine a fair hourly rate for yourself and multiply this by the number of hours a week that you will be working at producing your crafts. For example, if you pay yourself $12 an hour for a forty-hour week, the cost of your labor would be $480.

Next, calculate how much the supplies cost to make one item and how many items you can produce in a week. Multiply the supply cost per item by your weekly number. For instance, if your costs are $2 per item, and you can make 100 per week, your total would be $200.

Add these two numbers, and they come to $680. Divide this figure by the number of items you can produce in a week (which we said above was 100), and you arrive at $6.80 per item. This is the price you would have to charge to earn $12 an hour if you sold every piece you made. You should compare this price to what others are asking for similar items and adapt your calculations accordingly to be competitive in the marketplace.

Copyrighting Your Crafts

If you are concerned about chicanery among your crafting colleagues, you may want to copyright your work. Just as writers and others can register their work and intellectual property with the U.S. Copyright Office to protect against people stealing their ideas, crafters can register their work to receive the same protection. Copyrighting your work does not actually prevent theft, but it will prove that you came up with the product first, which gives you the legal grounds to sue for copyright violation.

You can find a list of craft manufacturers, distributors, and suppliers at *http://artsandcrafts.about.com*. The list is conveniently broken down by state so you can find the resources nearest you.

You must register your product if you fear that the above may happen. You can learn how to do this at the Library of Congress Web site at ✐*www.loc.gov*. For a craft item, you go to the Visual Arts section. Then you will open and print Form VA, fill it out, and mail it to the address listed with one physical copy of your handmade craft and a nonrefundable $30 fee. Taking this action does not mean that the Copyright Police will be out looking for thieves who have stolen your idea. That is your job. If you come across a suspiciously similar item in your crafting travels and determine that its existence is more than mere coincidence, it is up to you to sue the idea thief.

You can put a copyright symbol, followed by the year, on your item without registering it with the copyright office. All original works are, in theory, automatically copyrighted. However, no legal action can be taken unless it is officially registered.

Quality Assurance

In this age of declining professionalism and fading quality, the best thing you can do is make your crafts with care and with love and the highest caliber of raw materials you can find. If you use cheap materials, your product will look cheap; the consumer will notice and be disinclined to purchase your craft. A quality product will enhance your reputation through word of mouth and keep customers coming back for more. This is more important than all the business plans and advertising you can devise. People want good stuff. If you make it, they will buy it. Ⓔ

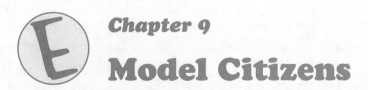

Chapter 9

Model Citizens

Have you dreamed of making a living on a runway, but don't have any interest in working at the local airport? The other notable runway profession is modeling. Like acting, writing, dancing, and the other "glamorous" alternative careers, modeling is difficult to break into. But it's not impossible. In this chapter we will take a look at the modeling business.

Have You Got What It Takes?

There are realities that you have to face if you want to pursue a career in modeling. Do you have "the look?" You know what it is. Peruse the fashion magazines. Are you tall, skinny, and beautiful? That is the required look for those creatures called "supermodels." You may disagree with it, and you may believe that it creates an impossible dream for the typical woman to aspire to. And indeed it does. It can damage a girl or young woman's self-esteem to see the supermodels on the runway. Precious few people even have "the look." There are specific requirements you will have to meet. As unpleasant as this reality is, it is nevertheless a law of the business and there is nothing you can do about it.

Supermodels

You probably have a slightly better chance of becoming a supermodel than winning the lottery, but just barely. According to *www.modelnews.com*, one person in a million is born with the possibility of joining the select club that includes Tyra Banks, Cindy Crawford, and a precious few others. If you are a woman who is 5'9" or taller, and you fit society's notion of perfection in face and form, then you have a chance.

High-Fashion Models

Below the supermodels on this hierarchy of appearance are the high-fashion models. There are the women and men you see on the major magazines and in the print and other media ads for the big designers. They are well paid for presenting their pristine mugs before the camera, and they also have to have a certain look. A woman must be 5'9" or taller, no more than 115 pounds, and young. A man can be a little older, though at thirty-five he is ready for retirement. He has to be at least six feet tall. Men must be in excellent shape, but they have the luxury of not having to be facially perfect. Handsome is not discouraged, of course, but different looks are not immediately discounted. A man can be "ugly" and still considered sexy if he has a certain magnetism. A high-fashion model can make a million dollars for one advertising campaign. Your odds of making it in this category are a little better—only about 250,000 to one.

On the Runway

Runway models are essentially animated coat hangers who model designer fashions live, on the runway at fashion shows or sometimes at designer boutiques for individual customers. They are supposed to show the clothes in their best light, but they don't need to show how the clothes complement a lush "real woman" figure. Runway fashion shows happen twice a year on connection with the spring and fall fashion lines. The circuit for runway shows is Milan, London, Paris, and New York. Women have to be over 5'9" and slim. Men must be tall and fit. A runway model can make anywhere from $500 to $5,000 a show.

In the Catalogs

Catalog models run the gamut, from the supermodels in the Victoria's Secret catalog to the woman in the girdle in a local department store's ad in a small town paper. Women should be 5'8" and a size six. Men must be, as usual, 6' or taller and fit into a size forty regular sports coat. Most catalog models are in their twenties. The top echelon makes $10,000 to $15,000 a day, and the lower levels make $100 to $150 an hour.

The Web site *www.models.com* is an excellent resource for those who want to learn about the modeling business. It lists the top agencies and a professional directory of photographers, makeup artists, and more.

If you have "the look" to make it as any of these kinds of models, then you can give it a shot. It is no less a noble use of your God-given gifts than becoming a scientist. If you do not possess the look and are at peace with the fact that you are never going to be the next Tyra Banks, there are other types of modeling work that you can do.

If you are a regular guy and not the buff and hunky young studs with six-pack abs and a full head of hair that you see in magazines and on television, you need not despair either. There is modeling work to be had even for the average-looking Joe.

You Can Do It, Too

These descriptions of the requirements to enter the exalted stratosphere of the modeling world can be intimidating, but fear not! If modeling is your dream, do not give up hope just because you don't fit this tight mold. Observe your fellow citizens the next time you are walking down the street or at the mall. None of them looks like a supermodel. Yet there are more modeling assignments than there are supermodels. There is work to be had for the 99.9 percent of us who do not make it to the Mount Olympus of the fashion world.

Promotional Modeling

Promotional models come in all shapes and sizes, male and female. There are no specific requirements to do this kind of modeling. These are the people you see greeting passersby at trade-show or convention booths, at grocery stores or at the mall, handing out literature and promotional freebies such as T-shirts and caps. They answer questions and generally represent the organization in an articulate and attractive manner. A charismatic and comely promotional model can increase traffic to a company's booth and thus increase business. A good promotional model who is seen at a trade show or other venue is invariably noticed by representatives of other businesses, and he or she gets more assignments this way.

Sophisticated Ladies (and Gentlemen)

Although modeling is considered a youth-oriented business, there are in fact modeling jobs for mature men and women. These are known euphemistically as sophisticated models. These models are thirty and up. They appear in print and other media that cater to the mature population, who are have the disposable income that advertisers would love to get their hands on.

Fitness Modeling

In this health-and-fitness conscious time, there are more and more opportunities for people who are in good enough shape to model their excellent physical condition. These are fitness models, and they range from bodybuilders to the rugged outdoors types. They can be seen on catalogs that cater to workout clothes and gear, as well as clothing outlets like L. L. Bean.

Commercial Modeling

This is a very general umbrella term that encompasses the various types of modeling that are outside the realms of fashion and glamour. Product modeling, character modeling, lifestyle modeling, and corporate modeling are all examples of the kind of work a commercial model can expect to perform. There is no official look required of a commercial model. The look depends on the product or the client the model is representing.

Product modeling involves selling a product. The advertising agency working on a campaign for a client looks for men and women who can help sell the product. An ad for a pharmaceutical company may want a serious-looking mature man to dress in a white lab coat. A computer company may want a pocket-protector-wearing nerd. In the world of auto sales, there is nothing like an attractive woman languorously lounging on the hood of a car. The men and women who model in this category are a diverse lot. They are like actors with no dialogue. In fact, they are called character models.

Similarly, lifestyle models are used in advertising that tries to appeal to a particular age group or economic class. For example, an older couple strolling in the park would be used for an ad dealing with retirement issues. These models can be of varied ages and looks, though they are usually what Madison Avenue deems attractive.

Corporate modeling is an offshoot of this, and the models must conform to the advertiser's vision of what a cross-section of the business world looks like.

Product Demonstrators

Many models get their start demonstrating products. These models are needed everywhere, not just in the big cities and fashion centers of the world. They typically work in front of or inside stores or at tables in malls, and they give out free samples of a product or hand out literature about a service. This is a good ground-floor opportunity to build your confidence and become accustomed to working around people.

Product demonstrators have to be attractive and personable. In addition, they must be able to knowledgeably discuss the product or service they are demonstrating. Basically, they act as salespeople in addition to being models. They generate public interest in the product, initially by the way they look. An attractive woman in sexy clothes selling a wireless phone plan will attract a crowd, but so will a portly middle-aged man dressed as a chicken handing out samples of buffalo wings.

If the product is a piece of merchandise or machinery, product demonstrators must be able to show the assembled throng how the product works. Sometimes they take the names or e-mail addresses of people who want to be contacted with additional information. They must be attention-getters, either by their looks or their manner or their accessories—or by a combination of all of these elements.

Glamour Modeling

These models are men and women who pose for images of a sexual nature. This includes but it is not limited to pornography. Porn is the poor relation of glamour modeling. Most glamour models appear in lingerie and bikini advertising, provocative calendars, posters and "cheesecake" images.

The physical requirements for a glamour model are obvious. Unlike an emaciated supermodel, a glamour model is usually curvaceous. And the men range from pretty boys to brooding hunks. Success as a glamour model is a slippery uphill slope. On their way back down, many—but certainly not most—of the glamour models have done things they are not proud of. This brand of modeling, if you have the look, is one of the easier to break into. However, it is also one of the hardest to break free from.

Where to Start

As is true with any highly competitive field, certain rules apply to the pursuit of a modeling career. Steel yourself against rejection and discouragement. If you are in the right place at the right time you may be discovered, but do not count on it. Learn as much as you can about the industry. Read the magazines, and watch the many cable television programs about fashion and style. Attend fashion shows, and talk to as many people as you can. Ingratiate yourself. Talk to the photographers and designers. Finagle your way backstage if you can, and talk to the models.

QUESTION?

Are beauty contests demeaning?
Many women who went on to bigger, better, and respectable things competed in beauty contests when they were younger, including Michelle Pfeiffer and Oprah Winfrey.

Modeling Schools

The merits of modeling schools is the subject of ongoing and vigorous debate. Some find them to be a valuable training ground. Others see them as a waste of money. If a modeling agency likes your amateur portfolio and wants to work with you, you will receive all the training you need and will be in very good hands. Remember that a modeling school is in business to make money. Check them out thoroughly if you want to go that route. See how many graduates have gone on to greater things.

Inquire if they are associated with modeling agencies and have placement service that can provide an entry point into the modeling world. Do not fall for an aggressive sales pitch and promises that sound a little too good to be true. On the fringes of all glamorous and creative careers there are charlatans and con men out to exploit the ambition of the inexperienced and naïve.

Many modeling schools across the country are franchises of the famous modeling agencies. That is, the agency lends its well-known name to a chain of schools, which teach the basics of modeling. This is a profitable sideline for the big agencies. The best course of action is to take the steps to get hooked up with an agency, where they will work with you and teach you all you need to know for free. If they see potential, they will invest in your training. This is better than your paying for training with no guarantee of work down the line.

Beauty Contests

If you are interested in becoming a model, you have probably been thinking of it for a long time, maybe since you were a little girl or boy. If you are a woman, you may even have appeared in a beauty contest or two over the years. If you have not, and you find the whole beauty contest atmosphere to be offensive and sexist, then why are you thinking of being a model? Your main asset in this career is your body and your looks. These are the commodities that you are, in essence, selling. If you find this mindset appalling or even offensive, then a career as a model is definitely not for you.

FACT

For a comedic look at the dark side of beauty contests, rent the movie *Drop Dead Gorgeous*. You will laugh, but it may also change your mind about wanting to participate in this very competitive, often catty atmoshere.

Entering a beauty contest is often a good way to break into the modeling world. Many times, the prizes even include a modeling contract. Scouts from the big modeling agencies often attend pageants in the same way that major league baseball scouts attend college and other amateur games. If you do not think that wearing a one-piece bathing suit and high heels is a tad silly, then you may want to check out the small beauty contests that occur across the country all the time.

There are also the less formal beauty contests, like swimsuit and bikini competitions. You may find these to be about as dignifying as a wet T-shirt contest during spring break, but it is another way to get noticed by industry professionals. It is not the top tier of the industry, but there are plenty of swimsuit and lingerie catalogs and magazines that, although not in the same league as Victoria's Secret, are nevertheless widely disseminated.

Beware of the Scam Artists

Like aspiring actors, neophyte models are often young, mostly female, and usually innocent in the ways of the business world. The intensity of their desire to make it in the fashion world makes them vulnerable to the many predators and the scams they run to make money off people's dreams and desire for success. A good rule of thumb to follow is that if it sounds too good to be true, it probably is.

Key things to note when evaluating a photography agency are that the fee is low, the model keeps the negatives, and the photographer has a seal of approval from the Better Business Bureau. These are all things that should be prerequisites when looking for a professional photographer.

Obviously you should report any person who offers to advance your career in return for sexual favors. This does occasionally happen, and sadly some women (and men) are foolish enough to fall for this scam. No reputable modeling agent would ever risk his or her career by engaging in this kind of unethical conduct.

You must also be wary of any photographer who insists you need to spend thousands of dollars for a photo shoot. A couple of hundred ought to be enough for a presentable fashion test. Nor should you ever get involved with an agent who wants money up front. Agents in any field are paid by commission. Their paycheck is a percentage of your earnings. An agent will work with you if it is apparent that you have potential to make money down the road.

The Road to the Runway

There are two essential ways to pursue a modeling career—or anything in life, for that matter. You can do it by yourself, or you can look for a person or persons to help you. In the modeling business, this means you either try to become affiliated with an agency or opt to go freelance. In both cases you will need to be prepared with a modeling tool kit.

Like any professional, you have to have your act together and compile an arsenal of accoutrements to present to agencies when you are seeking modeling work. A very important part of this is your portfolio. You can walk into an agency and have every head pop up out of its cubicle like a series of jacks-in-the box, but you had better have with you a series of photographs of what you look like in a variety of costumes and poses.

An ideal portfolio should include modeling work you have done. If you are just beginning you will not have an extensive resume, of course, so you may have to hire a professional photographer take some pictures of you. Do not spend a lot of money on this. It is not necessary, and you probably do not have thousands to spend if you are just starting out. Find a photographer, and have him shoot a few rolls of film. This is called a fashion test. Wear different outfits and hairstyles. Pick the best of the lot and have them blown up into 8 x 10s, and invest in a professional portfolio binder. Now you can go into an agency with confidence.

Composites and Cattle Calls

The composite is a two-sided single page that has a head shot on one side and more pictures and vital statistics on the back. After you get this professionally done—if you have desktop publishing knowledge, you can do it yourself—you can make the rounds with your portfolio and leave the composites with interested parties. If you have an agent, he or she will send your composites out. If not, you will be obliged to do the research as well as the legwork.

Some photographers who are interested may want to see you individually; on other occasions, you may be obliged to endure the dreaded cattle call. It is as unappealing as it sounds. You may feel like a commodity rather than a person, but that is the nature of the business. You might as well get used to it sooner than later. If you want the brass ring, there will be indignities you must endure. If you do not have an agent, you can find out about the cattle calls and other auditions by making cold calls to photographers, ad agencies, design companies, casting agents, and public relations firms. The big modeling agencies also hold open calls. These are cattle calls where the prize is signing with an agency, something that will save you a lot of time and effort in your quest for success.

ALERT!

The John Casablancas Modeling and Career Center (✍ www.johncasablancasmodels.com) is one of the many modeling schools. When researching for your career, please note that these are independently owned franchises that have purchased the name of this and other famous modeling industry giants. They are not the actual modeling agencies, which are usually located in New York City.

From A to Z

If an agency does not hold open calls, you can call them and see if they accept photo submissions. One of the ways to do this is to print what are called zed cards. This is a resume and photo on a small card that is an easy reference. It is smaller than and an alternative to the composite. Any printing/copy shop should be able to do a professional job. Bring the photos you want to use, and the staff in the store will advise you on designing the layout. The card should have your name, measurements, and contact information. These resumes are a little different than the format used to get a job in corporate America, where it obviously would be inappropriate to list your bust, waist, and hip size among your assets. If you have computer skills, you could even do your own zed card yourself (using a program like Microsoft Picture It! Publishing). Be sure you print it on quality cardstock.

Send your zed card with a cover letter that asks about opportunities and requests an interview. Be patient about waiting for a response. Then, after a reasonable period of time has elapsed, make your friendly follow-up call.

What agencies should you contact? The most famous agencies are the Elite, Ford, and Wilhelmina agencies, which are based in New York, and L.A. Models in Los Angeles.

Every major metropolitan center has reputable modeling agencies. There are working models all over the country, not just on either coast. As in other forms of media and entertainment, New York and Los Angeles are considered the major leagues. But you can be a working model in many other cities. There are always photo shoots and fashion shows going on. They may not be for the cover of your favorite women's magazine, but there are opportunities. It is likely that you will start out as a small fish in a small pond, and that may be advantageous in that you are more likely to get noticed.

Contests

Some modeling agencies sponsor contests. These are good way to get noticed. They are always free to enter. Never enter a modeling contest that charges an entry fee.

The Ford modeling agency sponsors the Supermodel of the Year contest. Information can be found at their Web site (*www.fordmodels.com*). Through the Elite agency, you can compete to win the Model Look of the Year. Further information can be found at elitemodel.com.

Internet Models

A relatively new phenomenon, only as old as cyberspace, is the Internet model. There are many men and women who have established personal Web pages with images and vital statistics to pitch themselves to the industry. Most modeling agencies still want a professional portfolio in hand and to see you in person, but more and more models are going the Internet route. It is an inexpensive and easy way to get free publicity.

You still have to personally contact the big modeling agencies. They do not sit in their offices surfing the Web in search of new talent. That talent is desperately attempting to get their feet in the door the old-fashioned way. A model with a Web site may get many hits a day, but chances are they are going to be from teenage boys and not modeling industry professionals.

However, more and more modeling agencies will accept a portfolio submitted by e-mail. A resume is easily sent as a text document and a jpeg is as easily viewed as an 8 x 10" glossy. The Internet is reshaping every aspect of the world, including the modeling business.

Though there are plenty of Web hosts that provide a free e-mail address and a small amount of space to make a personal home page, if you want to make the best impression, you should have your Web site done by an expert. Create and secure a unique domain name and hire someone to create your site. The more professional the page looks, the more seriously you will be taken. With all due respect to AOL, one of their free home pages, though perfectly easy to set up all by yourself, will not quite cut it.

ALERT!

The Web site ✐ *www.modelingadvice.com* has a section on the many modeling scams that seek to take advantage of would-be models for monetary gain, or worse. You can avoid a lot of heartache by becoming aware of the warning signs of a con artist who is out to deceive you.

There are a lot of geeks and even more menacing characters out there with nothing better to do than surf the Web looking for pretty people. You can therefore expect a lot of sometimes silly, sometimes scary e-mail. For this reason you should not list your home address or telephone number on the Web site.

Nobody's Perfect

If you do not meet the physical requirements to be a supermodel, you will not be on the catwalk with the other divas. This is sad but true. One of the worst things you can do is use unnatural means to try to transform yourself into something you are not. Diet and exercise is one thing, but binging and purging, popping pills, and submitting to various forms of cosmetic surgery in an effort to look like what Madison Avenue tells you that you should look like is destructive to both body and spirit.

There are other types of modeling careers that will be discussed in the remainder of this chapter. Those do not require the elusive and illusory perfection that the goddesses on the Mount Olympus are purported to possess. When you read a little bit about the lives of some of the world's famous models, you will find that they do not have picture-perfect existences. There is much in the way of sadness, substance abuse, eating disorders, failed relationships, and heartache in the lives of what the media calls "the beautiful people."

Do not judge your inside by other people's outsides. You have to find happiness with who you are in body, mind, and spirit. Of course we should always be striving to improve ourselves and grow in all these areas. The true key to happiness and fulfillment is loving yourself, not in the egotistical way of a prima donna, but in a positive and self-nurturing fashion.

Other Modeling Opportunities

Saddam Hussein is not the only person to use body doubles. If you admire the hands or legs or perhaps another, more erogenous, part of a famous actor or actress in a movie, there is a good chance that the part is not actually theirs! There is a dirty little secret in Hollywood that is not so secret anymore. Many men and women make a nice living substituting their assets for those of your favorite stars. Chances are very good that the body parts of the performers in a nude scene are not those of the superstars.

Body-part modeling is another specialty category that, as the name suggests, uses just part of the body in advertising. A person may have the supermodel equivalent of great hands or feet, while the rest of them may be rather ordinary. Such a person can make a career out of modeling shoes or gloves or hand soap—things that involve only that part of the body. Body-part models produce the same composites and portfolios as other models, though the pictures are only of the body part in question.

Plus-size models are, no pun intended, the largest growing group in the industry. This is because designers and advertisers are finally targeting the majority of women in America. One in three women is a size sixteen or larger, and this group has been largely forgotten when it came to stylish and sexy clothing lines. This is happily changing and also creating more opportunities for large and lovely women to work in the modeling business. There are more and more agencies popping up that work exclusively with plus-size models.

ALERT!

The Web site *www.plusmodels.com* offers plenty of practical advice on how big, beautiful women can get started in the modeling business. It also includes plus health and beauty tips, warnings about the many scams and con artists who prey on naïve models, and a discussion board to communicate with other models and industry professionals.

Everyone has strengths, and there is likely a modeling venue for you to display yours. Be flexible and open and make the requisite rounds and you may find your modeling niche. (E)

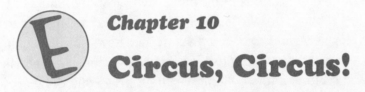

Chapter 10

Circus, Circus!

Running away to join a traveling circus has been a romantic notion that has captured the imagination of people for generations. It is not a fanciful daydream from a bygone era—many people still do it. In this chapter we explore the many ways you can seek a career cavorting under the Big Top.

Run Away and Join the Circus

For many, the circus evokes a certain magic. This magnetism might be inspired by childhood memories, but there's also a powerful draw in the seemingly adventurous and bold move of pulling up stakes, saying good-bye to a stagnant and all-too-predictable life, and touring the country as a wandering vagabond. Circus performing is wholesome family entertainment, perhaps a little corny to many in this so-called sophisticated era. The clowns, jugglers, and trapeze artists do not have the hip cutting edge of today's popular performers, yet the ringmaster in his garish outfit, the sights and sounds and smells under the Big Top still draw crowds as they hark back to a simpler time.

FACT

CircusWeb (✎ *www.circusweb.com*) is an interesting Web site that gives you a history of circuses and circus life, plus a list of links to the many circuses operating in America today.

You may think of the circus arriving in a small town in the heartland as something uniquely American, but circuses have been around as a form of entertainment for thousands of years. Julius Caesar spoke of giving the masses "bread and circuses" to keep them fed and entertained and thus passive and not inclined to revolt.

In today's high-tech world, the ringmaster in top hat and tails, the brass band playing the lively strains of John Philip Sousa, the parade of animals, jugglers, acrobats, trapeze artist, and of course the clowns are anachronistic and passé to many. But there are plenty for whom the smell of sawdust is still thrilling, and the circus will forever captivate their imaginations.

As in all forms of entertainment, there is a lot more going on behind the scenes, and very little of it is as glamorous and romantic. Let's take a look at some of the more mundane and earthy aspects of the circus world.

Life Under the Big Top

As in any business, the unskilled laborer may have to start at the lowest rung of the totem pole, hopefully showing the aptitude and initiative to rise within the ranks. That is, it's good to have a skill if you do not want to spend your career cleaning up after Dumbo. (Don't knock it—the spiritual among us will tell you that there is nobility in every profession.)

For those who consider the circus to be inhumane, one must admit there has been some improvement since the days of ancient Rome, when animals were pitted against each other to the death, and also got to feast on the occasional Christian.

There is a lot more going on in the operation of a circus than the hijinks that delight the cotton-candy-consuming spectators. Like any of the performing arts, there are stagehands, set builders, ticket takers, concessions people, and many more. You may find yourself doing a little of everything, especially in the smaller circuses. An ideal circus employee is a jack of all trades.

A Day in the Life

A typical circus day begins in the middle of the night, driving into the next town where the circus will perform. Arriving at the empty lot where the circus tents will be set up, the staff can catch a catnap before rising at dawn to assemble what is essentially a small town. This is physically demanding work that has to be completed in a few short hours. There is a lot to do. The canvas crew pitches the tents. The seats are put in place, the concession stands are put up, and the electrical crew sets up the generator. The performers are responsible for preparing and testing their own rigging. A trapeze artist usually wants to supervise his or her own setup and does not trust it to others. Their life may depend on it, particularly if they are working without a net.

There are usually two performances on weekdays, three on weekends, and immediately after the last show the whole thing is broken down, packed, and off they go to the next venue.

A circus community is like a family, with all the joys and dysfunctions that family life entails. Since they spend all their time together, close bonds are formed. They celebrate holidays together, and children are home-schooled by their always-traveling parents. Given the nature of show business in general and the eclectic citizens it attracts, circus folk are a tolerant and diverse group of people.

Though there is ritual, rote, and routine, no two days are ever the same. There are always problems that arise, whether it be accidents, temperamental animals, damage to the tents by the forces of nature, or myriad other crises large and small.

This life goes on uninterrupted on the average of eleven months a year without a break. Circuses typically take a hiatus for a few weeks around the Christmas holiday, but otherwise it is a nonstop grind with no days off.

ALERT!

Mooseburger Camp is one of the many clown schools across the country that will give an aspiring clown the training and skills they need to go out into the world and entertain and amuse children of all ages. You can find them on the Web at *www.mooseburger.com.*

People do not enter this life to make their fortune. They do it for love. Some performers can make a nice living, and it is reported that the concession stand owners can make a nicer living through popcorn and cotton candy. But is the smell of the greasepaint and the roar of the crowd that draws a certain type of person to the circus world.

If you do not want to do the grunt work and clean the cages, and you have your sights set on the performance element of the circus world, then you will need to seek training. It is just like any other career in the entertainment field. There are schools for aspiring circus performers.

Clowning Around

You have probably known many a person that you called a "clown" in your time. You may not have known it at the time, but you did a disservice to an old and venerable vocation when you called someone whom you thought was foolish or annoying a "clown."

Being a successful clown takes more than an ability to make people laugh through pantomime and rubber-faced mugging that rivals the early films of Jim Carrey. The great English actor Edmund Keane is reputed to have remarked on his deathbed, "Dying is easy. Comedy is hard."

The Clown Resource Directory (✑ www.clownville.org) posts a comprehensive list of links to clown classes, camps, events, workshops, and more. Anything you need to know to aid your clownish quest can be found here.

Clowning around is serious business for its practitioners, and a mini-industry all its own. For generations, since the first clown put on makeup and a red nose, clowns have followed in a family tradition, or learned the old-fashioned way—by doing. Young people with an interest and aptitude were mentored by a veteran clown. In the 1960s, clown training programs started to pop up over the land. One of the reasons that this occurred was the growing loosely knit confederation of noncircus clowns. Some folks were journeymen solo clowns, performing at birthdays and other private functions. Another reason was to preserve the tradition of the great American clowns of the early twentieth century, most of who were dying off. Irvin Feld, one of the men behind the famous Ringling Brothers Barnum & Bailey Circus started the Clown College to pass on the classic routines of the grand masters. The major clown networks extant today are the Clowns of America International, the World Clown Association, Shrine Clown International, as well as many other smaller associations.

There are many clown schools across the country. Simply entering "clown school" into any Internet search engine will return many results. They all offer more or less the same courses. The basic curriculum of a clown school should include a basic set of courses, as described in the next section.

Clown Curriculum

Any respectable clown school should have an introductory course on "the way of the clown." This might include a brief history of clowning and should definitely include the basics in makeup and its application, costumes, and other elements of the professional clown's arsenal of whimsy.

Another course might be an introduction to the physicality inherent in being a clown. Clowns walk and move a certain way, and they have to be able to slip, slide, trip, fall, and get knocked around without hurting themselves. You have to learn all aspects of physical comedy. This is an area in which a natural aptitude must be present. You must have a knack for physical hijinks that can be nurtured and refined by a professional.

ALERT!

You can learn more about clowning on the Internet and in the trade magazines *3 Ring News*; *Clowning Around*; *Clown Alley*; and *Tops and Calliope*. These periodicals are for clowns what the *Wall Street Journal* is to the financial community and what *Variety* is to the theatrical world.

Learning about how to work with balloons and how to perform magic tricks are other things you need to know in order to be a successful clown. All through this process, you should be encouraged to create your own "clown personality" based on your strengths and interests. Your course of study, which usually lasts from three days to one week, should conclude with a public performance.

Make sure that one of the courses offered is a practical look at the business of clowning. This will teach you how to find work, set up your own business, learn what fees to set, how and where to advertise, and the other essentials to being a happy clown.

There are also other categories of clowning you may be interested in. Some clowns specialize in performing in hospitals. This can be difficult, but it's also poignant and rewarding work if you are there to lift the spirits of the very ill, especially sick children. You might also want to learn how to build your own props, incorporating music, puppets, and ventriloquism into your act. There are even courses in Christian clowning that teach you how to sing, dance, and pratfall your way to salvation.

FACT

Princess Stephanie of Monaco (Grace Kelly's daughter) found freedom from her royal responsibilities by running away to marry a man who was an acrobat with a French circus. By all accounts she was much happier under the Big Top than in the palace.

The Man (and Woman) on the Flying Trapeze

Did you ever want to fly through the air with the greatest of ease? Trapeze and high wire acts have been thrilling circus-goers forever. This is an area of expertise where skill and split-second timing mean more than the difference between a great show and an embarrassing display. Trapeze artists have died in the long history of the art, particularly those daredevils who have sought to thrill the audience by plying their trade with no safety net beneath them to break their fall. The expression "Don't try this at home" is painfully applicable to the art of the flying trapeze. If you have no experience in this field, then professional training is a must, both for your own safety and your ability to land a job.

Flying High

There are many trapeze schools out there. It is possible that you may find one in your area, though some hopefuls will probably have to travel a distance to find one. But if you have an overwhelming desire to leap off a platform twenty-three feet in the air to catch a swinging trapeze, or the hands of your aerial partner, you will find your way to a training center.

Those who have never flown before are likely to find the experience both frightening and liberating when they attend their first class. The instructors are sure to be patient, encouraging, and always safety conscious. If not, get your money back and try another school.

You will start slow. First you get used to hanging from a low bar by your hands, and then you learn to hang by your knees. You will not be far off the ground at first. When you do ascend to the platform, you will be equipped with a safety harness. The greatest obstacle will likely be your fear and your survival instinct. To leap from a great height is not a natural act for humans. It goes against instinct. If you take that leap of faith, knowing you are in no real danger, the result will be exhilarating.

In the second lesson you will practice hanging from the trapeze by your knees. Hanging high above the ground is one thing; doing it upside down is another experience altogether. This is the position where you will function as a "catcher." This means just what it sounds like. Another person, probably the instructor, will leap from the platform into your waiting hands. Timing is everything. Don't despair if it does not work the first few times. Practice makes perfect, and no one will be hurt.

FACT

Ludwig's Flying Trapeze Resource Page (✑www.damnhot.com) includes links to trapeze schools, not just in the United States but all over the world. It also has job listings, a chance to chat with other high flyers, video clips of trapeze artists in action, and a lot more.

Eventually you will be working without the safety harness, but there will always be a net beneath you. You will be learning tricks called the pull over, uprise shoot, and forward over. Before you know it, you will be doing double somersaults and twisting tricks. You will work individually, in pairs, and in teams. You will be taught exercises and stretches to do at home to make you more limber and graceful. You will learn about the rigging and other equipment used.

Once armed with the essentials, you can set about going on auditions to circuses. Inquire if the school has job placement and/or assistance programs. Many do. The instructors will certainly have contacts in the industry. It will be difficult but not impossible to get your foot in the door. If you are prepared and able to give a soaring audition, you can look forward to enjoying the natural high provided by a cheering audience.

Some trapeze schools to check out are the Trapeze School of New York (at ✍ *www.trapezeschool.com*), and the San Francisco school Trapeze Arts (at ✍ *www.trapezearts.com*). These schools will give you an idea of the typical curriculum that fledgling flyers need to learn before they can swing above a cheering crowd.

Animal Handlers

If you have a love of animals, you might be considering a career as a circus animal handler. You really have to love them if you want to make a living at it. It can be very hard and sometimes heartbreaking work. You can start at the entry level and work your way up through on-the-job training and continuing education.

If you have a kitty cat imagine caring for a lion or tiger or bear (oh my!). It is a little different and definitely more dangerous. If you want to work with the animals in a circus, you cannot be squeamish about bodily functions. Animals have them, and you will have to clean up the byproducts. You will also have to feed, water, train, groom, bathe, exercise, and clean up after them. You will also keep them company, bond with them and, with the occasional exception, come to love them. You will have to be able to recognize behavioral changes that might indicate a problem or an illness. And, if you have a heart, you will weep when they get sick and die, or have to be put to sleep.

If you work with horses, your title will be groom. You will be doing the same things you would with other animals in addition to cleaning and organizing the various equestrian accoutrements, called tack (bridle, saddle, harness, and so on).

Training

If you are new to all this, an experienced trainer will have to serve as *your* trainer in animal training. The circus animals in your charge will need to be trained on performance ability, obedience, riding (for the horses and elephants), and more. You will need to accustom the animal to your voice and train it to respond to verbal commands. Another training technique is called a "bridge." When the animal responds positively to a command it is immediately given positive reinforcement in the form of a treat of some kind. This takes a long time. Months and months of repetition are needed to train an animal. Circus animals are not always domesticated when you begin to work with them. Working with a horse is very different from training one of the big cats.

QUESTION?

Are circus animals often mistreated?
The Humane Society of America's Web site, at ✍www.hsus.org, includes information that offers a critical view of the way circus animals are treated. (Enter "Circus" into the site search field.) It claims that there is much cruelty to the animals that perform in circuses. The Ringling Brothers Web site has a section that assures the reader that their animals are not treated badly. Read both and form your own opinion.

Conditions

You need to be very careful when interacting with circus animals. They can turn on you even if you have worked with them for years. There is a reason they are called *wild* animals. They can be disagreeable at times, just like the human animal. Some of the duties will be smelly, icky, noisy, and dangerous. You are bound to have a few scratches and bites along the way in your career as an animal handler.

The hours are irregular. The creatures have to be fed at specific times that do not always fall within regular business hours. You will sometimes be called upon to work nights, weekends, and holidays. It is a physical job as well. Lots of bending and kneeling and crawling and squatting and lugging heavy sacks of feed and hay and other supplies.

Formal training is not necessary, but you should have a high school diploma or the GED equivalent. There are some exceptions. Those who work in an aquarium or marine park might need a degree in marine biology and know how to swim and have SCUBA skills.

The main prerequisite remains a love of animals. The rest can be learned along the way. If you truly love the creatures, it can be an extremely rewarding job. Ⓔ

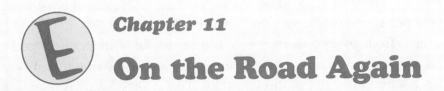

Chapter 11
On the Road Again

If the four walls are starting to close in on you and the open road is wailing a siren's call, maybe it is time for you to look for a job on the road. There are plenty of jobs that will keep you traveling from place to place. You may not be upwardly mobile, but you will always be on the move.

Living out of a Suitcase

Not everyone is suited for living out of a suitcase. Others thrive on it. If you are not a homebody and do not have any attachments, or you feel the need to get away from it all from time to time, there are ways you can be paid to travel. If you have never spent a lot of time on the road, it can be a difficult adjustment. As we are learning about alternative careers, it is not all about glamour. In fact, there is precious little glitz. The reward comes from going your own way and the sense of independence and satisfaction this brings. Though this can bring peace of mind, it is not always free from stress and boredom. This is particularly true of those people who spend a lot of time on the road. There are common factors of this life and specific ways to deal with them.

Fighting Boredom

You will experience a lot of downtime if you are a frequent traveler. Whether it entails waiting around an airport or traversing the heartland on a Greyhound bus or your car, a lot of the time you will feel like you are in a tedious limbo en route from point A to point B. This time will be less grueling if you can use it productively. If you are not behind the wheel and have the luxury to turn on the radio and go into that meditative rhythm that long-distance drivers enjoy, you have to find a way to keep yourself occupied. When you leave the driving, or flying, to someone else, the loss of control can be frustrating and the downtime especially maddening.

ALERT!

Being on the road is not for everyone. If you have a family, you are going to miss them (unless you come from a dysfunctional family). If you are a free spirit with few attachments, life on the road may be more to your liking. Rather than a monotonous grind, each day is a new adventure.

If you have a laptop computer, bring it along and use it to check e-mail, surf the Web, get some work done, or have some fun. If you are not equipped with a computer or the means to get online, then entertain yourself the old-fashioned way and read a book. This is a novel idea in these times, but a good way to pass the time. Bring a portable tape or CD player, and listen to your favorite tunes or a book on tape. The worst thing you can to is to just sit there waiting to get to where you are going. It will feel like an eternity before you arrive.

Do Not Be Burdened by Stuff

It is wise to pack light when traveling. Of course a long trip means you need more things, but in general most people bring more than they actually need when going on the road. Traveling pros suggest that 90 percent of the contents of your suitcase should be what you need for the length of the trip, with 10 percent allotted for a potential delay that requires another change of clothes. Take a look at what you needed and did not use on your last trip, and this will help you pack more economically for the next adventure.

Check the weather forecast of where you are going in advance of your trip to see what you may need to bring. Of course the weather is subject to change, but you will be a little more prepared if you have a basic idea of what the conditions will be when you arrive at your destination. The Weather Channel will tell you what you need to know, and it is very easy to check weather conditions around the country over the Internet—just enter "Local weather" into any search engine. You can click on that and will be given the option to enter the city, state, or zip code of where you are and where you are going.

Do not rush the packing process before you go. Allot ample time to pack briskly yet methodically. Hastily throwing stuff in your bags is a sure way to leave the house without bringing critical items.

Home Sweet Home

There is no place like home, or so they say. And no matter how far or how often you travel, at some point you will return there, even if only for a short stay. You may get into a pattern in which much of the time spent at home is nothing more than planning for the next trip. You get home and crash, do laundry, and get ready to go back on the road.

If you are lucky enough to have a spouse or significant other, and that person is not also always traveling, they can take care of the little things like housecleaning and paying the bills. If not, you had better make the time to take care of these mundane but essential tasks.

Since you will be away from your house or apartment for extended periods of time, you should unplug your computer, television, and other appliances to prevent the damage that an electrical storm can cause. If you have a house, do not completely shut off the heat in the winter, or you may come home to find your pipes have frozen and burst. You might also consider a timer than turns the lights in different rooms on and off periodically to maintain the illusion that your empty space is inhabited.

Now that you have an idea how to be prepared and stave off boredom, we will now take a look at some different ways you can make a living on the road.

Roadies

A roadie is a person who does much of the grunt work that is involved with a touring concert. When you go see a musical star at a local venue, the roadies have done all the work to construct the stage or set, make sure the electricity is working, and hundreds of other tasks to ensure that the performance goes off without incident.

There is a pecking order among roadies, which is a career with a hierarchical structure just like any other business. Mules are workers who do the hard-core, down and dirty manual labor. They need to be in good shape and handy in matters of construction and carpentry. A mule that proves his mettle can be promoted to a managerial position supervising the other workers.

Some roadies also function as security for the performers. They keep unwelcome visitors and swooning groupies away from the band—and no doubt also sometimes escort a select few swooning groupies to the band's dressing rooms. Others function as drivers who transport the band and the equipment from one venue to the next. Real go-getters with an ingratiating manner can become personal roadies to the performers. This is a glorified gofer position, but it enables a person to rub elbows with the stars, if that is one of your goals. Roadies, after all, seek to get a taste of the limelight and catch the crumbs that fall through the cracks in the stage. Perhaps this is why roadies endure the long hours and the backbreaking work. It is an opportunity to be on the periphery of the entertainment world. Roadies live in a world that is a combination of blue-collar sweat and glamorous glitterati.

ALERT!

The Web site ✐*www.roadie.net* is "a resource for all Roadies, Ex-Roadies, or anyone who ever dreamed of being a Roadie." The site includes fun stuff like "Roadie Recipes," "Want to be a Roadie?" and "Roadie Lingo," including both American and British roadie slang.

Couriers

Air travel couriers, also known as casual couriers, are people who get to see the world for a fraction of the cost that most tourists pay. It is not a career in the traditional sense, but if you have the time and the inclination, it is a great chance to travel at a substantial discount and visit many parts of the world you might otherwise never see.

Believe it or not, it is sometimes cheaper for a courier company to send a human being along with the material they want delivered. Via this method, a person checks the freight as luggage, rather than having it shipped as cargo. A passenger can collect his or her luggage quickly (usually) and deliver it to its destination. Freight shipped as traditional cargo can take forever to get there and languish in a customs warehouse.

If you are over twenty-one, you are eligible to be a casual courier. Most courier companies expect a clean-cut appearance. Besides, your nose ring and tongue stud will set off the metal detectors. A casual courier travels like any other passenger, except that the bulk of his or her luggage is a company's freight. You can save up to 85 percent on a round-trip airline ticket, and once you have delivered the goods to a company representative, you are free to go off and explore the country for at least seven days, sometimes longer. On your return trip you will probably be accompanying freight back to the United States.

If a company desperately needs something to absolutely, positively be there they might spring for a free round-trip flight, but usually a discount is all that's offered. It is a better deal than you are likely to get from any airline or travel agency.

When you are registered with a courier agency, they pay for the ticket, and you pay them for your share. You pick up the ticket at the airport from a representative of the company. You pick the place you would like to visit and check to see if any couriers are needed to travel to that area. You should inquire at least two weeks in advance, sometimes as long as four to six weeks in the summertime. During the off-season, Europe in the winter for example, you might get a call within twenty-four hours to prepare for takeoff.

You return ticket is usually for seven days, but sometimes longer. You could arrange to spend as long as six months overseas and be guaranteed a return ticket. Of course you are on your own once you are over there.

FACT

The International Association of Air Travel Couriers (✐ *www.iaatc.com*) promises a 100-percent money-back guarantee if they are not able to place you as a casual courier. The registration fee to join the association is currently $45. When you want to make your trip, you simply telephone the appropriate reservation number to schedule a flight.

This is an aboveboard business. You do not even touch the merchandise. The courier company representative deals with customs at your departure destination and another one collects the manifest from you and deals with the customs people at the arrival point. You do not have to fear that you will be the fall guy in a smuggling operation. You are not responsible or liable for the merchandise in any way. You are not a bonded agent.

Tour Guides

If you like working with people—and you *really* have to like working with people—you might want to look into being a tour guide. As a tour guide, you escort a group of people through locales and give them the background and history of various points of interest.

It is not easy shepherding a group of as many as forty people from place to place and educating them about the culture and geography of the region. A tour guide does even more than this. As a tour guide, you should plan to spend all day, every day, for about a week with a cross-section of the population, each with their distinct personalities and quirks. There will be the loudmouth who questions and challenges at every turn, the timid soul plagued with motion sickness, and the inevitable noisy children whose obnoxious behavior is interpreted by their parents as positively darling. Emergencies will also arise from time to time, and a tour guide must be able to deal with them as well.

A tour guide is also the travel coordinator. The guide handles all aspects of the trip, including checking the group in and out of the hotels, planning the itinerary and dealing with the locales, be they the human animal or the wildlife and the elements if you are guiding a tour in the great outdoors. You have to be able to compromise, improvise, and not get rattled by any problems and obstacles that are sure to occur from time to time.

A Typical Work Schedule

Remember that for the tourists on the trip, it is a vacation. For the guide it is work, and often the work is very hard. You may have as little as two days off a month in the busiest seasons. The work can be sporadic, so you may find yourself with too much time off during winter months. Your home may fall into disrepair, and your social life may suffer. If you are thinking that the romance of brief encounters with those in your charge may be a nice source of companionship, you may find yourself on the unemployment line in short order. People who travel for a living often tire of it eventually, and tour guides can and do become victims of burnout. There is a high turnover in the industry as a result.

If you are a full-timer with a travel service, you may be expected to pitch in during slow periods and the off-season with office work and other less glamorous chores. If you do not want to do this, then you should budget yourself for the periods when the work is not forthcoming. In these instances you will be "on call," which means you are required to be ready at short notice.

A tour guide meets their group at the starting point, which is usually the airport in the tour company's hometown. The guide flies with the tourists to the destination, and there they board a bus equipped with a special seat and microphone for the tour guide at the front of the bus next to the driver. Public speaking is a requisite for the job. If you are not comfortable with this, you will have to learn fast or find another line of work. You have to become well versed with the territory you are touring. For most guides, poise and confidence builds with each successive tour until they become unflappable, seasoned professionals.

There are both year-round and seasonal opportunities for tour guides. The larger the tour agency, the greater the potential for diverse assignments. An agency that handles tours of national parks in the summer, foliage-viewing trips in the fall, and tropical excursions in the winter could keep you busy all year. It could also expose you to that big wide world beyond the cozy confines of your neck of the woods. There are more than 300 land tour companies in the United States and Canada that hire tour guides and managers.

Princess Cruise Lines, one of the major ocean liner companies, lists available jobs in such areas as boutiques, casino, entertainment, front desk, and photography on its Web site, at *www.princess.com*.

A Real-Life Love Boat

Perhaps you prefer the sea breeze in your hair to the claustrophobic atmosphere of a bus. If so, you will want to investigate jobs with one of the many cruise lines that traverse the seven seas. Life at sea, like most alternative careers, has an element of drudgery that goes hand in glove with the romance of the nautical life. But since your current position no doubt has its share of drudgery, why not enjoy your down time on the Love Boat?

A cruise ship has a hierarchy that is similar to the navy. The captain and officers expect to be addressed by rank and treated with deference and respect. A captain of a ship at sea is one of the last truly autonomous jobs around. He or she can either wear their power like a loose garment or swagger and strut like a twenty-first-century Captain Bligh. You will be asked to remove your "Question Authority" button when you come aboard. There are rules and regulations unique to the maritime tradition that must be followed. There will be frequent lifeboat and other safety drills, and you will need to be versed in how to handle the singular emergencies that may arise at sea.

ALERT!

If you have never been on the high seas, you should find out if you are prone to seasickness before taking a job on a cruise ship. A ship is rolling and bouncing even in relatively calm seas. The ocean creates an undulating effect that can surprise those unaccustomed to the constant motion. And if the ship encounters a storm, the uninitiated can become quite ill.

Life on a cruise ship is one of teamwork and close quarters. You may have to bunk with another worker. It will seem like you are back in your old bedroom that you shared with a brother or sister, or perhaps you will be reminded of the college dorm. While accommodations for the guests are often plush, cabins for the staff are not. If you stick around long enough to gain seniority, you will probably be bumped up to better quarters. The food is not the quality served the passengers, either—but there is an upside to working like a dog, and that is that you will sometimes get the scraps from the captain's table. Some, but not all, cruise lines have televisions in the staff rooms or at least a recreation lounge.

Your skills as an actor will be required in that you always have to be pleasant despite your mood. Remember Julie and Isaac, the perky cruise director and bartender on the television show *Love Boat*? The difference is that they were on a one-hour television show. You will have to be "on" during all your waking hours for the length of the cruise. Staff members frequently sign contracts for three to eight months, and that involves a lot of smiling. The passengers you will be serving are paying a lot of money for what may be a once-in-a-lifetime experience, so they do not need to be subjected to cranky, glowering staff. You are considered on duty any time you are in a public area, which is just about everywhere but your cabin.

Meals and laundry services are included, unless you work in the kitchen or the laundry room. When the ship is in port, and the passengers have disembarked, staff can use the pool and other facilities, but commingling socially with the guests is verboten. Unlike the romances featured on the television Love Boat, becoming romantically involved with a passenger can lead to your dismissal if discovered.

Typical workers on a cruise ship include bartenders, shore excursion guides, retail clerks, youth coordinators, child care staff, musicians and entertainers, casino staff, cruise staff, aerobics instructors, restaurant staff, and hosts. Depending on what you do, the average salaries are between $1,500 and $3,000 a month. Some ships offer a bar allowance of $75 a month. The ability to save is greater than a lot of other jobs since expenses like commuting, laundry, and meals are covered.

Cruise ships are constantly sailing here, there, and everywhere, so you can sail the seven seas and visit exotic ports of call from the Caribbean to the fjords of Norway, from Asia to Africa, and from the Baltic Sea to the port of New York City.

FACT

Norwegian Cruise Lines posts job listings on their Web site (✍ *www.ncl.com*), including positions in a variety of specialties: casino, hotel and food and beverage management, housekeeping, purser's department, cruise staff, shore excursions, dive-in entertainment, music, medical, information technology, gift shops, photography, beauty salon and spa, and Internet café.

Road Rats

We have all seen the large trailers on the highway carrying brand-new cars to the dealerships across the country. But how do larger vehicles like RVs, school buses, vans, FedEx and UPS trucks, limousines and other vehicles get to the destinations? They are driven by people who have come to be known as "road rats."

The requirements are minimal. You need to be over eighteen and have a valid driver's license. It is estimated that more than 100,000 road rats traverse the United States on any given day. Some do it as a paid weekend road trip and for others it is a full-time job.

Part-timers can earn from $100 to $250 for a weekend, while experienced, full-time drivers can make between $35,000 to $52,000 a year. People can sometimes get a plane ticket home or a free trip to the pick-up location. There are several ways you can do this.

The Web site ✍ *www.roadrat.com* gives you more information on this potentially liberating and lucrative career. The founder of the site coined the phrase "road rat" and has been doing it full-time since 1977.

Make a Few Phone Calls

There are more than 3,800 automobile manufacturing sites in North America. Cars and trucks can simply be put on a trailer and shipped to dealerships and buyers, but larger and uniquely shaped vehicles cannot. You can check your local Yellow Pages or do an Internet search to find the manufacturers and dealers near you and inquire about any opportunities. Of course you can expect your background to be thoroughly checked out before anyone hands you the keys to a brand-new vehicle.

Transporter Companies

If you find that you are encountering roadblocks in your independent quest to find work as a road rat, you can try applying to a transporter company. Transporter companies supply vehicle manufacturers with drivers. These companies have full-time drivers, but they often need additional drivers as well. There are opportunities to work part-time, seasonally, and to be an on-call driver. Of course, the pay is less than working as an independent contractor since the transporter company will take their cut. The average rate is eighteen cents a mile, as opposed to a possible thirty-three cents when working directly for the manufacturer. You can find a list of auto shippers at *www.moves4u.com.*

DPUs

Another option is to contact your local RV dealership to find out if they employ drivers to do dealer pickups (DPUs). You can make more money than with the transporter companies (twenty-eight cents a mile on average). Manufacturers and transporters usually fly you home when you have delivered the vehicle to the dealership. Dealers fly you to the manufacturers and you drive the vehicle back to them. DPU drivers usually work for the dealership. Some may also contract freelancers to make deliveries.

Going Both Ways

Once you have been doing this for a while and have established a trustworthy track record and networked with many companies, you can devise a schedule that allows you to pick up a second vehicle from the same or different manufacturer or from a transporter company to drive back to your area. This is additional income and keeps you on the road more. If you are considering this as an alternative career, on the road is where you want to be.

Requirements

As mentioned earlier, you have to be over eighteen and have a valid driver's license to work as a road rat. There are circumstances in which you may need a special type of driver's license to drive a particular kind of vehicle. Under federal law, you only need a regular license to drive any vehicle less than 26,000 pounds. Anything more than that weight requires that you have a commercial driver's license (CDL), the type of license that truckers have. Acquiring this license requires that you go for additional driving lessons in larger vehicles in order to become certified. You will also need to check with your prospective employer and your state's department of motor vehicles to see whether they require you to upgrade to a chauffeur's license.

Demographics

Almost anyone can become a road rat at any stage in his or her life. It is estimated that one-third of the rats on the road are retirees and other senior citizens. Many people fear age discrimination and a decrease in career opportunities as they get older, but this is not the case for potential road rats. Statistically speaking, older folks are among the safer drivers in the road, and that is what matters to those companies that hire drivers. As long as you have a good driving record and are in good health, age will not be a factor in your eligibility to be a cross-country driver.

Many students and teachers also work as road rats in the summer months. For teachers, this job is a nice way to make extra money, and for students it certainly beats working at the local fast food eatery.

Couples often take out two vehicles and stay close to each other on the road. This way they double their income. There are some companies that do not mind if you bring along your children. Proceed at your own risk when doing this—just imagine how many times you will have to hear the familiar cry, "Are we there yet?" (E)

Chapter 12

E

Working at Home (or Close to It)

There are many reasons why you might consider working from home these days. Perhaps you have children, or maybe you are tired of your time-consuming commute. Perhaps you simply prefer working in your underwear. In this chapter, we look at the many opportunities to make a living without venturing far from your humble abode.

The Home-Court Advantage

Working from home, if you find something that is rewarding and generates a decent income, can be a wonderful experience. You will not have to deal with traffic, and you can spend more time with your family. You can avoid office politics, irascible supervisors, and the 1,001 headaches that go along with the traditional working life. Do not think you will be spared headaches as a person who works from home. There will be different kinds of problems and obstacles to contend with, but by and large they will be your headaches, not those imposed on you by the boss.

For some of the careers in this chapter, such as a cleaning service or personal companionship, you may have to go over to someone else's home to ply your trade. For others, such as working in a kennel, you may start out working at someone else's business for experience before eventually opening up your own establishment at your own home sweet home.

Caring for Children

If you want to work at home and you like children, you might want to consider a career in childcare. If you do not want to work for someone else, you can start your own day-care center. The growing number of mothers who are obliged to go to work because of the economy or the fact that they are single parents keeps day-care centers in demand.

Opening a Day-Care Center

There is a great responsibility to running and/or working in a day-care center. Not only are you accountable for the physical safety of the children, day-care workers will be the primary adult in the child's life for most of its waking hours. Ages one to six are important in a child's development. Much of what makes us who we are is forged during this time. Even though most of us do not have clear memories of those years, what happens to us during that time stays with us forever. More is expected of day-care center staff than to be mere babysitters. There must be structure and some preschool educational activities and games in addition to naptime.

You have to check with state and local regulatory agencies and find out the requirements for running a day-care center in your area. While you may not look forward to dealing with a big bloated bureaucracy, day-care centers are a business that can benefit from government intervention in the free-market economy. Some state governments offer grants, subsidies, and other funding to people who want to open a day-care center. Big government never gets smaller despite the campaign promises of politicians, and programs for childhood education and before- and after-school programs are expected to increase in the coming years.

Some states have a mandatory space allotment for each child. You cannot crowd too many kids in a small space. Child development experts suggest that an individual day-care worker should be responsible for no more than three or four infants less than one year old, or five or six toddlers from one to two years old, or ten preschool-age children between two and five years old.

The mandatory training requirements and necessary qualifications vary from state to state. Some require college degrees, while others need nothing more than a high school diploma. Some states will insist that you take continuing education courses in the field once you begin working in it. Check with your state and local governments to find out the particulars.

Check out the licensure information posted on the site ✍*www.busykids.com*. It lists the individual state regulations that one needs to know in advance of opening a day-care center. You will be able to see how easy or not-so-easy the process will be in your state.

Other requirements may include one hot meal per day, the presence of a licensed teacher for every fifteen to twenty children, and a nurse on the premises. You have to make sure you are well versed in the local regulations or you may be shut down and subject to litigation.

Getting Started

You can start off small by offering a baby-sitting service as you learn and prepare for a more ambitious day-care center. You will probably have to begin this way unless you have deep pockets or venture capital. All you need for a baby-sitting service are good references. Remember we live in an age where there seem to be more villains who prey on children, so parents are going to want to check you out thoroughly. As your baby-sitting service grows, you need to investigate finding a space for your potential day-care center. If your residence is not an ideal site, you should look at large vacant properties in your community. You can also approach local churches and other organizations in your community with whom you can go into partnership. This will save you the hassle of finding a place and having to deal with the local bureaucracy about things like zoning laws.

Many novice day-care center operators find space in vacant stores in shopping malls. This too will not violate any zoning laws—in many areas, it is illegal to operate a business in a residential neighborhood. And there will be plenty of parking space. Parents can pull up in front of the storefront and quickly drop off Junior.

Hours of Operation

Day-care center hours are usually from 6 A.M. to 6 P.M. If you do not have help, you will have to be there all day. Even with help, you will probably be there for the duration, early to set things up and late to accommodate the inevitable parent who is running late. You also need to decide if you want to offer breakfast. You are definitely going to need kitchen facilities of some kind, and may have to offer at least a lunch-hour meal per child per day. You might want to let the parents know that they are on their own for breakfast. If you choose to offer it, make sure you factor this into your fee. The midday meal should include fruit and juice and not a steady diet of junk food.

A Typical Day-Care Day

A day-care center is a less formal form of preschool. The day usually begins with a play period from arrival to about 9 A.M. You will need toys and a television, but plopping the kids in front of the tube all day is unacceptable. From 9 to 10 in the morning, the children are grouped by their age and there is a story time. The midmorning snack is between 10 and 11 A.M. If you can get them, try to have guests come in to entertain the children after the snack time. The local police and firemen will usually send volunteers. Your local chamber of commerce will be of assistance for getting local educators and entertainers to occasionally drop by.

The noon hour to 1 P.M. is reserved for lunch, followed by another learning session. You can invite college students and retirees to come in to lend a hand, and you may be required by law to have a certified teacher on site during business hours. Nap time and another afternoon snack time round out the day. By then, you will probably be happy to see the parents arriving in the late afternoon.

Some states demand that a registered nurse be on the premises. If not, you definitely need a basic knowledge of first aid. Be sure you have a first-aid kit on hand. Despite your best efforts, little ones will bang into things and fall down on occasion. You will also need written instructions from parents about the special needs of their kids.

To learn about the eligibility requirements, and to find a description of what constitutes the official designation "Certified Childcare Professional," you can contact the National Childcare Association, 1016 Rosser St., Conyers, GA 30012. Their Web site is *www.nccanet.org*.

Day-Care Fees

The going rate for day-care centers is $35 to $65 per child for a five-day week, with an extra charge of $5 to $10 for meals. In some areas of the country, fees can be significantly higher. It is not out of line to ask for the money in advance. In fact, it is a very good idea. This will eliminate the problems of collection and ensure that you have working capital on hand. Asking parents to pay by the week is better than by the month. A month is considered to be made up of four weeks, but every third month has five weeks. You do not want to be giving away a free week of service four times a year.

Advertising

Day care is in demand. Statistics reveal that most are operating at 90 percent capacity within six months of opening. This is because there are plenty of families who need the service and also because of the advertising campaigns of the owners.

One easy method is good old-fashioned fliers distributed throughout the community and on telephone poles. You can either go to a printer or do it yourself. Your home computer probably came preloaded with a software program that produces basic fliers and brochures. This, coupled with a color printer and quality paper, will enable you to produce quality fliers.

You should also place ads in the local newspapers, magazines, and the Yellow Pages. Creating a press release and sending it to the same papers will probably get you mentioned in the community news section of the paper, maybe even a feature story. This is valuable free publicity.

FACT

You can find out about the eligibility requirements and a description of the child development associate credential at the Council for Professional Recognition, 2460 16th St. NW, Washington, D.C., 20009-3575. Their Internet address is ✎ *www.cdacouncil.org*.

Advertise in advance of your opening. Put on a splashy grand opening party, inviting members of the press and the community. During this open house they can see your place as well as meet with you and any staff you may have. Make a good impression, and the parents will be pulling up in front of your day-care center bright and early on Monday morning.

Pet-Care Careers

You may love animals, and maybe you think it would be fun to work with them all day. It is hard enough work caring for your personal pet, but if you think you have the right stuff, there are many ways to make a living in the pet-care industry. Once you are experienced enough, many of these careers can be based from your own home. Before you open a kennel or pet-grooming parlor, just make sure that zoning regulations will permit you to do so (and that you don't live in a small studio apartment).

ALERT!

A word of warning to those who are thinking of working with other people's pets as a career: Pet owners are a unique demographic that can be quite devoted to their furry and feathered friends. Their pets are precious, often more so than the humans in their lives. Keep this in mind when taking someone's pet in your care. It is more of a responsibility than you might imagine.

Kennel Workers

Kennel attendants care for dogs and cats whose masters and mistresses are going on vacation or need to board them for some other reason. If you work as an entry-level kennel worker to gain experience you will be responsible for feeding and exercising the animals. Do not forget about cleaning their cages. If you are not comfortable with this aspect of an animal's natural biological functions than you should reconsider your career choice.

The American Boarding Kennels Association (ABKA) has a home-study program available for those interested in the field. It involves the basic and advanced aspects of animal care and the business side of running a kennel. If you complete the course and pass both a verbal and written test, you will earn the title of certified kennel operator (CKO).

For more information on jobs in animal care and control, as well as the animal shelter and control personnel training program, you can contact The Humane Society of the United States, 2100 L St. NW, Washington, D.C., 20037-1598. Their Web site is *www.hsus.org.*

Groomers

Groomers tend to the personal appearance of a pampered pet just as beauticians and people who work in nail salons tend to their preening human clientele. Groomers work in kennels, veterinary offices, pet supply stores, and animal hospitals. Some eventually start their own business. Groomers are often the first to notice a problem like a rash or infection on the pet and will refer the owner to a vet for treatment. Grooming a pet entails washing, brushing, and clipping the fur and the nails. A good groomer can intuitively handle a cranky canine or frenetic feline that becomes agitated during the process.

Most groomers study under a veteran groomer to learn the trade. They are put in charge of one facet of the process, such as bathing the animal, while observing the experienced groomer at work. Gradually they are given more responsibility until they become seasoned professionals themselves.

ALERT!

To get a list of state-licensed grooming schools, you can send a stamped, self-addressed, business-size envelope to the National Dog Groomers Association of America, P.O. Box 101, Clark, PA 16113. Visit them on the Web at ✍ *www.nationaldoggroomers.com*.

There are also numerous state-licensed grooming schools across the country with courses of study ranging from one to four months in length. There is an organization called the National Dog Groomers Association of America that gives a certification in dog grooming. The test is both written and practical. After answering the 400-question examination, you groom a pet under the watchful eyes of the examiners.

Dog-Walking Services

People love their pets, some to the point of obsession. They treat their beloved best friends better than most people they know and as well (one hopes) as they would treat their children. They feel badly that they have to leave their pet alone during the workday. This has created the growing business of dog walking and pet sitting.

Some pets may also have special needs. They might have a medical condition that necessitates taking medication or shots during the day. Or they may need to "go to the bathroom" (to be polite) more than the average dog.

Dog day-care centers are a thriving business, particular in large urban centers where the animals are cooped in small apartments and deprived of a back-yard. Dog day-care centers are different than kennels in that they operate during the weekday. With some exceptions, there are no night or weekend hours.

FACT

Pet Sitting.biz (*www.dog-walking.com/dog_walkers.html*) is a site where pet sitters and walkers can learn how to start a business, get pet-sitting insurance, fill out the necessary forms, and find out what to put in a contract with the pet owners you will be dealing with.

A dog day-care person walks clients' dogs, feeds them, plays with them, and keeps them company. The dogs also gets to gambol and interact with other members of their species. If you are interested in this field, you have to be in good enough shape to handle a number of dogs on leashes while navigating a city street. In most cities there are now laws that you must clean up after your dog, so you have to be prepared to pick up a lot of waste and deposit it in the nearest trashcan. You will also be dealing with a diverse group of personalities, as uniquely individual as any humans you have encountered in your travels. You must also know animal first aid in the event of an emergency.

Depending on where you live, pet owners will pay as much as $30 an hour to see that their dog is not lonely and remains active and entertained during the day. If you have several dogs a day as your "clients," you could make a nice weekly living as a dog walker/sitter.

Cat sitters have it a little easier. Cats are much more low maintenance. They use the litter box and do their own thing. It would not be a demanding job to sit in an apartment and keep kitty company for a few hours. If the cat wants some attention, it will trot over and let you know. Dog sitters are much more in demand than cat sitters and will make more money simply because the work is more arduous.

To receive career information and information on training, certification, and salaries of animal control officers at federal, state, and local levels, you can write to the National Animal Control Association, P.O. Box 480851, Kansas City, MO 64148-0851. They can be found online at *www.nacanet.org*.

Personal Companions

Children and pets are not the only creatures that need care and feeding during the day. Many elderly and disabled people rely on personal companions to help them during the day and keep them company. This can range from a person who will run errands or accompany them to the store or a couple of hours in the park to health-care professionals who will administer medications and physical therapy.

If you do not have health-care or nursing credentials you can work as a home care aide. Also known as caregivers, companions, and personal attendants, the job usually involves housecleaning, laundry, cooking, shopping, and other domestic chores. They may also have to move the client from bed to bathroom to other rooms in the house as needed.

Some personal companions will stay with one person for months, even years, and develop a close bond with their charge. For others it is just a job and they may visit more than one client a day, spending a couple of hours taking care of business and going on to the next person. The empathetic personal companion often serves as a friend who will talk with the person and listen to them. In other cultures, the elderly are respected for their wisdom and insight gained from a long life of experiences. We have lost this regard for the graying members of our American society, and that is too bad because there is much to be learned from senior citizens.

A personal companion can anticipate encountering a true cross-section of the aging and disabled populace. Some will be nice; some will be nasty. Some of their homes will be quite tidy; others will be much less pleasant. You have to be able to handle the many moods of your clients.

As with most of the positions described in this chapter, you need to research if the state has put any restrictions and requirements on your ability to work as a personal companion. Some states will leave you alone to work as a self-employed personal companion. Other local governments will be more intrusive and require certification and formal training, and possibly a physical examination and a screening for tuberculosis. This disease, once all but eradicated in the United States, has been making a comeback of late. You can become a certified personal and/or home care aide through National Association for Home Care. This is not mandatory to work in the trade, but those who get the certificate have something to show a prospective client during the interview process.

Personal companions will be in greater demand as the years go by. People are living longer and thus will stay alive long enough get serious health problems that require constant attention. In the old days when the mortality rate was high people died before chronic medical problems could occur. The fact that health-insurance plans are more inclined to kick people out the hospital more quickly than in years past has created a greater need for personal companions.

Tutoring

If you were good in school, and you have a love of learning coupled with an ability to effectively impart your knowledge to others, you could find work as a tutor. If you are a teacher, you could tutor for the extra money. If you do not have the inclination to deal with the education system as it stands today, you may want to do your tutoring as a self-employed contractor.

Like other small home-based businesses, you can start off simply. Put ads in the local paper, fliers in store windows, and notices on telephone poles. Chances are you will be getting calls in short order. The sorry state of the school system in most parts of the country will work in your favor. Kids are being graduated without being able to read and write, so concerned parents who cannot do the job themselves know they are going to have to supplement their children's education if they want to give them a fighting chance in the competitive world of college and career.

FACT

If you think you need additional advertising in your tutoring business, use services like TutorNation (✍ *www.tutornation.com*). Businesses like this hook up parents looking for tutors with tutors seeking work. This service charges a lifetime membership fee of $45 for tutors, and it is free for those looking for tutors.

When a potential client contacts you, be prepared to provide a resume, references, and academic transcripts or a diploma. You may also want to offer the initial lesson for free. This will ingratiate the client to you, and you can see if you and the child will work well together before you settle into a routine. Here are the going rates, as of this writing, based on your level of education and specific subject matter:

- **Master's degree or Ph.D.:** $25–35 per hour
- **Bachelor's or education degree:** $20–25 per hour
- **Undergraduate students:** $15–25 per hour
- **High school students:** $8–15 per hour
- **English as a second language:** $15–25 per hour

Cleaning Services

The cleaning business is ideal for someone interested in starting a small business. There is always a demand for good cleaning services, no matter what the economy. Some people can afford to have their homes and apartments cleaned, and even those who are not in the high-income brackets employ the services of cleaners out of lack of time or lack of motivation.

Home and apartment cleaning requires no special training or equipment. Of course, if you are the sloppy half of *The Odd Couple,* you have to ask yourself if you have what it takes. On the other hand, many thorough, borderline-obsessive cleaners do not keep their own places in pristine condition at all times.

There is almost no overhead and no start-up fees other than the basic advertising as described throughout this chapter (ads, fliers, word of mouth). You can start part-time and build to full-time as you collect a loyal clientele. A steady stable of regular customers can generate a nice income.

Tax Information for the Self-Employed

This brief introduction into tax information should not constitute the last word on the subject. All self-employed people should consult an accountant at tax time. The fee an accountant charges will probably still save you money in the long run, and it will diminish the dreaded possibility of an audit.

Make sure your home is not zoned in a "residential only" area. It could be illegal to operate a business where you live. This is probably not the case, and even if it is, many people get around such zoning laws. At the same time, zoning is important, and it is something you should at least be aware of before setting up shop in your home. If you want to do business by the book, and of course you should, you should find out if you need any special permits. If you are selling products, you may need a vendor's license. This means you will be obligated to collect sales tax.

Tax Deductions

The tax laws are no longer as beneficial for home-based businesses as they once were. Still, there are some deductions you can make, after confirming this with your accountant, of course.

You can deduct part of your home or apartment if it is used for business purposes or as a home office. The IRS is picky about this. It has to be a separate space dedicated and designated as a working space. If you have a television in your home office that your children watch in the evening, the IRS says this is not a deductible office space. And people who live in studio apartments are out of luck entirely.

Keep good records in the event of an audit. The Feds will scrutinize your domicile for anything that does not jibe with what you claim in your tax return. Make sure that the percentage that you claim accurately reflects the space in your home used for business. If you have a home with four rooms, and you use one of them as an office, you may be able to deduct 25 percent of the rent/mortgage and utilities as utilities. Depending on the size of your rooms, you could instead figure a percentage based on the amount of total floor space your work area encompasses. Obviously, you'll want to use whichever legitimate percentage is higher.

Avoid That Audit

You also have to prove that the business is in business to make a profit. If you are in the red (that is, operating at a loss) for a few years in a row, the IRS will decide that your business is a hobby and disallow any deductions. You can also deduct things like a percentage of the utilities, phone and Internet bills, and other expenses. Check with your accountant.

The IRS maintains that they do not give extra scrutiny to people who claim deductions for a home business, but one H&R Block tax preparer would not deduct the phone bill on a certain freelance writer's tax return, claiming that it would be a red flag for the IRS. Keeping accurate records for at least seven years remains a good safety measure. The tax form you use to claim business deductions is Schedule C, Profit (or Loss) for Business or Profession.

Rather than get socked with a whopper of a tax bill on April 15, many self-employed people pay estimated taxes, usually on a quarterly basis. The form for that is 1040-ES, Declaration of Estimated Tax.

Establishing an IRA (individual retirement account) is a good way to both plan for your retirement and save some money on taxes. This is called a tax shelter, and your accountant will have further details and specifics on the many plans available.

Chapter 13

Internet Opportunities

T he Internet is changing the world, including the way we do business and make money. There are numerous opportunities to make extra income and even a living through the miracles of modern technology. This chapter will show you how to ease on down the superhighway to success.

Superhighway to Success

More and more people are using the Internet as more than a means to send e-mails to long-lost relatives or to download naughty pictures. The word "e-commerce" has entered the language to describe this growing trend. Most major businesses have an online presence. Many retailers give you the option of buying their products over the Internet.

People are working from home and using the Internet for business in greater numbers. For some it is a sideline to generate a little extra pocket money. For others, it has become their livelihood.

With the better and faster connectivity available for e-mail and the Internet, you may be able to work at a job that would traditionally be done in an office (maybe even your current nine-to-five gig) from your home as a telecommuter. Or you may decide to start your own Internet-based business.

Consumer Reports magazine is a good reference source to use when shopping for a computer or when making any other major purchase, for that matter. Their experts rate various products to assure that you get the best deal for your money. You can also find them on the Web at ✍ *www.consumerreports.org*.

The advantages of either plan are that you can work from home, avoiding the annoyances and pettiness of office politics—not to mention the long commutes. If you take the time and learn the ropes, all you need is a computer and a modem. If you can afford them, you can also treat yourself to other ancillary accoutrements, like a printer, scanner, and digital camera. With these tools of the trade, you can forge an alternative career that can be rewarding and profitable.

The Right Computer and Internet Connection

If you are going to be spending a lot of time online, you must have a good Internet connection. You are going to be online most of the day, and you cannot afford the busy signals, freezes, and getting the boot when you are right in the middle of an important project.

Your Computer

If your computer is several years old, you really need to trade up if you want to work from home and on the Internet. Back in the day, a desktop computer was very expensive, and 32Mb of RAM was considered a lot. Such a device is essentially obsolete if you want to navigate the World Wide Web and do business today.

The prices have come down, and the power has grown dramatically in personal computers. You can get a desktop model with all the bells and whistles for under $1,000. Most computer retailers will offer special deals like throwing in a free printer and/or a CD burner or DVD drive for free. If a laptop is more to your liking, they are a little more expensive, but they also come fully loaded with extras added to inspire the sale.

DSL

There are plenty of people still getting online by the increasingly antiquated method of dial-up. They call the access number of their internet service provider (ISP) and are connected at a maximum speed of 56K. This speed is more and more ineffectual and frustrating now that Web sites are becoming complex and graphics-laden, with audio and video elements. If you are going to work from home, you will definitely need a faster connection.

Digital subscriber line (DSL) services enable an ordinary phone line to function like a high-speed digital service. The DSL modem gets up to 99 percent more performance out of your phone line without disrupting your phone service; you can be both online and on the Web at the same time. This is essential for a home business, as potential clients and customers will not take kindly to constant busy signals.

Most DSL services are not much more expensive than dial-up services, and many services come with an e-mail address and other features.

Broadband

Broadband is a general term used for high-speed Internet connection. Strictly, however, a broadband connection strictly refers to Internet access via a cable modem, which transmits information over the same lines used to send and receive cable television. DSL is known as a kind of broadband service, but real broadband providers are usually cable television providers, rather than telephone companies.

FACT

Your local phone company probably offers DSL service. You can read reviews of the various companies offering DSL and broadband Internet connections at the Web site *www.dslreports.com*. This site could be called the *Consumer Reports* of the broadband world.

Many broadband customers get Internet access as part of their cable television package. This connection is even faster than DSL. It can also be on around the clock without incurring hourly charges, and it enables you to surf the Web at high speeds, downloading documents and audio and video files almost instantaneously. If you have digital cable and you do not have accompanying Internet access, you should definitely sign up if you are planning to use your computer and the Internet to work from home.

Telecommuting

Telecommuting is another way of saying that one is working from home for an organization based elsewhere. When you think about it, those in white-collar jobs could probably do the same thing from home that they do in their cubicles if they had the right equipment. Even meetings can be handled through conference calls and the increasing use of video conferencing over the Internet. Telecommuting, whether we like it or not, may become the wave of the future. In addition to being beneficial to the worker in many respects, companies large and small may carry their cost cutting to include the elimination of a physical office. We are living in less and less of a material world and more and more of a virtual world as each day passes.

Office Space

You had better make the office area in your home worker-friendly. If it is too much like the rest of the house and not separated in space and ambience, you may not be able to psych yourself into the altered mindset needed to be productive. Some ritual may be required. One famous author would put on a suit and tie and go into the office space as if he were going to a nine-to-five office job. It was his way to set the structure he needed to give him discipline.

Even those of us who are not versed in the Asian practice of feng shui know that your home environment can affect your mood. If your home is sloppy, chances are other aspects of your life are messy and in disarray. It is wise to keep your workspace in order, as if you had a pesky manager on your back to complain about your messy cubicle. There will be no custodial staff to tidy up when you go home. It is your home, so keep it neat and clean.

Telecommuting Jobs (☞ *www.tjobs.com*) is an Internet service that connects telecommuters with employers. You can post your resume and view and apply to job offerings.

Make sure you have the required equipment and that the area you choose has the necessary electrical and cable outlets and phone jacks. These are some of the many little things that seem obvious in hindsight, but many people do not think about them when setting up their home office.

You must also make sure that your residence can handle the added burden of the computer, phone/fax, copier and any other equipment. You do not want to be constantly blowing fuses or to create a fire hazard. If you own your own home, and it is an old house, you may need to upgrade the wiring. If you rent, you should ask the landlord or superintendent about making modifications. A surge protector is an essential, and you may need more than one depending on how much equipment you have. If you have wires all over the place, you should use twist ties to keep them under control so you do not keep tripping over them.

Keep the climate controlled. If it gets too hot, you will get cranky, and if it becomes too cold you will not want to stay in the space. Do not have a television in the room unless your job requires it. Make every effort to minimize outside noises. See that you have good lighting. Headaches and eyestrain will diminish productivity.

Independent Contractors

You do not have to officially have "independent contractor" status to telecommute for a living, but it is to your advantage. An independent contractor is a person who is self-employed, but who has not necessarily gone through the legal paperwork to establish themselves as a small business.

Informal deals and "gentleman's agreements" are all well and good, but you cannot make a deal based on a handshake over the Internet—at least not yet. It is always good to have a contract, sometimes less formally called an agreement with your employer.

You can keep it simple. Include what is expected of each of you, payment arrangements, and conditions under which the agreement can be terminated. The employer may ask you to agree to a "noncompete clause," meaning that you cannot work for other companies at the same time you are working for your current employer. This is to protect the employer but can be restricting to the independent contractor. Do not agree to this unless you are guaranteed a sufficient income from the employer. If you are only working for them part time, you cannot be expected to subsist solely on what they pay you.

Less controversial is the confidentiality clause you may be asked to sign. This is fair and reasonable on the part of the employer. They do not want the independent contractor to share company business with rivals. If you do so, it can be interpreted as industrial espionage and that is a crime that can lead to jail time. It is your obligation to respect your current employer's right to privacy.

Paying Taxes

There is more work required on your part if you are an independent contractor. You are your own boss and your own human resources person. There is usually no income tax withheld by your employer. At the end of the year, you receive what is called a 1099 Form and are responsible for squaring things with the taxman. You should put some money aside specifically for this purpose. Thirty percent of your income is recommended. If not, you are likely to get a terrible surprise on April 15.

The law can be very daunting and baffling for the average person. Lawyers like it that way, just like accountants love the complex and confusing tax codes. The legal reference site Nolo, on the Web at ✑*www.nolo.com*, has a wealth of free legal information, including resources for independent contractors and entrepreneurs.

The money you owe can be substantial, but as an independent contractor you can deduct certain things that a person with a regular job cannot. As a general rule, you can deduct a certain percentage of your rent, utilities, Internet and phone bills, business lunches, and other expenses if your home is also your office. It is strongly recommended that you have an accountant do your taxes when you are in this situation. You do not want to be subject to an audit from the IRS. With freedom comes responsibility, and those who experience working as an independent contractor usually prefer it that way and are loath to return to a traditional office job.

Good News and Bad News

The good news is that independent contractors make more than salaried employees who do the same job. Employers pay 20 to 40 percent more an hour. Companies can afford to do this because they are not paying for other things that an office worker takes for granted. This includes things like the cost of your office space and equipment, utilities, and so on. And it also includes things like unemployment compensation, half of the Social Security taxes, worker's compensation, medical benefits, and sick days. The bad news is that as an independent contractor you have to pay for all this or do without.

FACT

Visit ✍ *www.ebay.com*, and see the thousands of items being auctioned by millions of people every day. Registration is easy, and you can begin unloading your life of clutter while simultaneously lining your pockets.

You also have no job security as an independent contractor, but no one really does anymore. However, a salaried employee can still shuffle papers and look busy when things are slow and still collect their regular check. When things are slow for an independent contractor, they make less money. Also, you will not be eligible for federal or state unemployment insurance during periods of downtime.

Buying and Selling on eBay

The online auction site eBay began as a small cyber presence several years ago. What began as a service that auctioned things like used and rare books, movies, and collectibles grew to auctions of things like cars, boats—even a small town has been put up on the virtual auction block. Some unscrupulous auctioneers even try to sell items like wreckage from the space shuttle *Columbia* and other bizarre and lurid memorabilia. Those folks are booted off and reported to the authorities. For the overwhelming majority of eBayers, it is a great way to make a few bucks. Some people have even given up their day jobs to become full-time eBay auctioneers. It can be done.

How eBay Works

In order to sell on eBay, you have to sign up and create a seller's account. You can elect to accept payments by credit card via a service called PayPal, which electronically wires money from one account to another. The funds can remain in the PayPal account (in case you want to make purchases of your own), or you can transfer the proceeds to your checking account.

The next step is to write a description of the item you want to sell. Use your salesmanship to make the item appealing, but do not exaggerate its value or condition. False advertising will come back to haunt you. It is not mandatory to but definitely helpful to take a picture of the item. For this you need a digital camera, or a traditional camera and a scanner. If you intend to become a serious eBayer, you should invest in a digital camera, since this eliminates a step that will save you time.

PayPal.com is a common method of payment on eBay. The service works by wiring a customer's money to the PayPal account of the seller. Both buyer and sellers must sign up for the service. It is a convenient way to do business on the Internet.

Make sure you list your item in the appropriate category so the consumers who are surfing eBay for an item like yours can easily find it. Then click the "Sell" button, and fill out the form that will appear. You determine how many days you want the item to remain available for bidding. The standard time period is one week. You set the minimum bid accepted, and you also have the option to create a "Buy It Now" dollar amount. A bidder can bring the auction to an end if he or she opts to pay the "Buy It Now" price right away.

Auction Fees

There are two selling fees that eBay collects for providing this service: an initial insertion fee for posting your item, and a final value fee at the end of the auction. Here is the general fee structure:

Opening Value	Insertion Fee
$0.01–9.99	$0.30
$10.00–24.99	$0.55
$25.00–49.99	$1.10
$50.00–199.99	$2.20
$200.00 and up	$3.30

Insertion fees are based on the starting price, though for a reserve price auction the insertion fee you pay is based on the reserve price you set.

The final value fee is figured from the amount of the winning bid (that is, the high bid at the auction close) using this formula:

Final Value Fee	Final Sale Price
5.25%	up to $25
Additional 2.75%	on any sales amount
	ranging from
	$25.01 to $1,000
Additional 1.50%	on any sales amount
	greater than $1,000.01

Let's say you sold your old BMW on eBay for $1,500. You would pay a final value fee of 5.25 percent on the first $25 of the sales price ($1.31), then an additional 2.75 percent on the amount ranging from $25.01 to $1,000 (that's 2.75 percent of $974.99, or $26.81), and finally 1.5 percent on the remaining sales amount above $1,000 (that's 1.5 percent of

$499.99, or $7.50). Add those three together, and you find that it cost you $35.62 to sell your BMW on eBay—a lot less than a dealer would have charged to do the job for you.

End of Auction

When the auction ends, the seller and buyer should contact each other within three business days to seal the deal. Be flexible, and allow for unforeseen problems. Sometimes buyer and seller don't hear from each other in the allotted time. You and the buyer will exchange the pertinent information—where and how the buyer will send the payment and where and how the seller will send the item.

After the transaction, both customer and seller are encouraged to leave feedback. Feedback shows up in you eBay information and is accessible to all. Positive feedback shows that you are a reliable seller or a buyer who pays promptly. Negative feedback is a big red flag to potential buyers and sellers. Do not leave negative feedback without first trying to resolve the situation with the buyer/seller you are dealing with.

Do not blame a seller for the vicissitudes of the United States Postal Service. If you wanted an item shipped via Media Mail (the cheapest way to send a package) do not blame the shipper if it takes as long as three weeks to reach you. Media Mail is notoriously inconsistent. Packages sometimes get across country in forty-eight hours; others can take weeks to get to a neighboring state.

What to Sell

Many eBayers hunt through their attics, book and video collections, and other little-used nooks and crannies around the house for items that are taking up space and that they would like to unload. Others turn an initial avocation into a full-time business. If you are a manufacturer, you can sell your products; you can also sell your used car. There is even a "Mature Audience" category for naughty merchandise and a "Weird Stuff" section for odd and hard-to-classify material. The majority of eBay categories are more traditional, including the following:

- Antiques
- Movies & DVDs
- Cars & Other Vehicles
- Cars & Other Vehicles
- Jewelry & Watches
- Real Estate

Yes, you read that right: real estate. You can buy everything from a farm to a timeshare in a Caribbean getaway. Even if you do not have the family farm to sell, there are other things that you can get pretty cheap that command big bucks in online auctions.

If you go to garage and yard sales, you can pick up stuff that people are eager to part with just to free up space in their homes. Most of them have no idea that there are hidden gems among what they think are nothing but old junk. Old paperback books are generally considered not especially valuable, but there is a market for certain kinds of books. There is a small but enthusiastic minority who goes crazy for pulp art from the 1930s through the 1960s. Pulp fiction has a romantic appeal among collectors; the colorful, lurid art that graced those covers conveys an odd combination of raciness and quaint innocence that collectors love. In used and rare bookstores in New York, old pulp paperbacks can sell for $50 and up. By combing the garage sales in your area you can pick up these kind of books for under a dollar from people who do not know their value.

ALERT!

Yard Sale Search (✍ *www.yardsalesearch.com*) offers tips, tools and techniques about where to look for great deals, how to have your own yard sale, a live-chat forum, and more to help you get the most out of the world of yard and garage sales.

Dolls and doll paraphernalia are also big business. People have been known to pick up dolls and doll dresses for next to nothing at yard sales and make a bundle during heated bidding wars on eBay. These and other collectibles are out there for the cagey bargain hunter to find and sell on eBay. In addition to garage and yard sales, another venue to search are estate sales. When an elderly person with a lifetime of possessions passes on, their heirs often try simply to clean house and get rid of stuff after they have chosen their heirlooms and keepsakes. If these people are not collectible and antique savvy, they are probably throwing away thousands of dollars worth of items that could be auctioned on eBay.

Selling on Amazon.com

If you want a simpler way to sell your stuff than on eBay, you can try Amazon.com. Amazon, in addition to having an auction feature similar to eBay, has a very user-friendly process by which you can sell new and used products.

Every product page has a new and used link that you can click on to see the items that Amazon Marketplace sellers are offering. Signing up to be a Marketplace seller is easy, and the process is even less complicated than it is on eBay. The buyer purchases your item just as they would buy anything else from Amazon. Their credit card is billed, and the funds are deposited in the seller's Amazon account. Every two weeks, the money in your Amazon account is electronically transferred to your bank account.

If the item you are selling is in stock, you can only sell it at or below Amazon's price. If the item is out of print (as books, videos, and DVDs often are), the sky is the limit. Check your shelves and the boxes in your closets and garage. You will be surprised what collectors are willing to pay for an out of print (OOP) movie. If you have been a pack rat all your life, you can lighten your load and make a tidy sum selling your stuff online.

Naturally Amazon is not doing this out of kindness. They get a fee for this service. Amazon takes a ninety-nine-cent closing fee, plus 15 percent for the privilege of using their service. On the plus side, they issue a shipping credit to help you defray the cost of packing and shipping the item. An item is listed for sixty days. If it does not sell within that time, the listing expires, and you are charged nothing. If you have to issue a refund to a customer, Amazon refunds you its percentage.

The seller is obliged to pack securely and ship within two business days. All sellers are required to offer standard shipping (Media Mail). They can also offer expedited shipping, such as Priority Mail. The standard shipping credits are $1.84 and $2.26. (A single DVD in a padded envelope is actually cheaper to send first class mail than Media Mail. However, a video tape is not.)

Providing Computer Services

Believe it or not, there are still plenty of computer-illiterate people out there. Many people do not own a computer, have never surfed the Web, and have no idea how to send an e-mail. In this high-tech age, these people are at an increasingly great disadvantage. Some are older people who simply cannot adapt to new things. This is not true of most graying Americans. Many grandparents exchange e-mails with their grandkids. Nor is it necessarily a trend associated with the older population. There are some very stubborn people in the world who vow to exist without this modern convenience. And there are some people who cannot afford a personal computer.

At some time or another, any and all of the above-mentioned demographic groups are going to need services that only a computer and access to the Internet can provide. That is where you can come in by providing these services for a fee. There are plenty of people in your community who will need your help on occasion.

So how do you contact these people? You cannot send them an e-mail. You go about it the old-fashioned way. Run a small ad in the local paper. Print nice-looking fliers, and place them in the windows of amenable neighborhood merchants and staple them on telephone poles. You will attract the fringe underground of out-of-touch souls who sometimes need to a deal with a business or bureaucracy. You will be their lifeline to the digital age.

Some people still need forms filled out on that increasingly antiquated of devices, a typewriter. If you still have yours, take it out of the closet and dust it off. Some mailing and faxing business charge as much as fifty cents *a line* to type text on a document. You can also expand your business to include doing people's resumes and the many other little things that technologically challenged people need done. Positive word of mouth will increase your business.

This is probably not something that can turn into a full-time income, but combined with other home business enterprises it can supplement your income nicely if you market yourself properly and build a reputation.

Spam and Scams

Your e-mail box is probably filled with messages that claim that they can make you hundreds, if not thousands, of dollars a week at home with just your computer. If most of them sound a little too good to be true, that is because they are. While there are legitimate ways to make money on the Internet, there are many more scams that come in the form of unsolicited e-mails, fondly known as "spam."

Here are some popular scams to avoid at all costs, before they end up costing you plenty:

1. Never get involved in a business that requires you to assemble crafts like toys and dolls at home with the promise of money for the finished product. This is a classic scam. You pay for a start-up kit, and when you send back the finished product the company tells you they are not any good. The company makes its money selling start-up kits with no intention of buying back the results.

2. Medical billing scams convince people to pay several hundred dollars for software and a list of clients to start a home-based medical billing business. Most clinics take care of their own billing or farm it out to large firms, not individuals. The software may not be state of the art, and the list of clients is likely to be bogus.

3. The e-mail processor scam will charge you for their kit on how to get started in this "new and exciting" business that you can do from home with the promise of getting $25 for each e-mail processed. The only thing you receive is instructions on how to spam other people with the same con you fell for yourself. A similar scan is the promise of a "typing at home" business.

4. Never pay for a list of companies seeking home workers. You will get a list of companies, but it will be nothing more than a list. If you contact the companies, you will discover that they do not want home workers, and they will wonder how you got their contact information.

5. Never follow up on an e-mail that tells you to call a 900 number for more information. The only thing you will learn is that you paid a lot of money for the 900 call when you get your phone bill.

6. While there may be some legitimate multilevel marketing (MLM) businesses, most are what are known as "pyramid schemes." Climbing the ladder becomes the objective; the products and services become secondary.

Chain-letter e-mails and envelope-stuffing scams have been around for a long time before anyone ever "went cyber." The chain-mail scam usually directs you to forward an e-mail on to more people, and then to send money to the top names on the list. You add your name to the list, with the promise that when you move to the top, everyone on the list will be sending their cash to you. Sound likely? No, it does not!

Envelope-stuffing scams promise you will be paid one or two dollars for every one that you stuff, all from the comforts of home. At 1,000 envelopes a week you can make a nice living, right? Wrong! The real deal is that after you send the money you receive a manual with flier templates that you are told to post around your community advertising the work-from-home scheme.

Checking Out Online Opportunities

As you can see from the previous section, there are a lot of con artists on the Internet, all promising something for nothing. You have to perform due diligence on any organization or offer that sounds appealing. You will find when doing a search that most of the results are for somebody trying to sell you something, a book or series of tapes, or software that will make you lots of money. Most likely they are the people making the most money on the Internet, exploiting the ambitions of the needy and the greedy.

Do not even bother with an Internet company that does not have a seal of approval from the Better Business Bureau. Double-check with the BBB to see that they are indeed registered with them. The regrettable reality is that you have to separate a whole lot of chaff to get to the precious little wheat in the Internet moneymaking world.

BBB Online (*www.bbbonline.org*) is the Internet wing of the Better Business Bureau. Here you can learn about the many scams on the Net and the red flags you need to recognize, lest you fall prey to a cyber-con.

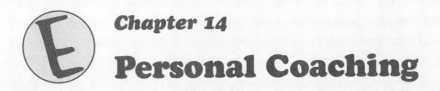

Chapter 14

Personal Coaching

Do you have empathy, insight, and patience in abundance? Are you interested in working from home and commanding a high hourly rate just to listen to someone's woes? Are you willing to offer a sympathetic ear and practical counsel? If so, you will want to learn more about the new and booming business of personal coaching.

Get in on the Ground Floor

Personal coaching is a large and growing industry. It is also a very new profession. Personal coaches make a lot of money and do not put in long hours. The path to becoming a personal coach requires a certain kind of personality, plus patience and perseverance in establishing a clientele. If you have what it takes and can survive the growing pains of starting from scratch, it can be a rewarding and lucrative trade.

FACT

There are courses of study you can take to get certified as a coach. But this is an unregulated field. Anybody can simply be a coach— all you have to do is say that you are one and set out to get clients. As the field becomes more competitive, any maverick coaches will need to get some letters after their names.

Coaching benefits the practitioner in more ways than simply generating an income. It helps people become better communicators, thus improving their personal relationships. Doing something positive for someone else increases the sense of satisfaction on the part of the coach. It is always the best of both worlds when you are doing something you that you can be proud of and that helps others.

A Source of Motivation

A personal coach is a motivational force for people who find that their lives are in disarray and that they are not fulfilling their potential. Perhaps they want to start a business, change careers, lose weight, or simply clean their apartment. The personal coach is both a supportive shoulder to lean on and a practitioner of tough love. Unlike a psychologist, who in most schools of psychoanalysis maintains a detachment from the patient, a personal coach is a pragmatic cheerleader. The personal coach is willing and able to give the client a figurative pat on the back or a kick in the butt when either is called for.

A coach is a kind of consultant, but not in the traditional sense. The coach does no research or legwork on behalf of the client. To paraphrase Shakespeare, "Therein the clients must minister to themselves." A personal coach helps the client identify their goals and then achieve them.

A coach is not a therapist. A coach's role is not to delve into the client's troubled psyche—nor is the coach qualified to do so. Coaching is a practical approach to problem solving and both personal and professional fulfillment.

ALERT!

If a coach determines that the client's problem is one of substance abuse, depression, or serious mental illness, he or she should terminate the relationship and recommend another form of counseling and treatment.

A coach should never offer advice on financial or relationship matters. Most forms of therapy deal with discussing the past and uncovering hidden motivations for one's self-destructive and counterproductive actions. A coach deals with things "on a going-forward basis" as they say in contemporary corporate-speak. A coach does not have to be a "power of example." The cliché "Do as I say, not as I do," applies to coaching. Coaches use their skills to motivate and inspire, but unlike a sponsor in a twelve-step program, coaches do not have to have done all the things they prompt their clients to do. Seasoned coaches should have the names of other professionals in their Rolodexes so that they can refer their clients to those experts whose provinces are outside their purview.

Growing Popularity

Coaching is becoming increasingly popular in this self-help-oriented age. People feel that they are overwhelmed by life. Often, it takes an objective outsider to help them look at the world from a different angle and put things in a proper perspective. As we will see, personal coaches are well paid for their skill. This is a luxury service for people who have the disposable income to spend. Most but not all of the people who seek out personal coaches are business executives, creative types, and other professionals. There are also corporations with plenty of money that often hire personal coaches to work with their personnel.

There's Money to Be Made

People hire coaches for short-term or long-term projects. Coaches usually ask for a three- to six-month commitment. It is not recommended that a coach demand that a contract be signed. It is best to be flexible and accommodating. And as for the money, a coach who has worked to establish a clientele can command $200 to $450 a month for one half-hour telephone conversation a week. This fee rate applies to individual clients. If a personal coach is working for a corporate client, with the attendant corporate expense account, he or she can ask for and receive between $1,000 and $10,000 a month.

FACT

The Web site ✍ *www.findyourcoach.com* is a service that helps individuals find the right coach for their needs. Do you need a life coach, business coach, executive coach, personal coach, or sales coach? You can even be contacted by a coach who will consult with you free of charge.

Look at it this way: law school costs an average of $125,000. The median salary of a young lawyer is $165,000. These ambitious men and women work an 80- to 100-hour week. This averages to $3.43 *an hour*, far below the minimum wage. If a personal coach has twenty clients who pay $300 a week for the service, they can make $6,000 for thirty hours of work *a month*. Not bad.

Are You Cut Out to Be a Coach?

You do not have to have any special educational background to become a personal coach. They come from all walks of life. They do not have any medical or psychological training. The Coach Training Alliance (at ✎ *www.coachtrainingalliance.com*) lists the qualities of a successful coach as the following:

1. Have a strong sense of self, value themselves intrinsically, are confident, and show up authentically.
2. Willing to evolve and develop themselves.
3. Listen at the deepest levels, know how to filter out their own emotions, judgments, and conclusions.
4. Genuinely curious about people, have a healthy sense of humor and humility.
5. Live from high personal integrity, walk their talk, tell the truth, know how to get their own needs met.
6. Open to, not attached to outcome, can make themselves blank for the client's agenda and solutions to emerge.
7. Financially stable, think and act like an entrepreneur and business owner.
8. Balanced in life, have a strong support system.
9. Have good boundaries, knows that the client knows what is best for them.
10. Intuitive, courageous, creative, willing to take the chance of being wrong.

The Coach Training Alliance (✎ *www.coachtrainingalliance.com*) provides general information in this new industry. It offers information about the many programs available and the training required to become a certified coach.

Getting Started

Personal coaching is something you should ease into. You should keep the job you have until you are working with enough clients to generate a living wage. Then you can phase out your current job and become a full-time coach. You do not need to be certified to begin coaching clients for a fee. But you *do* need to get noticed and build a reputation. Most coaches begin by working with willing friends. Practice makes perfect, and if a friend agrees to serve as a guinea pig for your coaching skills, take full advantage and use them to hone your skills. Fledgling coaches often have the equivalent of Tupperware parties. They place ads and post fliers in their neighborhood and invite people over to their home to dazzle them with their coaching acumen. The hope is that some of the guests will be interested in retaining their services and will recommend them to their friends. Since the hours a coach works are not demanding, it is easy to do this while working at your current job. Novice coaches also offer their services for free at first, then later at a deep discount, as they work their way up to being able to charge the going rate.

While it is important to be accommodating in the beginning, you should not allow yourself to be taken advantage of. Most professional coaches ask for payment in advance on a month-by-month basis and postpone the first call of the month if the check has not arrived. Personal coaches are also wise to get some kind of personal liability insurance, which is a form of malpractice insurance. This is a litigious society, and you never know if a disgruntled client may try to sue you for giving bad advice. If they can go after McDonald's for making people fat, shyster lawyers will readily try to make a buck at the expense of a personal coach.

Building a Business

Those who are new in the personal coaching game not only must have empathy, compassion, and all that warm and fuzzy stuff, they must also be aggressive entrepreneurs who will do what it takes to build a business from the ground up. You have to be willing to work very hard to build your fledgling venture. Many coaches who go through all the requisite training and have the innate skills have a hard time drumming up a paying clientele. It takes a couple of years to build up a steady stable of paying customers. It is easy to get pro bono work and maybe even a few clients who will pay a cut rate. The objective, of course, is to move beyond this low-income period as soon as possible.

The main reason for this is not the state of the economy but a lack of confidence on the part of the new coach. Many of us have been discouraged from an early age from tooting our own horns. Assertive salesmanship is regarded as unseemly and bordering on the obnoxious. However, if you do not want to live as a clock-punching man or woman who works for someone else their whole life, then you have to let the world know that you are alive and kicking. You have to be able to shift the focus from your self-centered insecurities and think about the service aspect of your new industry. If you can get over yourself, as they say, and place the emphasis on your present and future clients and *their* needs, you can surmount the shyness and timidity that all too often sabotages many a self-starter.

FACT

The best personal coaches have their own personal coach. Just as a therapist usually has their own therapist, and a priest has his confession heard by a fellow man of the cloth, so too a good coach seeks counsel from another member of the craft. This is usually a person with more years in the field and is often the coach's mentor who guided them through their early days.

A Typical Session

A typical coaching session takes place over the phone and lasts about half an hour. After an initial consultation—which a coach, especially a new one, should offer free of charge—the coach and the client begin identifying and working on whatever the problem or problems that inspired the client to seek out the coach.

The client usually calls the coach, but often the coach calls the client so he or she can be in more control of the call. That way the coach can start it and finish it according to his or her schedule, without having to sit and wait for a tardy client. There is a structure to this timetable for a reason. Coaches cannot have clients calling whenever they feel like it. There has to be a regular appointment, like visiting the doctor or dentist. Though just as those professions will accommodate emergency cases, an obliging coach will permit the occasional quickie call or brief e-mail outside of the parameters of their regularly scheduled appointment.

During the consultation, trust and comfort must be established. A coach must assure confidentiality. Once the coach and client have decided that they have a rapport and will begin a relationship, the initial session will involve discussing the problem or problems at hand. The coach will inquire about how the client is feeling, what they are looking to change, and how they can go about it. The coach will suggest three things that the client can do to work toward achieving their goals. Since looking at a life change in its totality can be intimidating, coaches try to help the client make changes incrementally. The little things add up, until eventually a major change has occurred.

In subsequent sessions, the coach and client review what has happened in the week since the previous session. They discuss any breakthroughs and insights the client may have, his or her progress in the goals and objectives, and any obstacles the client may have encountered during the week. The coach offers advice, challenges the client to fight their natural resistance and make things happen. The coach helps the client brainstorm solutions and come up with a plan of action. As each goal is achieved, the coach and the client continue the process as they take on new objectives to achieve and new opportunities to pursue.

In sum, a typical coaching session can be broken down as follows:

1. Client gives a brief recap of the week.
2. Coach listens to the client's success concerning struggle with the action steps they have completed since the last session. Coach offers input.
3. Coach and client discuss what the client is currently working on and the challenges client faces.
4. Client and coach identify the next steps to move successfully forward.
5. Coach and client determine the skills and strategies client needs to implement the next steps.
6. Coach and client work together to build a plan of action for the week ahead.

Coaching should not be a long, codependent relationship. Rather, it's more successful as a short-term commitment of a few months to one year that allows clients to reshape their world and be able to function independently of the coach. The coach should not be a crutch for a person. He or she should be a professional motivator whose goal should be the same as a mother bird in a nest—to help their fledgling chicks learn to use their wings and fly.

The Web site ✍*www.coachville.com* is called the "McDonald's of coaching" by others in the industry. The good news is that this service is much cheaper than the other coaching schools. The bad news is that you cannot get an accreditation from them. You do not need one to practice the profession, but as more and more people are drawn to it, accreditation will be more and more important.

Certification

There are several training organizations that offer certifications in this new industry. Coach U has a training program that, as of this writing, costs about $4,500 and takes an average of two years to complete. The Coach Training Institute (C.T.I.) offers the certificates personal certified coach (PCC) and master certified coach (MCC). The PCC requires 750 hours of training, and the MCC takes 2,000 hours of training. Most of these hours are earned online and in group telephone conference calls. The majority of the organizations that offer coaching certifications operate this way. Since the telephone is the means of communication between coach and client, the telephone and the Internet are logical methods to conduct training.

The average coaching program includes thirty to forty required "teleclasses" and another thirty to forty elective telephone courses that are usually completed, depending on the ambition of the student, in anywhere from twelve to twenty-four months. Each class consists of four one-hour sessions and is conducted by an experienced coach. There are about twenty to thirty fellow students on the conference call. These courses include the basics on how to become a working coach. The elective courses include specialty subjects such as developing your intuition, how to ask probing questions, and more. Although most courses are on the phone or online, there are also weekend seminars that count toward your certification. These are an opportunity to place a face with the disembodied voices you have been hearing on the phone during the teleclasses.

Different Philosophies

The world of coaching is not a monolith. Just as there are different schools of psychology, there are different approaches to coaching. For example, the Coach Training Institute operates on the philosophy that the client has the answer. Like forms of therapy that do not believe in telling the patient what is wrong with them, this coaching philosophy draws the answers out of the client by asking artful and probing questions. It is a spiritual belief that we have within us all we need to know to not only survive, but also thrive in this world. For a variety of reasons, our instincts have been dulled and blunted. The right mentor can help the clients to search within themselves to find the solutions to their problems and the independence to slay any metaphorical dragons in their path.

The institution called Coach U believes that the answer is somewhere out there and can be found through the interaction between coach and client. This philosophy is based on the belief that the solution should be reached by any means. They feel that as long as a desired result is achieved, it does not matter if the coach suggests the answer, the client comes upon the solution, or they both discover it through brainstorming.

If you have the temperament and the inclination, this alternative career can be a personally rewarding and also profitable livelihood to look into. You can make a difference, make a nice living, and have an abundance of leisure time on your hands. That sounds like the best of all possible scenarios for anyone's working life. (E)

Chapter 15

E Law Enforcement Careers

If you fantasize about being a smooth private eye or a suave super spy, you can find work in these professions. They are going to be dramatically different than they are depicted in books, movies, and television, but can nevertheless be rewarding jobs that make a difference.

Detective Work

If you have read plenty of mystery novels and have seen every episode of *The Rockford Files*, then you probably have fantasized about what it would be like to be a private detective. You probably also know that the reality is far less glamorous than the fiction. The romantic image of the gumshoe as a modern knight errant with tarnished armor, helping damsels in distress in the neon-lit urban jungle, is a glorified image that does not represent reality. Nevertheless, many people are drawn to the work, and they do make a living as private detectives.

FACT

You will want to check more than one school for private detectives, and there are plenty out there. The Private Investigator Training School (✑*www.detectivetraining.com*), for example, bills itself as "the most comprehensive home study course in private investigation available." Private investigators do much more paperwork than their literary counterparts. There is a lot more mundane fact-checking through research and phone calls than there are car chases and encounters with sultry, dangerous dames.

What Detectives Do

Detectives do background checks on people, verifying employment history, income, and character references. This work might be done at the request of a potential employer or on behalf of a suspicious fiancée. Other services include assisting attorneys in civil lawsuits, which includes assignments like following a person making a personal injury claim to see if the claimant takes off a back brace when they think no one is looking to dance the night away. "Premarital screening" is a growing aspect of the private investigation business. Women want to check out Mr. Right to see if he is indeed "all that," and husbands and wives often have each other followed to see if they are remaining true to their marriage vows.

There is also a lot of sitting around as a detective. You are likely to spend many long hours in a car or a van across the street from a location observing the home or business of a suspect. The low-end private eye will sit in his car; an investigator with a more elaborate setup will have a van loaded with the latest surveillance equipment.

If you want to be a detective, you had better decide what you are willing to do and what may compromise your ethical code. You may find yourself wallowing in the underbelly of human affairs when working as an investigator. A literary example is Raymond Chandler's hero Philip Marlowe. He refused to handle divorce cases, finding them quite unsavory.

Less Legwork

The Internet has made life easier for the detective as it has for everyone. An investigator who knows where to look can find out much of what he or she needs to know from computer research. This saves the legwork long associated with the life of a private detective. An Internet search can reveal enormous amounts of information about a person. In addition to an address and telephone number, a detective can find out an individual's arrest record, vehicle registration, and more. A detective working with an unscrupulous hacker can find out even more personal information, though this is illegal and would not be admissible in a court of law.

American Detectives (✍ www.americandetectives.net) is a California-based organization. Their Web site can give you a very good look at the many aspects of private detective work. This agency handles areas they call "WWW relationships," "corporate countermeasures," and "cheating spouses."

Areas of Expertise

Private detectives often focus on one aspect of investigations and become specialists in that field. Legal investigators are retained by a law firm or individual attorney. They gather information that the lawyer needs to either prosecute or defend an individual. They locate witnesses who are hard to find or in hiding. They interview witnesses and help gather evidence. Sometimes detectives are called upon to testify during the trial.

Corporate investigators work for particular businesses, doing everything from determining who is stealing the sticky notes and paper clips from the supply room to who is selling company secrets to the competition. They also may investigate charges of drug abuse among workers and check to see if an employee is padding his or her expense account.

ALERT!

All Criminal Justice Schools (⌨ *www.allcriminaljusticeschools.com*) gives you a host of schools across the country that offer courses and degrees in subjects like private investigations, forensic science, criminal psychology, and many others.

Financial investigators check out individuals who are in the middle of large financial negotiations and transactions. These investigators are hired by the other negotiating party, and they often have a background in accounting. This may not sound like the most thrilling aspect of detective work, but we should recall that the gangster Al Capone was not sent to prison for the many murders he committed. He was ultimately convicted of income tax evasion. Digging into a person's financial dealings can often produce plenty of incriminating evidence.

Loss prevention agents are detectives who work in retail stores and prevent shoplifting by both customers and employees. Hotel detectives keep an eye on the comings and goings in major hotels making sure there are no unauthorized persons wandering around the halls and that working girls are not conducting their business on the premises.

Life As a Detective

Like many alternative careers, being a private investigator is not a nine-to-five job. You may be conducting surveillance for days at a time at all hours of the day and night. You will divide your time between deskbound duties and footwork that will probably not fall within regular business hours. Those who run large detective agencies may be able to keep regular hours, but their staff will not. You will be doing most of your work alone, though sometimes associates may be necessary. A detective needs colleagues if they are conducting twenty-four-hour surveillance on a person. If you work alone, you will need to hire a trustworthy operative to assist you.

Ready for Anything

Not as often as in the movies, but every once in a while, a detective finds himself in a confrontational situation. A detective should have some basic training in self-defense and be in decent physical shape. A violent situation may never arise, but you need to be prepared if one does. This is a job where a lack of preparation can be fatal. Some, not all, detectives carry guns. These, of course, need to be licensed by the local authorities. In some parts of the country it is harder to get licensed to legally carry a gun than others.

Packing.org (✍ *www.packing.org*) lists the many rules and regulations involved to carry a concealed weapon. You can do a search by state to see how easy or difficult it is to get licensed to carry a gun.

Requirements to Be a Detective

There are no education requirements for a private detective. Many have a background in the military or law enforcement. Lots of cops put in their twenty years on the force and then "go private." This is true in the movies and in real life. The fictional detective is often a former policeman who was a lone wolf and did not take orders well from "the brass." People rarely go right from school to being a private detective. They usually have worked at other types of jobs.

Do not let a lack of previous law enforcement experience deter you if you really want to be a private detective. Like most careers, you can start at the bottom with the hope of advancement. You can inquire about an office job in a large detective agency. There might also be low-level operative work available, such as computer research and maybe even surveillance duties. There is a possibility that something in your work history can be of use in detective work. In addition to law enforcement experience, people enter the private investigation game from occupations such as insurance, credit and collections, journalism, and other diverse careers. Every once in a while a college graduate with a degree in criminal justice may go right from the classroom to the detective agency, but this is rare.

FACT

The Global School of Investigation (✍*www.pvteye.com*) is another home-study school that promises to turn you into a gumshoe in twenty-five easy lessons. Check this or any online school out thoroughly before enrolling.

Licensing

A private detective must have a license of some kind, with some exceptions. There are six states in the union that have no licensing requirements. In Alabama, Alaska, Colorado, Idaho, Mississippi, and South Dakota, a person can simply call himself a private detective and hang out a shingle. In most states, however, the rules are pretty strict. More and more states are making training programs mandatory.

In California, the Bureau of Security and Investigative Services of the Department of Consumer Affairs requires that private detectives be eighteen years of age or older and have an educational background that includes criminal justice and police science and 6,000 hours of previous investigative experience. They also have to be evaluated by the U.S. Department of Justice, submit to a detailed background check, and take a two-hour written exam. This does not include the added process of getting a license to carry a weapon. Convicted felons will be denied a license.

A qualified private investigator needs to have excellent interviewing and interrogation skills, not be afraid of the possible physical confrontation and have a persistence and dogged determination to see a case to its conclusion. They must be able to think quickly and adapt to any situation and be good communicators, since they will at times be called upon to explain themselves to the police and to testify in court.

QUESTION?

How realistic are TV detective shows?
On the whole, not very. For example, Jim Rockford of *The Rockford Files* is an ex-con who went on to become a private eye in sunny California. But in the real world, being a convicted felon would have precluded him from getting licensed.

Schooling for Sleuths

If you are considering this field, it would be a good idea to take some courses in criminal justice. There are schools specifically for investigators, but you need to check these out carefully. Make sure the school is accredited and not some fly-by-night operation that will take your money and run. If you are a college graduate who has been in the workforce for awhile, and you are thinking of switching careers, a degree in business or accounting can help you secure a position as a corporate investigator.

Some professional organizations confer certifications that will come in handy when looking for work. Through the National Association of Legal Investigators (NALI), you can become a certified legal investigator. This will help you find work as a legal investigator where you will primarily work with lawyers in civil and criminal investigations.

You will find a lot of competition when you begin looking for work as an investigator. Odds will favor candidates with a law enforcement background. A retired cop can still be a vigorous forty-something person who wants to supplement their pension and keep busy. Entry-level positions will be available usually on a part-time basis. If you prove your mettle, you will be given more work and more responsibilities (and of course, more money). Another entry-level route is that of the department-store detective. While this may seem nothing more than a security guard position, you have to start somewhere and build credentials in order to advance.

G-Men (and Women)

The "G" in G-Man stands for government. The term was coined by gangsters and refers to any federal law enforcement officer. There are many branches of law enforcement under the federal umbrella, not just well-known institutions like the FBI and CIA. The famed "Untouchable" Eliot Ness was a treasury agent working for the U.S. Bureau of Alcohol, Tobacco, and Firearms. People complain about "big government," and it is indeed getting bigger. This also means more opportunities for careers in federal law enforcement.

Opportunities

There are more than 188,000 law enforcement officers in forty different job types currently employed by Uncle Sam. There is also a new agency, the U.S. Transportation Security Agency (TSA), whose staff is responsible for screening passengers and packages at 429 airports nationwide. This new agency has created more than 30,000 new jobs. All these law enforcement jobs have minimum and maximum age requirement. It varies slightly, but the average is a minimum of twenty-one and a maximum of thirty-seven years of age. United States citizenship is a prerequisite, along with a battery of screenings and background checks.

Here is a brief list and thumbnail sketch of various federal law enforcement agencies. Every government agency has its own Web site (usually the agency's initials, followed by the domain designation ".gov"), and they all post employment opportunities.

1. The U.S. Department of State Bureau of Diplomatic Security special agents fight the war on terror. They manage the security and protect the personnel in America's many embassies and consulates abroad.
2. U.S. Secret Service special agents protect the president, vice president, and their families; presidential candidates; former presidents; and foreign dignitaries visiting the United States. Secret Service agents also investigate counterfeiting, forgery, and credit card fraud.
3. U.S. marshals and deputy marshals are stationed in federal courthouses. State and local courts also employ court officers.

4. The U.S. Drug Enforcement Administration (DEA) employs agents in the war against illegal drugs.

5. Customs agents investigate smuggling, money laundering, and international child pornography rings. They inspect cargo, baggage, and people entering or leaving the United States on planes and boats and trains.

6. The agents of the U.S. Immigration and Naturalization Service (INS) track and deport illegal immigrants, patrol the borders, and man the facilities though which people enter the country legally.

Other agencies of the federal government that employ agents who can make arrests and carry firearms are U.S. Postal Service, the Bureau of Indian Affairs Office of Law Enforcement, the U.S. Forest Service, the National Park Service, and federal air marshals.

Spy Games: The CIA

The CIA began its existence during World War II as the Office of Special Services (OSS). It was the espionage unit that worked behind enemy lines to sabotage enemy facilities and supported resistance movements within occupied countries. After World War II, when tensions rose between the United States and the former Soviet Union, the OSS became the Central Intelligence Agency. Those interested in a career with the CIA should note its own words about what it takes: "It demands an adventurous spirit . . . a forceful personality . . . superior intellectual ability . . . toughness of mind . . . and a high degree of integrity."

Members of the CIA do not like to use the word "spy." They prefer titles like operations officer, staff operations officer, and collection management officer. Of course there are many other job opportunities in an organization of such size and scope. The CIA needs scientists, engineers, and technologists; clandestine service providers; foreign language experts; and even people in the less-glamorous positions, such as custodians and secretaries.

You must be a United States citizen over eighteen years of age. A college degree is not mandatory for consideration, but it is highly recommended. For many positions, particularly those overseas intelligence-gathering "clandestine" jobs, a college degree is necessary.

People in the military cannot transfer to the CIA to fulfill their enlistment obligations. Though they are usually on the same page in the geopolitical playbook, the CIA is not a branch of the armed forces.

Needless to say, the CIA employs a thorough screening process, including drug tests and background checks. All CIA employees need to be vetted for a security clearance. There are several levels of clearance, depending on the responsibilities of the job. Be warned: When they say "thorough," they mean it. The CIA describes the process as follows:

> Applicants must undergo a thorough background investigation examining their life history, character, trustworthiness, reliability and soundness of judgment. Also examined is one's freedom from conflicting allegiances, potential to be coerced and willingness and ability to abide by regulations governing the use, handling and the protection of sensitive information.

A polygraph test and a thorough physical examination will be included in this screening. This process can take as little as two months to more than a year.

To learn more about the many employment opportunities available at the Central Intelligence Agency, you can visit their Web site at ✍ *www.cia.gov.*

Working for the FBI

Just as the CIA is—theoretically—supposed to be involved with external matters and not allowed to do its thing within the U.S. borders, so the Federal Bureau of Investigation (FBI) deals with matters inside the United States. There is a blurring of responsibilities these days, and perhaps there always was. The mission of the FBI, established in the early 1920s, according to the organization itself, is:

> . . . a noble one. It entails upholding the law through the investigation of violations of federal criminal law; to protect the United States from foreign intelligence activities; to provide leadership and law enforcement assistance to federal, state, local and international agencies; to provide the Executive Branch with information relating to national security—and to perform these responsibilities in a manner that is responsive to the needs of the public and is faithful to the Constitution of the United States.

Like in the CIA, there are many types of job opportunities in the FBI. For our purposes, we will look at the duties of the FBI special agent. You have probably seen enough episodes of *The X-Files* to know that these are the men and women who fight the bad guys, meet the space aliens, and all that fun stuff.

In actual life, an FBI special agent is involved in investigations that include organized crime, white-collar crime, public corruption, financial crime, fraud against the government, bribery, copyright matters, civil rights violations, bank robbery, extortion, kidnapping, air piracy, terrorism, foreign counterintelligence, interstate criminal activity, fugitive and drug-trafficking matters, and other violations of federal statutes.

Recruits train at the FBI Academy in Quantico, Virginia. If they make it through the sixteen-week intensive training that includes physical fitness, firearms, self-defense, and classroom academics, they enter a two-year probationary period. They are assigned to one of the many field offices across the country. A new agent may voice his or her preferences, but the final decision will be based on the FBI's staffing needs.

Requirements

In order to qualify as a special agent, you need to be between twenty-three and thirty-seven years old, pass a physical and background check, and have a valid driver's license. You must also be a college graduate. Currently, the following critical skills are needed, and candidates with experience in the following will go to the top of the list:

- Accounting/finance
- Computer science and other information technology specialties
- Engineering
- Foreign language proficiency (Arabic, Farsi, Pashtu, Urdu, Chinese [all dialects], Japanese, Korean, Russian, Spanish, and Vietnamese)
- Intelligence experience
- Law-enforcement experience
- Law-enforcement or other investigative experience
- Military service
- Physical sciences (physics, chemistry, biology)

If you do not want to be a special agent, but you still want to work for the FBI, there are other opportunities if you have the necessary skills. These are called professional support roles, and they include this far-from-comprehensive selection: computer specialist, crime scene specialist, linguist, fingerprint expert, intelligence research specialist, laboratory tech, accounting professional, laborer, and secretary. Details about these and many other job opportunities at the FBI can he found at the agency's Web site, ✐ *www.fbijobs.com.* (E)

Chapter 16

Giving Something Back

Are you in a position to do some good in the world? We're not just talking charitable contributions, valuable and altruistic though they are. Are you interested in giving something back on a more dramatic scale, changing the world and maybe yourself in the process? Then read on.

So You Want to Do Some Good

If you have a desire to help others and see another part of the world, there are many opportunities open to you. If you feel that there is plenty to do in your own country, there are plenty of places and ways to serve the greater good in the good old U.S. of A.

You can contribute in all sorts of ways to make the world a better place. The Zen philosophy tells us that every job has value, no matter how menial it may seem to our often-spoiled Western sensibilities. Zen also teaches that if everyone tended their own garden with care, then all the parts would be a harmonious sum of the whole.

Alas, humanity does not do a great job when it comes to tending to our respective gardens. If you want to do work that enriches the many and diverse gardens in the world, one place to look is the Peace Corps.

FACT

Cross Cultural Solutions bills itself as an alternative to the Peace Corps. You can learn more at ✍*www.crossculturalsolutions.org*. This organization operates volunteer programs in Brazil, China, Costa Rica, Ghana, Guatemala, India, Peru, Russia, Tanzania, and Thailand.

The Peace Corps

The Peace Corps was an idea in the mind of President John Kennedy that became reality when the U.S. Congress passed legislation that formally authorized the organization in 1961. Its mandate is to "promote world peace and friendship." The goal of the Peace Corps is "to help the people of interested countries in meeting their need for trained men and women; to help promote a better understanding of Americans on the part of the peoples served; to help promote a better understanding of other peoples on the part of Americans." There are now almost 7,000 volunteers serving seventy countries.

Typical assignments are two years long after a three-month training period in the country you choose. Most postings require a college degree. In some cases, several years of comparable (and often more valuable) life experience will be accepted. You must be over eighteen and a United States citizen. There is no age cap, and retirees are welcome.

A Word of Warning

If you are thinking of joining the Peace Corps, you need to be aware of the sometimes-unpleasant realities of being an American abroad. The corps operates in some of the most underdeveloped countries in the world. In addition to being a culture shock to most Americans, there are security, safety, and health risks that a Peace Corps volunteer will have to face. Though accidents and mishaps are rare, and most people do their two-year hitch without incident, sometimes tragedies occur. If you statistically break it down, however, the chances of such an event happening are very small. Nevertheless, you should be aware of the risks before signing up, while also resting assured that the Peace Corps does everything in its power to ensure the safety of its members.

ALERT!

The organization I-to-I is another organization that sends volunteers abroad on what it calls I-Ventures, Mini-Ventures, and Earning-Ventures. The last category includes paying jobs that are available overseas, if you meet the requirements. Check out their Web site for details, at ✎ *www.i-to-i.com*.

Fitting In

When you first arrive at your Peace Corps assignment, you will truly be a stranger in a strange land. During the three-month training period, volunteers are placed with a host family in order to acclimate them to the culture and language of their temporary home. Most of the natives will be welcoming, but some may voice the sentiment, "Yankee go home!" There may be some tensions and conflicts at first. One of the things you can do is not swagger into the region like the stereotypically brash American. Play it cool, and try to blend in as much as you can. Respect the culture of the host country. Do what you can to make a good impression. After all, you will be an unofficial ambassador.

Female Peace Corps volunteers may have the most difficult time. Women should do their homework regarding the countries they might like to visit. If it is a culture that does not have a stellar record on the treatment of women, know what to expect going in. If you do not want to deal with it, pick another country.

The corps tries to ensure volunteer safety though a system of what it calls "building relationships, sharing information, training, site development, incident reporting and response, and emergency communications and planning."

Job Opportunities

Paying job opportunities within the Peace Corps are country director (CD) and associate director (APCD). The Peace Corps also recruits MDs (medical doctors) or DOs (doctors of osteopathic medicine) for area Peace Corps medical officers (APCMOs) for the Africa region. Job postings for APCD and APCMO positions can be found on the Peace Corps Web site, at ✍ *www.peacecorps.gov*. Some jobs require that you have a working knowledge of French, Spanish, or Portuguese.

FACT

If you want to read what former Peace Corps members have to say about the experience, visit Peace Corps Writers (✍ *www.peacecorpswriters.org*). The writings of these returned Peace Corps volunteers are their way of educating Americans about the world, fulfilling the third goal of the Peace Corps, which is to "bring the world back home."

The Peace Corps divides the world into three areas: Africa; Europe, Mediterranean, and Asia (EMA); and Inter-America/Pacific (IAP). There is a time limit of five years for which you can be an employee of the Peace Corps. After that time you are expected to move on to the next adventure of your life and leave open the opportunity for someone else.

Candidates will be obliged to have a medical screening and background check in order to be given a security clearance. If you fail the physical and/or the security check, the offer of employment will be rescinded. Your housing and relocation expenses are paid by the Peace Corps.

There is a philosophical concept that there is no such thing as a completely altruistic act. Even people who volunteer are getting something out of the experience. When thinking about where you might like to volunteer, go to the place that can simultaneously enrich you as well as those you serve. Volunteerism is meant to be a mutually rewarding arrangement.

Education Volunteers

Peace Corps volunteers are divided into three categories: general, secondary, and advanced. If you are a general education volunteer, you need a bachelor's degree and hopefully some teaching or tutoring experience. Many education volunteers will find themselves working in local schools, teaching English as a second language (ESL). English, math, and science teachers are in high demand.

Secondary education math instructors teach basic addition, subtraction, multiplication and division, plus geometry, algebra, statistics, probability, and calculus. They will also be involved with after-school and library programs. The curriculum of secondary education science teachers includes general science, biology, chemistry, and physics at the high school level. They also provide health information.

Advanced education volunteers need an education degree and teaching certification. They work with college-level students who want to improve their English language skills and learn about literature, medicine, engineering, business, and other disciplines. Other duties of advanced education volunteers include teaching English grammar and conversation, American literature and culture, creative writing, and linguistics. They also establish English-language clubs and develop resource centers.

Special education volunteers work with local teachers on developing new techniques. They provide one-on-one tutoring, work with parents and community, and promote a public awareness of persons with disabilities, who often do not fare well in developing nations.

Business Volunteers

Business volunteers fall into the same categories as education volunteers. General business volunteers should have a business or public administration degree, though comparable life experience can be an acceptable substitute. They work with private and public businesses, local and regional governments, nonprofit organizations, women and youth organizations, and agricultural businesses. They help the local citizenry with marketing and financial management. These volunteers write project-funding proposals and conduct business training seminars and workshops.

Advanced business volunteers must have a bachelor's degree in business or public administration. They can either have an M.B.A. or work toward one through the Peace Corps Master's International Program. These volunteers consult with local businesses, teach seminars and business courses, and assist local governments with economic development strategies.

Environmental Volunteers

General environmental volunteers require a bachelor's degree. Other than that, they need problem solving and leadership skills and a passion for conservation and environmental issues. They help the local population strike the balance between helping their developing nation grow while not destroying the ecosystem in the process. Many developing nations that seek industrialization have neither the ability nor the inclination to preserve the environment. They are similar to Europe during the Industrial Revolution of the nineteenth century. There was much technical and economic growth, but pollution of the air, water, and earth was devastating. Environmental volunteers show farmers how to work the land without ravaging it beyond repair.

Advanced environment volunteers have degrees in biology, ecology, forestry, and other environmental disciplines and/or related work experience. They help the communities preserve their natural resources, including "soil conservation; watershed management and flood control; forestry, including sustainable fuel projects, and wood and fruit production; biodiversity conservation near parks and other preserves; training park managers and technicians; wildlife surveys; and conducting community-based resource conservation of forest and marine resources."

FACT

From Russia, without love: On Christmas Day, 2002, Russia officially kicked the Peace Corps out of their country. The Federal Security Service, known as the KGB back in the days of the Cold War, accused members of the organization of espionage.

Other Types of Volunteers

Here are some other types of positions you can find in the Peace Corps:

- **Agricultural volunteers:** Help farmers in developing nations by introducing them to the latest agricultural techniques with an emphasis on environmental conservation. They also educate the people on dietary issues. For example, they encourage the cultivation of fruit and vegetable gardens to counter malnutrition and vitamin deficiencies, especially among children. These volunteers offer alternatives to the harmful pesticides still used in developing nations.
- **Health volunteers:** Work to promote health education among the population, both in urban and out-of-the-way areas. They educate women in pregnancy and child-care issues, nutrition, sanitation, water purification, and many other health-related issues, including, of course, AIDS awareness.
- **Engineering volunteers:** Assist the people with sanitation issues such as sewage and irrigation systems, waste disposal management, building dams and other ways to improve the infrastructure while promoting health and preserving the environment.
- **Community service volunteers:** Do a little of everything. This is a flexible program. These volunteers should have a college degree but it can be in anything. A social services or counseling background is helpful but not a prerequisite. Some work in youth programs and vocational training. Others work with what are called "at risk" young people: mentally and/or physically challenged youth.

- **Construction volunteers:** Roll up their sleeves and help the people build schools, medical centers, and other necessary structures where the other volunteers can ply their trade. They also train the locals in the building trade. Needless to say you should only apply for this position if you have experience in construction, carpentry, plumbing and other similar fields.

- **Information technology volunteers:** A new class of volunteer. Most developing nations are woefully behind when it comes to computer technology and the Internet. These volunteers are working to correct this and get the rest of the world computer literate and online.

FACT

As of the end of calendar year 2002, it is estimated that 38.6 million adults and 3.2 million children are currently living with the HIV virus throughout the world. The Peace Corps strives to promote AIDS awareness in the nations it serves.

You're Not Getting Older, You're Getting Better

Do not despair if your hair is graying or, worse yet, disappearing from atop your head. Do not lament the fact that you had to surrender your vanity and get that pair of reading glasses. Your maturity is regarded as an asset, not a liability, by both the Peace Corps and most of the people in the developing nations it serves. America has an unfortunate obsession with youth and youthful appearance, mostly perpetuated by advertising and the entertainment industry. In other countries, elders are usually respected and looked to as wise old sages and crones. ("Crone" is not a negative connotation for women in other parts of the world.)

The minimum age requirement for the Peace Corps is eighteen, but there is no age cap for volunteers. Age and experience are considered a net plus, and it's never too late to do some good in the world. It is not uncommon for people in their eighties to be serving in the Peace Corps. They do most of the things that younger volunteers do, and they carry a lifetime of experience and hard-earned wisdom with them.

Like any other volunteer, a complete physical and dental examination is required in advance. A volunteer's health care and medical expenses are completely covered when serving in the Peace Corps. There are Peace Corps medical officers in every country to assist volunteers, and medical evacuation back to the United States will be arranged if a condition arises that the medical facilities in the host country cannot handle. Working for the Peace Corps does not affect an older person's pension or Social Security benefits. If you need to return home for a family emergency, you will be given an all-expenses-paid, two-week leave of absence.

Married Couples

You and your husband or wife can join the Peace Corps together and serve in the same country. In fact, if you are married, the two of you *must* serve in the same locale. Married couples comprise approximately nine percent of Peace Corps volunteers. Couples can start the process when engaged, but they have to be married when they are assigned to a country. The Peace Corps does not accept couples that have dependent children. These accommodations are not applicable for friends or unmarried couples.

For more information about what the Peace Corps does, you can visit their Web site at ✍ *www.peacecorps.gov*.

Habitat for Humanity

It is believed by many that the postpresidency of Jimmy Carter has been more impressive than his term in office from 1976 to 1980. Not everyone agrees with all of his actions and public statements as an ex-president, but few can find fault with his association with the organization Habitat for Humanity.

Habitat for Humanity is a nonprofit and nondenominational Christian housing organization. Its members build what they call "simple, decent, affordable housing in partnership with those in need of adequate shelter." Since 1976, Habitat for Humanity has built more than 125,000 houses in more than eighty countries, including 45,000 in the United States. The houses are sold to the families who will occupy them for no profit and with no interest on the mortgage. The future homeowners and volunteers build the home together with professionals supervising the process. Private citizens, corporate donors, and faith groups provide the financial support.

Getting Involved

As mentioned, Habitat is not a charity in the strict sense. The houses are not built and given to people free of charge. Families who would like to participate in the program have to be able to afford a modest down payment and a low, interest-free mortgage, which varies from seven to thirty years. They also have to invest their time (in the form of 400 hours of sweat equity) to help build the house. The cost of a Habitat for Humanity house averages between $800 and $46,000. The mortgage that the residents pay goes back into building more houses. It is not a moneymaking enterprise.

The physical address of Habitat for Humanity International is 121 Habitat Street, Americus, GA 31709-3498. You can reach the organization by telephone at ✆ 229-924-6935.

Habitat for Humanity has more than 1,900 affiliate offices in eighty-three countries. There is also an office in every one of the fifty states, plus Washington, D.C., Puerto Rico, and Guam. The headquarters employs a staff of professionals and support people. If you want to work for them, you are probably going to have to start as a volunteer. Since everyone who wants to get involved with this organization will have an altruistic nature, volunteerism is a natural place to begin. You should contact your local affiliate and offer to lend a hand.

Poverty Theme Park

Yes, you read that right. Habitat for Humanity's latest project is a "theme park" that gives the visitor a realistic look at the most abject conditions of poverty and suffering that its workers have encountered while building homes around the world.

It is called the Global Village and Discovery Centre. It opened in 2003, and Millard Fuller, founder of Habitat for Humanity, expected it to draw in excess of 70,000 visitors in its first year. Instead of roller coasters and other rides, people can tour recreations of slums from Central America, Asia, and Africa. Then they will be able to see samples of Habitat for Humanity's handicraft and compare how the hovels are transformed into decent living accommodations. Rather than a petting zoo and arts and crafts, children can get their hands messy with brick-making and tile-laying. They can see what it is like to sleep in a shack infested with scorpions and snakes.

Does this sound like great Saturday afternoon fun for the whole family? Would you rather go to Disney World? Habitat for Humanity hopes to attract socially conscious citizens who will be inspired to join the organization.

ALERT!

For further information on Habitat for Humanity, visit their Web site at ✑ *www.habitat.org*. There you can search for the affiliate office in your area and learn more about job opportunities and volunteering.

Keeping the Faith

If you have a calling and a burning desire to share the faith that comforts you with others, there are plenty of opportunities to help people and spread your message. Only the truly dedicated need apply—this is mostly volunteer work. If the message is more important than the money, read on.

Do You Have a Calling?

If your religious faith is the primary focus of your life, and you feel that part of your reason for being here is to share your faith with others, then it is your duty to go out and spread the word. There are many parts of the world that are in dire straits and need all the help they can get. Missionary workers aid these people with the practical aspects of improving the quality of their lives, while preaching to them in the process. This tradition is as ancient as the organized religions themselves. There is an old saying that you have to pay for the free soup by listening to the sermon.

Different Opportunities for Different Faiths

When we think of missionaries we usually associate them with the Christian variety. Certain elements in all faiths feel obliged to spread the word, but the majority of people who call themselves missionaries are Christians. The various sects of Islam and Christianity practice some form of missionary work, while Judaism does not. The Jewish faith welcomes converts, but it does not have a tradition of aggressively recruiting them.

Anyone going to a foreign country can expect to experience culture shock. Many missionaries have trouble adjusting and quit within the first year. The Center for Intercultural Training (✑*www.cit-online.org*) helps prepare new missionaries to deal with the challenges of working abroad.

There are hundreds of short-term missionary opportunities through many different faiths. There is help needed in orphanages, working on Native American reservations, teaching English as a second language (some missions will even train you), and other teaching jobs. Health-care professionals are always needed, as are people with computer skills. These volunteers are in demand to help bridge the "digital divide" between poor nations and the developed lands. MisLinks (✑*www.mislinks.org*) is a good one-stop resource for learning about all elements of missionary work.

Something Old, Something New

There is a new missionary model for the new age. In the old days, the missionary was an ordained priest or minister that was sent by the church, usually from a Western European nation or America to an underdeveloped part of the world. Nowadays, the indigenous church is in charge, and the missionary functions as a clerical consultant of sorts. In the Lutheran church, 70 percent of the missionaries are lay people. Back in the day, a missionary devoted his or her whole life to service; nowadays people serve in short-term tenures. The longest average term of missionary service is eight to ten years; for most, it is one year or two.

ALERT!

If you have technical skills and want to serve, you can contact WebMissions (✐ www.webmissions.org), a Christian ministry that helps missionaries by building and maintaining Web sites. Their services are offered for free. Christian webmasters design sites, provide free Web hosting, and maintain the sites if their clients do not wish to do that themselves.

Missionaries serve as teachers, counselors, computer instructors, accountants, and many other jobs not normally associated with the ministry. The Lutheran mission's Web site (✐ *www.elca.org*), for example, lists current openings for long-term and short-term international mission appointments in forty-seven countries.

Frequently asked questions about many aspects of the missionary life are answered at Ask A Missionary. You can review this resource on the Web at ✐ *www.askamissionary.com*. If you are thinking of taking on missionary responsibilities, you can learn about what the lifestyle entails here.

All Ages Welcome

All this sounds like a young man's, or woman's game. It is true that many missionaries start off quite young, bursting with idealism and not yet subjected to life's slings and arrows. These people enter into the work with literal "missionary zeal." Yet just as George Bernard Shaw observed, "Youth is wasted on the young"; missionary work need not be restricted to the twenty-somethings. People with a lifetime of experience under their belts also go off to serve. After working for years and raising a family, retirees comprise a fair percentage of the missionary population. Often the older folks make up for what they may lack in youthful exuberance with endurance and hard-earned wisdom. No matter what your status on the path of life, you can serve in missionary work if you choose.

ALERT!

If you want to spread the word, people have to be able to read the word. Opportunities to teach people to read and then teach them about the faith can be found at Literacy Evangelism (✐ *www.literacyevangelism.org*).

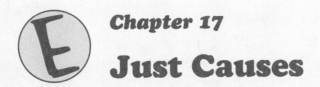

Chapter 17

Just Causes

If you have always had a social conscience and would like to combine your desire to make the world a better place while making a living, there are opportunities to do both. This chapter gives you several avenues you can travel to find a cause greater than yourself.

Making a Difference

There are many ways that we can make a difference in this world. We can start in our own back yard, or we can be more ambitious and take our desire to affect change on the road. What are your concerns? The environment, poverty, human rights? There is much to be done, and precious few are willing to devote the time and energy to making a difference. If you choose to venture down this path, you will always be busy and never bored.

Defending the Environment with Greenpeace

When you think of Greenpeace, you think of the brave souls who used to place themselves between whaling ships and their prey in an effort to save the whales from slaughter and eventual extinction. Those moments are some of the organization's finest hours, but there is much more to the organization than those seafaring heroics.

Greenpeace describes itself thusly: "Greenpeace is an independent, campaigning organization that uses nonviolent, creative confrontation to expose global environmental problems, and force solutions for a green and peaceful future. Greenpeace's goal is to ensure the ability of the Earth to nurture life in all its diversity."

Greenpeace would like to save the oceans and the forests, end our reliance on fossil fuels, eliminate toxic chemicals, and extinguish the threat of nuclear disaster and all manner of potential environmental disasters. In order to maintain their independence, they do not receive donations from governments, corporations, and political parties. Greenpeace gets its operational capital from donations from individuals and foundations.

Bearing Witness

Greenpeace began in 1971 when a small group of activists traveled in an old fishing boat to a small island off the coast of Alaska, called

Amchitka. The United States was conducting underground nuclear testing on the island. The intrepid environmentalists were concerned about the various endangered species on the island, including sea otters, peregrine falcons, and bald eagles. The area was also known for heavy seismic activity, meaning it has a lot of earthquakes. Logic suggested that this is a bad place to detonate a nuclear bomb.

The boatload of activists said, in Biblical language, that they wanted to "bear witness" to the blast. The craft was intercepted by the navy and turned around, but their actions shined much light on the activities on the island. Greenpeace took credit when the government ended nuclear testing on the island, which later became a bird sanctuary.

Some of Greenpeace's subsequent successes include influencing a moratorium on whaling, a ban on dumping radioactive waste at sea, and other positive initiatives to make the environment cleaner and safer. Greenpeace is based in the city of Amsterdam in the Netherlands and has offices in forty-one countries.

Working for Greenpeace

Greenpeace is looking for dedicated individuals who would like, in the organization's words, to "contribute to and be part of an important program of work to stop climate change, save the ancient forests, and protect our world's oceans, earth, and sky."

You can send a resume and cover letter to Greenpeace, but do not expect a response unless they are interested. In the old days, people received a polite rejection as a matter of course. Nowadays, there are so many applicants to job postings that responding to each one individually would itself be a full-time job. Greenpeace promises to keep your resume on file for six months. Send your resume to this e-mail address, putting "open application" in the subject field: *recruitment@ams.greenpeace.org*. Or you can send it via snail mail to Human Resources Department, Greenpeace International, Keizersgracht 176, 1016 DW, Amsterdam, The Netherlands.

The Greenpeace Web site also posts currently open positions. You can regularly visit *www.greenpeace.org* and subscribe to the mailing list to be alerted to new job openings.

Possible Positions

To give you an idea of the kinds of jobs Greenpeace advertises, a recent search returned results such as these:

- **Marketing manager:** Managing the external image and the integrity and effectiveness of the Greenpeace message.
- **Communications director:** Formulating and executing the global communications strategy for Greenpeace.
- **Office manager:** Managing and developing facilities, services, and support for the Greenpeace International office.
- **Crew manager:** Recruiting and developing seagoing personnel to ensure ships are manned as required.

Starting Out with Internships

Most organizations involved with the environment and other causes offer internships to qualified candidates, but these are more often volunteer assignments. You can the search the "paid internship" section of ✎*www.eco.org* to see what is posted. ECO annually places more than 750 students in paid internships across the country. The list is updated regularly, so you should check it often or subscribe to their free e-mail alerts. They are usually, but not always, summer assignments. A random sampling of jobs includes working with the U.S. Environmental Protection Agency (EPA) in Seattle, as a seismic and tsunamogenic hazards data processor in Woods Hole, Massachusetts, and a shipboard internship monitoring the water pollution of the Great Lakes.

FACT

The American site of Amnesty International lists current events and news, and information on how to get involved. The address is ✎*www.amnestyusa.org*. You can also get contact information for all of Amnesty International's global offices at ✎*http://amnesty.org*.

You can apply on the ✎*www.eco.org* Web site by following the instructions and cutting and pasting your resume in the body of the e-mail. This is a no-fee service. Although most internships are for students, you cannot be a full-time student since the assignments are themselves full-time positions. Like any job search, you should apply for as many internships as you like. Competition is fierce, so pick the ones that intrigue you and for which you are qualified—and good luck.

Amnesty International

Amnesty International has more than a million members in 140 countries. Their efforts are financed by donations from members and other altruistic entities.

The organization began in 1961 (the same year the Peace Corps was founded), when British lawyer Peter Benenson learned about two Portuguese students who had drawn a seven-year prison sentence for the "radical" act of raising their glasses in a toast to freedom. Apparently the powers that be found this to be a call to revolution. Benenson wrote a newspaper article about the incident called "The Forgotten Prisoner" that generated much publicity and offers of support. And so the human rights movement was born. Within a year, the organization had national branches in seven countries and had worked on 210 cases of human rights abuse.

ESSENTIAL

To take a look at job opportunities with Amnesty International, you can check out the U.S. Web site's employment opportunity (see above). The United Kingdom Web site also maintains a job posting board. In addition, there are also internships and plenty of opportunities to volunteer.

Amnesty International seeks to be strictly impartial. Hence, it does not only address what it considered human rights abuses in third-world countries and blatant dictatorships, but in all countries of the world. This includes the United States. The organization has recently cited the United States for its war against Iraq and its treatment of terrorism suspects as criminal acts of a rogue nation. If you find this proposition to be offensive, you may not want to be associated with Amnesty International.

Save the Children

Save the Children began in 1932, during the depths of the Great Depression. A group of New Yorkers decided to do what they could to help their fellow Americans in the Appalachian region of the country. They were inspired by the British Save the Children Fund, which was founded in 1919 after the horrors of World War I. From its humble beginnings in Harlan County, Kentucky, Save the Children now operates in forty-five countries, and its mandate is to provide communities with "a hand up, not a handout."

Committed Workers

Save the Children states that their goal is to "attract, motivate, and retain the best people in the right positions. We hire deeply committed, talented and experienced individuals who want to make a difference in the lives of children worldwide."

FACT

To read the United Nation's Universal Declaration of Human Rights, the document that continues to inspire the work of Amnesty International, visit ✍ *www.amnestyusa.org*.

This organization ensures that its employees work in an environment where cooperation and team building are fostered in a climate of empowerment. They offer a comprehensive benefits package, including medical benefits, a retirement plan, and relocation assistance for those who are assigned to work overseas. Given that their focus is children, they also offer flexible schedules and family leave. As with all service organizations, there are many opportunities for volunteers in their world headquarters in Westport, Connecticut, and in many other locations. Their needs vary, but they will eagerly find the right fit for you if you are motivated and have the right qualifications. There are also internship opportunities available.

The snail mail address to contact Save the Children is Save the Children, 54 Wilton Road, Westport, CT 06880.

ALERT!

The Save the Children Web site (⌨ *www.savethechildren.org*) has information about the history of the organization and what it does, how to sponsor a child for only $28 a month, plus how to volunteer and a section of employment opportunities.

Abroad and at Home

Save the Children says, "Our work is both inspiring and challenging, with real results for children and families in need. Today, Save the Children works in nearly fifty countries, serving 9 million children and adults throughout the developing world, the United States and areas of crisis. Save the Children is the only international aid agency that also works in the United States." Many forget that there are pockets of desperate poverty remaining here in America. In addition to working in Africa, Asia, the Caribbean, Eurasia, Latin America, the Middle East, Save the Children also works with families and children on Indian reservations, in Appalachia, and the Mississippi Delta.

Improving Your Own Neighborhood

There are many ways in which you can work in your neighborhood and serve the community. If you have an idea for a program or service, you may be able to hook up with AmeriCorps. This is a network of 2,100 nonprofits, public agencies, and faith-based organizations that work for their communities in a variety of ways. They tutor and mentor young people, build affordable housing, teach computer skills, clean parks and streams, run after-school programs, and much more. A quarter of a million men and women have worked with AmeriCorps since it was founded in 1994. AmeriCorps bestows grants to local and national nonprofit organizations and sends in trained professionals to help people at the local level function more efficiently. AmeriCorps grantees include national groups like Habitat for Humanity, the American Red Cross, Boys and Girls Clubs, and numerous smaller faith-based and community organizations.

AmeriCorps Projects

AmeriCorps VISTA has been in existence for thirty-five years. Its objective is to work to eradicate poverty. Members serve for one year on a full-time basis in nonprofit agencies and faith-based organization to improve the quality of life, teach kids how to read, help adults create small business, get people hooked up to the Internet, and more.

FACT

The U.S. Department of Health and Human Services (⌐*www.hhs.gov*) has a division called the Administration for Children and Families that lists many services at the federal, state, and local level. You can search there for employment opportunities.

AmeriCorps*NCCC is a ten-month, full-time residential program for men and women between the ages of eighteen and twenty-four. It is kind of a combination of the Peace Corps and the military. Members serve in teams of ten to fifteen people. The projects include public safety, public health, and disaster relief. Some of the types of projects include immunization programs, forest fire prevention, creating urban gardens, literacy programs, and many others.

AmeriCorps Requirements

AmeriCorps members must be United States citizens over seventeen years of age. They serve in full- or part-time positions, usually for a one-year term. Full timers receive an education grant of $4,725 toward college or graduate school or to pay back student loans. They also get health insurance, and some, depending on the job, receive a living allowance of $9,300. Not a lot of money, but if you are interested in this kind of service you are not in it for the money.

To learn more about joining AmeriCorps, visit their Web site at ✍ *www.americorps.org*, or call ✆ 1-800-942-2677 (TTY 1-800-833-3722).

The World of Politics

You can work for change and make a difference by becoming involved in the world of politics, though it may seem that today that few people who choose it as a vocation are so motivated. It is an area where you can affect change at the local and national level. Politics was at one time considered a true career in "public service," but sadly nowadays people enter politics to feather their own nests. Still, for the idealistic among us, it is a place to try to make the world, or at least your corner of the world, better.

The Corporation for National and Community Service has job postings that include both paying positions and internships (✍ *www.nationalservice.org*).

All Politics Are Local

If you want to pursue in a career in politics, first ask yourself this question: Do you know who your congressional representatives and senators are? For that matter, do you know the difference between a congressman and a senator, or how many of each you should have? You would be surprised—or maybe you would not—how many people cannot answer those questions. The answer is that you have two senators, and the number of congressmen depends on the population of your state. They all have offices in your area as well as in Washington, D.C. They all have a small staff of paid workers and a larger number of volunteers.

Learn a little bit about them, and see if you agree with their political philosophy. Pop in and say hello. See if they are hiring. If not, and you have the time and the inclination, volunteer.

There is a lot you can do in your community while working or volunteering for your local elected officials. On an altruistic level, you can help them work with the members of the community on projects to improve the quality of life. On a more self-serving level, you can work for their reelection campaign in the hopes of currying favor and advancing your own personal ambitions.

The Politix Group (✎ *www.politixgroup.com*) has a page of job resources if your ambition is to head for the nation's capitol to pursue a career in politics. You will find information on jobs in campaigns, internships in Washington, D.C., locally, and even in the United Kingdom.

Chapter 18

Staying Healthy

If you have a regular office job, chances are you have some kind of health insurance coverage. You may have to pay a certain amount each month, but it is a modest sum compared to those who have to pay the whole thing. Many alternative careers may not offer the best major medical coverage, so you will need to find a way to protect your health at an affordable price.

If You Have Your Health, You Have Everything

If you are self-employed or have an employer who does not offer a medical/dental plan, you have to fend for yourself with insurance or go without. Paying for your own health coverage is very expensive. Millions of Americans are without adequate health care, and not just those who live below the poverty line. Small business owners, entrepreneurs, and those in some of the alternative careers in the book are obliged to cover themselves or roll the dice and hope and pray that they stay healthy.

If you are going to go without health coverage for an extended period of time, be careful. You can't live like "the boy in the plastic bubble," but you can take sensible precautions to prevent any health problems from disabling you.

- **Watch what you eat.** You will find that you can eat healthily and inexpensively. Ironically, it is often the bad stuff that is more costly. Cook for yourself and do not eat out as much. This will be better for you and save you money.
- **Take vitamins.** A multivitamin and other supplements will help keep you healthy. If certain conditions run in your family, such as heart diseases and certain forms of cancer, look for supplements that can help prevent disease. For example, if you do not eat enough fiber, you should have some kind of fiber supplement to cleanse your digestive system.
- **Exercise regularly.** Even a small amount of regular exercise will help keep you fit and healthy. A couch potato without medical coverage is in an especially precarious position. Do not overdo it. You do not want to get an injury that requires medical attention.

Above all, be practical but not obsessive. Life is a risk, and you never know what is coming around that next corner. Whether you have coverage or not, being careful about your health is always a good idea.

The Right Plan for Your Needs

Take stock of your situation and your finances and find the plan that is best for you. There are several options available to you. Individual health insurance is the most expensive, and you may have to answer a detailed health questionnaire and have a physical by a doctor that is affiliated with the insurance company. If you fail the medical exam, your application will be denied, or you may only be eligible for limited coverage.

You can become part of a group insurance plan without submitting to a physical exam. The group insurer knows that some people will not be in the best shape and will use the plan often; others, perhaps most, will be in good health and not visit the doctor very often. Most people put off getting regular checkups for a variety of reasons (mostly procrastination and fear of what they may find out). Obviously, you should take advantage of your health coverage to find out about any health problems as early as possible.

Finding a Plan

Research the companies in your area thoroughly, and make sure you are well aware of what will be covered by different plans and what will not. You do not want to be surprised when you get a statement from the company saying they will not pay for a particular treatment.

It is also not advisable to buy a policy that does not honor pre-existing conditions. If you have a medical condition, such as asthma or high blood pressure, you do not want a health plan that will deny you necessary medication and treatment because you have had the condition before you signed up for their plan.

Types of Coverage

You should review your policy on an annual basis. For most people, especially those in an alternative career that may not have the best—if any—health plan, a group insurance plan is the best way to go. When you do the research, you can decide if you want what is called a "base plus plan" or a "comprehensive plan." A base plus plan has two parts: basic medical coverage for hospitalizations and surgery, X rays and laboratory tests. Depending on the plan, there will be some limits, but no deductible. The second part of the plan is called major medical. This is for routine check-ups and emergency trips to the doctor that are not so serious as to require hospitalization. A deductible is the amount you have to pay out of your own pocket before you start receiving reimbursements from the insurance company. The higher the deductible, the lower the overall cost of the health plan.

A comprehensive plan covers almost all medical services. Here, a single reimbursement formula is used after the deductible has been satisfied. Coinsurance is also applied to all covered expenses until your out-of-pocket limit for expenses is maxed out. Coinsurance is commonly figured with a formula of eighty-twenty. The insurer pays 80 percent of medical expenses, while the individual is responsible for the remaining 20 percent. Once you have paid all you are obliged to under the terms of the plan, all additional charges are paid in full by the health insurance company.

If you are relatively young and reasonably fit, you might want to consider a high deductible and pay low premiums, keeping the policy for peace of mind should a medical catastrophe occur. A prolonged hospital stay can be an extremely expensive affair.

When investigating health plans, find out what the covered expenses are. They should of course include visits to the your doctor, either for a routine checkup or a specific medical reason. This is usually a feature of coinsurance plans. Be aware of any caps that the insurer may have on the dollar amount they will pay for a particular procedure. All insurance companies have monetary limits on what they will reimburse. They will have a maximum number of days that you can stay in the hospital that they will pay for, and they set approximate amounts on what a procedure, an appendectomy for example, should cost. If your doctor or hospital charges more than the insurer decides in the going rate for the operation, then you will be responsible for the difference. This may necessitate shopping around for a doctor and hospital that will be in financial sync with the insurance company.

Should You Go with an HMO or a PPO?

HMO stands for health maintenance organization. They provide comprehensive health care to members who pay a fixed fee to the HMO in return for health care services.

You agree to receive treatment only from doctors and clinics that are part of the HMO. The only exceptions to this rule are emergency room visits and medical expenses that may occur when you are traveling.

An HMO is the 800-pound gorilla of health care. It does whatever it wants, so you must know as much about it before you sign aboard. Some HMOs even own their own hospitals and hire the doctors who work in them. Others are a network of doctors and clinics. The advantages of an HMO are that it provides all the services for the fee you pay. The negative element is that your choices are limited to those doctors and services affiliated with the HMO.

What to Look For

You have probably heard a lot of horror stories about HMOs. Some of them are pretty outrageous. Some will not cover certain treatments, even though they are life-saving. Given the preponderance of these horror stories, you should do extensive research before selecting an HMO.

There are several things you should look for. Does the HMO offer care and service in your area? Is your family doctor a member? If not or if you do not have a doctor, do doctors close to your home participate? Can you afford the various premiums, deductibles, and copayments? Find out the reputation of the HMO. Learn if it makes its payments on time. Find out if they have denied care or services to members and if there are any complaints against it.

PPOs

A PPO is a preferred provider organization. This is an organization that contracts with a collective of doctors, hospitals, and other health care providers to offer services at agreed-upon rates. The out-of-pocket expenses for members is low. The advantage is that you can go outside the network to other doctors and hospitals. You will have to pay more for doing this, but at least you can. An HMO may not pay anything if you want to see a doctor from outside the network.

FACT

If you are a senior citizen, soon to be one, or have one in your life, you can use the free service at HealthMetrix Research (*www. hmos4seniors.com*) to find the right HMOs for their needs.

Both PPOs and HMOs are known to be less than generous when it comes to treatments that they do not deem to be necessary. For example, you can forget about acupuncture or anything remotely "holistic." And if you become gravely ill and want to try an experimental treatment, neither a PPO nor HMO will offer any support.

Other Types of Coverage

One other kind of insurance to consider is dental coverage. It is not as essential as major medical coverage, but it can be very helpful. After all, for some of the careers in this book, an attractive smile is a basic requirement.

Dental coverage is rarely included in health insurance plans. Dental care is considered a separate entity. Civil service jobs, union plans, and most big companies offer separate dental plans in additional to major medical coverage. Most people hate to go to the dentist even more than they do the doctor, but if you have ever had a toothache in the wee small hours of the morning and discover that you need an emergency root canal, you know that dental bills can be extraordinarily high.

Most dental coverage is broken down into three levels. Level I covers routine examinations, X rays and cleanings, usually twice a year. Level II includes basic procedures such as fillings, extractions, root canals, and so on. Level III covers major work like bridges and dentures. Dental plans reimburse you more at Level I. Often the services are covered at 100 percent. The reimbursement is lower at Levels II and III, and like many medical insurance plans, dental insurance companies have a cap as to what services should cost. If their estimate of a root canal is lower than what your dentist charges, you have to make up the difference or find a dentist who will take what the insurance company pays. In the good old days, many a dentist in working-class communities would take what the insurance company paid them and leave it at that, but those men and women are a dying breed.

Dental coverage is expensive and usually involves a fair out-of-pocket responsibility, even with the coverage. Shop around for the best plan for your needs and your budget. If services are too cost prohibitive, make sure you brush and floss after every meal.

Like dental coverage, vision care is usually not included in major medical coverage and must be purchased separately. Vision plans usually pay a set amount for eye exams, lenses, and frames. If you are of a certain age and discover that you need reading glasses, you can buy an inexpensive pair off the rack in your local pharmacy. Even book superstores have a revolving rack of spectacles. If this does not solve the problem, or your eyes are not functioning as they used to in other ways, bite the financial bullet and get an eye exam. As with your overall health, neglecting your vision can lead to serious problems.

Life Insurance

Many people keep a small life insurance policy with the idea that it will be enough to pay for their funeral expenses. They do not want to burden their near and dear with that very expensive proposition. But there is more to life insurance than simply paying to bury a person.

If you are the head of a household with one or more dependents, you should definitely have a life insurance policy that will do more for your survivors. The amount and type of coverage you pick should be determined by you age, lifestyle, and other factors.

Term Versus Cash Value

The two most common forms of life insurance are called term insurance and cash value insurance. Term insurance provides coverage for a specific period if time and cash value insurance is permanent, until death do you part so to speak. Cash value insurance pays a death benefit plus the titular cash value for your beneficiaries. Term life insurance is more affordable, and, as the name implies, it is only for a finite period of time. Some insurance companies will allow you to convert a short-term to a cash-value policy.

FACT

One of the easiest ways to estimate how much life insurance protection you should buy is to use a life insurance needs calculator. One such calculator can be found on the Web in the life insurance section at ✍ *www.life-line.org*. If you are young and single—lucky you—you are probably not thinking about such things as life insurance. You probably still consider yourself indestructible and immortal. Not to burst your balloon, but life will gradually teach you otherwise. As you become more responsible and maybe even start a family, the need for life insurance will become more apparent.

How Much?

The life insurance policy you should buy depends on how much you want to leave your heirs. If you are married, both of you should have policies. You can buy a term insurance policy for a little as one and as long as thirty years. The premium you pay will be based on your age, health, family's health history, and whether you are a smoker. The premium will increase if you want to renew it when the term expires.

Research numerous life insurance companies before making your decision. Some companies are well known and have been around for over a century; others are less reliable and reputable.

You will have to fill out an application that will include questions about your health and lifestyle. Your responses on the application will determine the price of your policy. After you submit the application, you will probably be required to have a physical examination. This will definitely be the case if you are over forty. The insurance company will assign the doctor and pay for the visit.

Familiarize yourself with the policy. Know all the benefits and charges so nothing catches you by surprise down the line.

QUESTION?

How can you investigate an insurance company?
To find out what rating the company has received, check out the major ratings services, such as A.M. Best or Standard & Poor's. They evaluate an insurer's financial condition and ability to pay claims promptly. The insurance company giving you a quote should provide you with this information. Be wary of them if they do not. You can also contact your state's department of insurance to find out more about the company.

What Else Do You Need to Know?

Shop around when looking for insurance. The premiums range in price. There are plenty of Web sites that will give you an instant quote. This is not an exact science, however. You will still most likely need to have a physical from the company doctor before a final figure can be determined.

You should not buy more coverage than you need. There is no reason to be paying higher premiums than necessary. Stay healthy, because the healthier you are, the lower your premium will be. Of course there are better reasons to stay healthy, like living longer, but saving money is always a good thing too. On a related note, the longer you wait to buy life insurance, the more expensive it will be. Just as smoking and other factors work against you, so does the inexorable march of time.

After you've done all of the above and found the right life insurance, be sure to review your policy once a year. Do not file it away and forget about it. There will be events in your life that may require amending the plan.

Liability Insurance

Depending on your line of work, you might want to look into some form of liability insurance. This is similar to the medical malpractice insurance that doctors have to pay. This is a litigious society in which we live; people are more likely to initiate lawsuits than ever before. If you offer a product or service, there is always the possibility that a disgruntled or simply dishonest customer will take you to court. Self-employed individuals can get what is called general umbrella liability coverage to add a little peace of mind in these lawsuit-crazy times.

FACT

Even if you are working for yourself, you don't have to go it completely alone. The National Association for the Self-Employed (✍ *www.nase.org*), for example, is a valuable resource for entrepreneurs who run small and "micro" businesses. Membership benefits include discounted health and dental care, financial advice, and more.

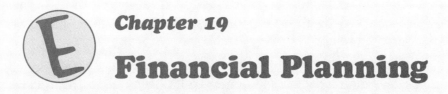

Chapter 19

Financial Planning

Everyone should have a sound financial plan in these less-than-sound financial times, but this is even more true for those who are looking for or already working in an alternative career. This chapter will offer advice and recommend resources for staying financially secure in an age of insecurity.

Don't Lose Your Cheese (A Fable)

Once upon a time there was a cute and cuddly little mouse who worked very hard to accumulate the cheese he needed to feed himself and his family. The cheese was eaten by one and all, but there was never any left over at the end of the month. They all ate as much as was available, even though their appetites could have been satisfied with less. They gorged themselves with no thought to a future when there might be a shortage of cheese.

Unfortunately, the head of the family of mice did not put enough cheese aside for what human beings call a "rainy day." This reckless rodent did not have a cautious or conservative outlook. He believed that there would always be plenty of cheese to go around.

Then, one day, after a period of what one might call "irrational exuberance," it started to rain and it did not stop for months and months. The "rainy days" become a monsoon season. The mouse's modest stash of cheese was quickly consumed. Then he had to go to the government for unemployment cheese, but that ran out and they would not extend his cheese benefits. He had to eke out a modest living for small allotments of cheese. His family struggled to get enough cheese to survive. It was difficult. One of the little mice began stealing cheese and found himself stuck on a glue trap. Another found a stash of cheese that was laced with rodent poison by a mean human. Still another was lucky to be caught in a humane trap and was released in a field, but he was soon at the mercy of cats and other predators.

ALERT!

Don't let the court jester hats fool you. The Motley Fool (*www.fool.com*) offers advice on many elements of financial planning including investing, insurance, IRAs, and other retirement plans.

Papa Mouse lamented the tragedies that befell his beloved family and blamed himself for not saving a stockpile of cheese to weather the occasional periods of cheeselessness that afflict both the rodent and the humans worlds from time to time. If you are a mouse with a small amount of cheese in your cheese account, don't let this happen to you.

Okay, so maybe the above won't sell 20 million copies like another popular fable about mice and their movable cheese, but you get the point. You have to prepare for lulls and gaps in an alternative career. Or any career, for that matter, particularly in these times.

Making a Budget You Can Live With

It is regrettable fact that most of us cannot buy whatever we want, go on extravagant shopping sprees with cavalier glee, or pay all our bills with plenty left over each month. Most of us have a limited amount of money to manage, and a seemingly ever-growing number of bills and creditors who do not like to be kept waiting. Everyone, and especially those seeking an alternative career, needs to get a handle on their financial life. A good place to start is to make a budget and stick with it.

Don't Put It Off Any Longer

Making a budget is something people tend to avoid, and sticking with one is something even fewer people manage to do. Like all things, if you do not control your money, your money will control you. When it comes time to actually sit down in with pen and a yellow legal pad and a stack of monthly bills, or in front of your computer with a spreadsheet document open, we often suddenly find something else more important to do. Perhaps it is a beautiful day, and you feel you should get out in the sun. Sitting and hammering out a budget is far too sedentary a task. Or maybe you suddenly feel the need to clean your closets or the attic if you have one. You have been putting that off too long. It is very easy to get distracted when confronted with examining your financial life in the harsh light of day.

Despite your facility for procrastination and delaying tactics, it must be done. The longer you put it off, the longer you are preventing yourself from the sense of freedom that comes from taking charge of your financial life. The freedom from financial insecurity is a liberating state of being that, in addition to reducing debt, reduces stress and opens all sorts of doors that you had no idea were available to you. Be brave, sit down, take a deep breath, and just do it.

FACT

Kiplinger (☞ *www.kiplinger.com*) is another respected financial organization. Their Web site has the latest financial news and stock market information, plus helpful hints and advice. There is a free section and a membership area, and you can sign up for free e-mail updates.

A Basic Budget

When making a budget, the obvious goal is to reconcile your monthly income and your monthly expenses. Of course, your monthly expenses should not exceed your monthly income. Ideally you should even have a little extra to save, but that is not always possible these days. The best many of us can do is to avoid descending into the deep dark void of desperate debt.

A budget is a fluid document, as are the ebbs and flows of the currents in your life. It will change as your circumstances change. Some expenses will be higher in a given month, while others may vanish through successful financial management and sound decisions. But before you can do anything you have to take the first step. You must, as the poet Dylan Thomas wrote, "begin at the beginning."

Collect all your financial paperwork—bills, bank statements, your checkbook, receipts, and so on. Create the following categories on your paper or your spreadsheet:

- **Savings:** This includes the money you put away, or try to, for the proverbial rainy day or your inevitable old age, plus any investment activity you may be paying into.
- **Food:** Include everything from the your grocery bills to restaurant receipts to the Big Gulp at the 7-Eleven. Try to get in the habit of saving your receipts even for the little things in life. If you forget, make your best guess.
- **Housing:** Rent, mortgage payments, and any property taxes or insurance associated with your home.
- **Utilities:** Water, electricity, heat, both landlines and cell phones, and online expenses.

- **Clothing:** Besides new purchases, don't forget to factor in laundry expenses and dry cleaning bills.
- **Medical:** Doctor's visits, dental and vision bills, and so on.
- **Entertainment:** You should include everything from a Blockbuster rental, to the cable bill, to a romantic weekend getaway, to a motel with a heart-shaped Jacuzzi.
- **Transportation:** All automobile expenses, as well as taxi, bus, train, and any other modes of transportation.
- **Other monthly expenses:** Credit card bills, life insurance, and all other monthly bills.

Personal Budgeting and Money Saving Tips (*www.personal-budget-planning-saving-money.com*) is a Web site of free advice for everything from planning a budget to record keeping to that most difficult of things—exercising fiscal self-control.

Hopefully you have saved bills or receipts for the last several months. If your bills and income are fairly stable, it would be good to make a budget for an entire year. With three to six months of receipts and bills, you can create an average monthly amount to work with.

Once you have a monthly average, you should determine your average monthly income. When you compare your monthly income with your average monthly expenses, it may be a deeply disturbing experience for you. Do not let it get you down. You can deal with it.

If your expenses exceed your income, create an "ideal budget" on another piece of paper, and try to tame the beast to conform to the confines of your monthly income. The objective is to reduce your expenses in order to be able to save more each month. When you are working in an alternative career, the work is sometimes seasonal and sporadic, so you need to have as much of a cushion as possible. You will probably be eligible to collect unemployment insurance during some down times (check with your state's department of labor), but that might not be enough to cover the lifestyle to which you have grown accustomed.

Helpful Hints

If your income is less than your expenses, a good first step is to do an across-the-board 5-percent cut of all categories. This will (hopefully) be a relatively painless method to save a few bucks. The less draconian your cost-cutting measures are, the more likely you will be to stick with the program.

The Financial Planning Association (☞ *www.fpanet.org*) has a search feature that will help you find a financial planner in your area. You can search by zip code, address, or mile radius from your location. The site will give you the names and addresses of certified financial planners in your community.

This can be a terribly unpleasant task, and it is more than a little overwhelming. We are often intimidated by the big picture. In such cases it is a good idea to compartmentalize. Look at each component of the whole enchilada while avoiding direct eye contact with its formidable totality.

There are many ways to reduce expenses without reducing your quality of life. Rent movies instead of buying them, or peruse the previously viewed bins of your local Blockbuster. Do your own laundry instead of lazily dropping it off at the "wash-dry-fold" service, and do not wear (or purchase) clothes that require dry cleaning very often. Avoid "fine dining," and eat at home more. Little things like this can go a long way to reducing your expenses and enabling you to save more.

Budget Counselors

If this procedure is simply too difficult for you for whatever reason, you can hire the services of a budget advisor. There are plenty of them out there. Just make sure you factor their fee into your budget. You will need to bring all the above-mentioned documentation to the person's office if they do not make house calls. They are experienced at this business and are likely to offer suggestions and recommendations that you might not occur to you.

ALERT!

The Quicken Financial Network (✍ *www.qfn.com*) has online tools such as a savings calculator and debt reduction planner and a loan planner. Quicken also sells financial and tax preparation software. Check the hard drive of your computer. It may have come preloaded with Quicken or another brand of financial software.

There are also software programs, like Quicken or Microsoft Money, that will make the process easier for you. Microsoft Money often comes preloaded on a new computer that has the Windows operating system. It might be on your computer without your being aware of it. There are also plenty of Web sites that will help you, some for free, others for a fee.

Working with a Financial Planner

Some people cannot deal with the facts and figures of their financial life, either because they have no facility with numbers or they find the task too daunting and depressing to deal with. For those folks, soliciting the services of a financial planner may be the way to go. Of course when the objective is to save money, why take on the additional expense of hiring someone to help you save money?

The truly frugal will do it themselves, even if it requires an intensive course of study. There is a lot to learn, but these days we are lucky to have the Internet. We do not need to attend seminars, visit libraries, or take courses, valuable though they are. Today you do not have to get out of bed (if you have a laptop) and the world comes to you. If you are intent on saving as much money as possible, this would be a good path for you. However, if you do not trust either your financial acumen or your motivation to do the necessary homework, then hiring a financial planner is best.

Finding a Financial Planner

There are many financial planners out there, and finding one may be a daunting task. Do not randomly pick a name from the phone book or a Web site. Word of mouth is a good place to start. Ask around among friends and coworkers. Chances are one or more of them have used the services of a financial planner at some point. If it was a positive experience, you will have someone to contact; if not, then you have a name to scratch off your list.

FACT

The free section of FinanCenter.com (*www.financenter.com*) has a lengthy list of consumer tools to help people with budgeting, estate planning, retirement planning, taxes, and many other aspects to secure a sound financial future. In addition to these features there is a section on how to apply for and receive financial aid through grants, scholarships, work-study programs, and more.

When you have a list of several names, you should set about interviewing them. Come to the appointment with any questions you have. During this getting-to-know-you session, you will determine if you and your potential financial planner have the rapport needed to work together—not necessarily a personal chemistry but rather a shared financial philosophy. If you are conservative with your money, you do not want to hook up with a maverick speculator. If you are willing to take risks, you do not want someone who will talk you out of bold moves at every turn.

You can conduct your initial interview on the phone or in person. In person is usually the best. There is nothing like looking into the eyes of someone who will be handling your money and getting a feel for their character. Also, this initial session should be a free consultation. A reputable financial consultant is confident enough that he or she will be able to sell their services to you. No payment should change hands until you decide that this is the person for you.

When you have a candidate in mind, do not feel funny about running a background check on them. They should provide verifiable references and be willing to show you a document called a Form ADV. This proves they are licensed to practice financial planning in your state. If the planner is a lawyer, check the state bar association; if he or she is a certified public accountant, you can consult the state accountancy board.

Do not forget to check with the Better Business Bureau to see if your candidates have been contacted about the financial planner's ethics.

Fees

The fees charged by a financial planner can range from $100 an hour to $300 to $700 for a comprehensive financial plan. You can decide if you want a fee-only planner or someone who works on commissions. Advisors who work for commission may advise you to make investments in which they have a vested interest, making these candidates less than objective. If that is a concern to you, then go with a fee-only financial planner.

Beware of the Credit Card Trap

So many of us have fallen into this terrible trap. It is a cunning, baffling, powerful, and insidious ambush that sneaks up on you, and the next thing you know you find yourself at the bottom of a deep dark financial dungeon. That may sound a little dramatic, but that's just how it feels. How did we get there, how can we get out of it, and how can we avoid it in the first place?

When you receive preapproved credit card offers in the mail, it is natural to accept them. They come in handy. You can buy things online, get some expensive necessities and maybe a luxury or two, and make small payments over time. A good deal, right?

Think again. If several credit card companies each send you an offer and you accept, you can quickly run up some big bills.

If you file for a Chapter 7 bankruptcy, this information will remain on your credit report for seven years. In the old days, you could not have a credit card during this period, but there are some companies who will issue cards within ninety days of a bankruptcy. Be prepared for loan-shark-style interest rates and no sympathy if you get in over your head again.

If you make your payments on time, the companies are likely to raise your credit limit, inspiring more charging. If times get a little tough, you might find yourself putting things like the rent and other bills on your cards. Maybe you were starting your own small business and ended up funding it with credit cards. Whatever the reason, it is a widespread fact that many Americans are carrying a lot of debt. Statistics suggest that the average American family has $2,000 in savings and is saddled with $8,000 in debt. For many this is not the case, but for many others the debt is a lot higher.

Once mired in the morass of debt, you can get out of it in a couple of ways. You can go through a credit counseling service, which will work with your creditors to reduce your high-interest rates and consolidate your bills into one monthly payment. Be aware that you will probably be paying this off for years to come and it will affect your ability to get more credit and other types of loans.

FACT

There are many companies that offer to help you work with your creditors to reduce your debt. Some charge a fee, others are nonprofit, and many are actually affiliated with the credit card companies themselves. It is a way for credit card companies to make sure that they get something back.

Another option is bankruptcy. As of this writing, this process is still easy and relatively painless. It is recommended that you get a bankruptcy lawyer to handle the case. These services will cost a minimum of several hundred dollars, but you have the relative piece of mind that it will be done right. This will clean your slate of all debt, but of course your credit rating will be damaged for several years.

The best way to avoid the credit card trap is to not get bushwhacked in the first place. Do not have more than two cards, and always pay more than the minimum. At the first signs of trouble, cut your cards up and stop using them.

Test Yourself

People in alternative careers, with uncertain and unsteady income, are more likely than many to be tempted to run into credit problems. Here are a few questions you should honestly answer to determine if you are on the road to credit card disaster:

1. You have plenty of credit card bills and next to nothing in your savings account.
2. You use one credit card to pay another.
3. You only make the minimum payment each month.
4. You use credit cards for things you used to buy with cash, such as groceries.
5. You have more than two or three credit cards.
6. When you do pay your bill in full, you max or near max the card out again in a short period of time.
7. Your balances always hover near the credit limit.
8. You've been denied credit line increases, and new credit card offers have stopped.
9. You miss the occasional payment and sometimes get collection calls.
10. You lie to your loved ones about the extent of your credit card debt.

If you answered yes to one or more of these, you should really do something about your credit card situation. If you answered yes to question 10, you are behaving not unlike an alcoholic, drug addict, or compulsive gambler. You are heading toward big problems if you don't own up to the problem and deal with it.

ALERT!

More and more people are digging themselves deeper and deeper in credit card debt. You should have no more than two credit cards and never allow them to hover near the maxed-out level. Pay with cash most of the time, and only use credit card on special occasions.

Weathering the Hard Times

Remember that if you choose to make your living in an alternative career, there will likely be lulls along the way. You may have even have to go back to less rewarding work to pay the bills from time to time. Do not burn any bridges in your old working world. Keep that network of contacts and sources in your phone book and e-mail address book and use them when necessary. You might have to rely on them from time to time.

If you have a spouse or loved one who supports you in your alternative career and also works, then you can help each other out during any hard times. That is what relationships are all about. If you are a singleton then you need to be take care of yourself and prepare for any eventuality.

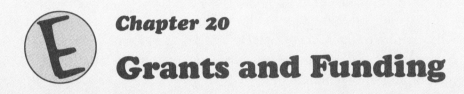

Chapter 20

Grants and Funding

Do you need a financial boost to get your alternative career going, or to take it to the next level? Many corporations and foundations regularly dispense monetary grants to individuals, small businesses and other organizations. Millions of dollars are given away every year. Some of it might as well be thrown your way, right?

Follow the Money

There are many sources giving out free money. These include major corporations, private foundations, and even the federal government. Some sources are altruistic outfits that have a mandate to make the world a better place by funding things like scientific research and the arts. And we have all heard of some of the projects that the federal government funds. Did you know that the government funded a study that determined that eating a steady diet of McDonald's and other fast foods will make people fat? *Hello?!?* For people who know where to look, there can be a lot of loot to be claimed.

Perhaps the most well-known person with his finger on the pulse of where to get grants is a fellow called Matthew Lesko. You have probably seen him on the television commercials in his suit covered with question marks. He has been on the Oprah Winfrey show more than once and many other talk shows as well. Or maybe you have heard Lesko's frenetic voice on his ubiquitous radio commercials. He also has a Web site, at the aptly named *www.matthewlesko.com.*

On Lesko's site, he makes the claim that more than "$1.1 trillion worth of grants are given out every year . . . Over 10,000 government and non-profit organizations offer grants . . . Over 30 million people receive grants each year!"

You see there is money to be had for vast and various reasons. Some are noble goals, some are selfish and self-aggrandizing. But if you can make your case in an effective and persuasive way to the people with their hands on the purse strings, then you can be given money to enrich your life. You can also be beneficial in the lives of those around you, or you might choose to take an lifelong daydream and make it reality.

Matthew Lesko is not one of the foundations dispensing free money— or free advice for that matter. He is selling books and tapes that will tell what you need to know. He is not giving the information away. The fact that he is in business for so long is a sign that the information he provides will get results. You can consider it an investment in your future. Though he is well known through his self-promoting showmanship, he is not the only resource out there.

Going to the Sources

An excellent source to find funding for is the Foundation Center Online (✑ *www.fdncenter.org*). Unfortunatley, it seems that your search for money is going to cost you some money, but overall this site is relatively inexpensive. You can try it for thirty days at a cost of $9.95, and a wealth of information, resources, and tutorials will be available to you.

ALERT!

You may need to go back to school to start your new career. Yahoo has a very thorough page of financial aid links at ✑ *http://dir.yahoo.com*. Here you will find dozens of organizations that bestow all sorts of grants in very eclectic subjects and disciplines.

What is it you would like to do? Would you like a government grant to help your fledgling small business get up and running? These and hundreds more foundations and institutions can be found on this site. You can do a detailed search and find the ones that are a good fit for what you have in mind. The individual Web sites of these organizations are listed, and you can go to them and find out their particular requirements and rules.

There are also online tutorials and information about products and services related to what is called "grantseeking." Another word for the foundations that offer funding is "grantmaker." The deeper you delve into the site, the more you will encounter "premium areas" that are not covered in your $9.95 trial membership. It is recommended that you fully explore what is available to you within the trial period before considering becoming a member.

A search of similar Web sites reveals that they all charge a fee. You have to spend a little money in order to make some. Welcome to the free-market economy.

Approaching the Benefactors

When you have done research, you will have narrowed your choices down to the corporations and foundations whose grant programs match what it is you are planning to do.

A foundation is a nonprofit entity whose whole reason for being is to make grants to other organizations or individuals for educational, cultural, scientific, artistic, or a variety of other reasons. There are private foundations and public foundations. The money bestowed by a private foundation usually comes from one source, often a wealthy philanthropist who has embraced a particular aspect of the culture and wants to promote and encourage it. A public foundation receives its money from a numerous sources.

You can also solicit corporations for grants. They disperse funds through two methods: company-sponsored foundations and direct-giving programs.

You do not have to pay for a list or special software to find funding opportunities from the federal government. Every division has a site, and most of them have grant-seeking listings, including the U.S. Justice Department's Office of Justice Programs (✑ *www.ojp.usdoj.gov*), the U.S. Department of Energy (✑ *www.doe.gov*), and the U.S. Environmental Protection Agency (✑ *www.epa.gov*).

Company-sponsored foundations are separate legal entities that are connected to the parent company, and the grants given are for things that reflect the company's mission statement. Corporate direct-giving programs are divisions within the company. While they do good, the company is also able to deduct 10 percent of its pretax income for charitable contributions. These programs are managed by the company's community relations or public relations departments. Other than money, other kinds of corporate gift giving may be in equipment and services. Things such as computers and other office services are regularly given to qualified applicants.

When seeking funding from a foundation, find one that fits in with your plans. When you apply to a corporation, reframe your proposal to show them how they will benefit in some way from your success.

RFPs

You will see the acronym "RFP" all over literature about grants and funding. The letters stand for "request for proposal." Sometimes governmental bodies or foundations will solicit proposals from qualified candidates. The RFP lists what is wanted and how to apply. Not all foundations advertise RFPs. Many still prefer to be courted by the applicants. You can subscribe to a free e-mail called the "RFP Bulletin" at ✎ *www.fdncenter.org.*

The Art of Grant Writing

Once you have decided what entities you are going to ask for money, the next step is to write a proposal. A good proposal should follow the general format described in the next few paragraphs. This template is not written in stone. You can be flexible and creative within these parameters. Needless to say, you need to make a solid case for yourself and your enterprise. However altruistic the corporations and foundations you approach may be, they will not be generous to a proposition that is not well-thought-out and clearly taken seriously by the person seeking funding. You need to make a good first impression and make the potential donor excited about doing business with you.

As in all things, patience is a virtue. You are not the only one sending out proposals. It takes perseverance and an ability to handle rejection. Be patient but persistent. Even an almost-perfect proposal could get shot down for any number of factors beyond your control. Or it could languish on someone's desk for years before being considered and approved.

You must also cast a wide net. Some foundations and corporations will dispense small gifts rather than bestow a large grant. Your goal should be to cultivate a network so that even if you do not get a large lump sum from one source, you could be getting regular gifts from a variety of sources.

ALERT!

Be aware that you should include the pertinent information in your proposal in the cover letter that accompanies it. Many foundations separate the cover letter from the application during the review process, and different pairs of eyes view each document. So unlike the cover letter that is sent with a resume, repetition in this kind of cover letter is not only encouraged, it is necessary.

Presenting Your Program

Adaptability is another essential component of any proposal. Just as you should tailor a resume to a specific job or company, so too you should tailor your proposal to a particular corporation or foundation. You should begin with a "master proposal" that is a fluid document that can be easily modified to accommodate many different potential funders.

The proposal must be compelling in its concept. You must make a case that will generate interest and enthusiasm. The best way to do that is to convey enthusiasm. And of course, you need to have done your homework. Half-measures get you nowhere in life.

Whatever your project may be, make sure you present a practical program so that your potential benefactors will know that you mean business. These are elements that need to be addressed:

- What the project is and how you will implement it
- The timetable
- The outcome
- The anticipated manpower (if you are not going solo)
- Expenses

These may have to be estimates, but you should provide some round figures. And do not be too ambitious—an expansive budget may make even the most generous foundation a little skittish, especially if you are an unknown quantity.

Elements of a Proposal

Your proposal should include some certain standard elements. First, the executive summary comprises the first page of the proposal and is a brief outline of what is to come. This is a very important element. You have to generate enough interest to get the person to continue reading. Make sure you include these factors in your executive summary:

- **The problem.** This should be one or two paragraphs explaining why you are contacting the foundation or corporation. It details what you want to accomplish and why their support will make for a mutually beneficial relationship.
- **The solution.** This is a short description of what you will do, how and who will benefit from what you do, how and where it will be run, and for how long.
- **Funding.** How much it is going to cost.
- **Expertise.** Why you are best qualified to make things happen.

The next part of the proposal is often called the statement of need. Hopefully, the funder has been sufficiently wowed by your introductory paragraphs. Now it is time to reel them in further with a detailed description of your goals and plan to achieve them.

FACT

And you think your phone company doesn't have a heart! AT&T has a foundation that awards grants in education, community service, and the arts. You can get further details from their Web site at ✍ *www.att.com*.

Like a trial lawyer addressing a jury, you need to be persuasive yet succinct. The people you are approaching are busy men and women, and any literary long-windedness won't help your cause.

The statement of need should include several key components. You should be "loaded for bear" with facts and statistics. You had better make sure your data is up to date. If the funder finds flaws in your facts and figures, they are not going to trust you with their money.

Making Your Case

Do not throw in everything but the kitchen sink to make your case. "Just the facts," as Sgt. Joe Friday more than once intoned. Avoid written histrionics. Do not try to sway your prospective benefactor with emotionalism.

Show how your proposal is unique, and demonstrate why it should be considered over similar entreaties the funder may have received. Strike a delicate balance here. You must come across as confident but not too cocky. Do not be critical of other people's efforts in an attempt to elevate yourself. This is bad form, and it will backfire.

Make your case the way students in Journalism 101 courses are told to write a story. Tell the what, where, who, why, and how. Describe *what* will happen, in detail, from the beginning to the end of your project. Tell *when* all this will happen, that is, the estimated time frame. The *why* should explain the reasons that what you are planning is of value and why the funder should bestow a grant upon you and your cause.

The Budget

We live in a climate that is result oriented. This is true not only in the private sector but also in the world of grantmakers and grantseekers. Even philanthropists are interested in the commercial viability of a project. They want to be part of a success story, just like a shrewd investor or venture capitalist.

In keeping with this new tone, you should prepare a thorough and realistic budget—thorough, but simple and succinct. It can be as short as one page or more complex. You can state it in the body of your proposal (in the section called the budget narrative) or include a spreadsheet. It is okay if these figures are estimates. If you are seeking funding for a project that will be a full-time occupation for a period of time, part of your budget will be your living expenses during the duration of your project.

It gets more complicated if you are working with a group of people, some of whom expect a salary. If it is just you, it is easier. Be honest and equitable. Do not give yourself an exorbitant salary. Only politicians can liberally give themselves generous salaries and pay raises with impunity and no accountability.

You should use your concluding paragraphs to reinforce your case. Write about the future as if the gift has been bestowed and your plans enacted. You might also write about how you would attempt to follow through with your plans even without funding. This will show your potential donor that you are determined to achieve your goals and will not be dissuaded by rejection. A determined person inspires confidence, and everyone wants to invest in success.

FACT

If you want a grant to do some scholarly research, one of the many places you can approach is the Getty Foundation (✎*www.getty.edu*). They have recently bestowed $40,000 grants for scholars to research such off-the-beaten-track topics as "Temple to Love: Architecture and Devotion in Seventeenth-Century Bengal," "Constructing the Cold War: Architecture, Urbanism, and the Cultural Division of Germany," and "Queen as King: Art and Political Propaganda in Twelfth-Century Spain."

The Short Form

If you are an individual seeking funding, chances are your proposal need not be as elaborate as if you were part of a nonprofit organization. In this case you can make your pitch in the form of what is called a letter proposal. When you do your research on the foundations and corporations you plan to contact, you will learn what kind of proposal they prefer. You will find that many prefer this short form. It is easier for them to read and digest.

The letter proposal should basically follow the format of the longer version, but it should not be longer than three pages in length. It can be less formal than the long form because it is, after all, a letter to someone. Take care in the writing; you must say much in a limited number of words. Here are the necessary components of a letter proposal:

1. Request for the grant. Why you are contacting the funder and what do you need.
2. Why there is a need for what you are seeking?
3. What you will be doing to achieve your ends.
4. Provide a brief description of yourself and/or your business of organization.
5. Submit a brief budget.
6. Make a convincing closing statement as to why the grant or gift will be advantageous to the potential funder. Be compelling, but not pushy.

In every grant proposal, you should be sure to be realistic and practical. The loftier the objective the more skeptical the potential funder may be. He or she has most likely made an unwise decision or two along the way. Again, though they are altruistic, they also do not want to feel like they are wasting their money.

In particular, even in a short proposal, be as specific as possible when stating your objectives. The competition is fierce. Say what you will do, how long it will take, how it will be done, and what you hope will be the results. You will be submitting a final report to the benefactor and if you have not delivered the goods, so to speak, you can forget about approaching that corporation or foundation again.

A final note on the short form—give as much thought and effort to it as you would a more detailed proposal. It is sometimes more difficult to condense a wealth of information than it is to write at length. Your letter proposal may therefore be more challenging to compose than a full request.

Presenting a Proposal

Multiple submissions are acceptable. You are not expected to contact one source and wait patiently for a response, which could take months or years. Funders expect you to be aggressively seeking funding from a variety of sources. If they ask you the names of other contacts, you should be forthcoming with that information.

As mentioned, the time from submitting a proposal to hearing back from them could be weeks or months or longer. The potential funder may contact you for additional information before reaching a final decision. This is called the review process. Be prepared to play this waiting game and try not to succumb to frustration and anxiety.

Another place you can look for information on funding and running your business is the Small Business Administration (at ✑*www.sba.gov*). They do not generally give grants to small businesses (only to organizations that support small businesses), but they do have a loan program.

If you are lucky enough to receive a grant, be sure to send a thank-you note. If you are turned down, do not despair. There will be other organizations who will be interested in helping you, and it does not mean that the funder who turned you down has shut the door on you forever. Contact the funder, and ask why your proposal was rejected. Perhaps you can amend the document to make a better case for yourself. Also, keep them in your database and do not hesitate to contact them at a later date with another proposal. Just because they do not like one idea does not mean they will reject another out of hand. You must not take such things personally, but instead see it as just one small bump on the road to your new career. Ⓔ

Appendix A

General Alternative Career Resources

The following Web resources on career, finances, and business may be helpful to you, no matter what particular type of alternative career you're pursuing. Appendix B contains resources appropriate to the specific careers discussed in this book.

FinanCenter.com

www.financenter.com

The free section of this site has tools to help with budgeting, estate planning, retirement planning, taxes, grant applications, and more.

Fundsnet Services

www.fundsnetservices.com

A page of links and other information on grants in the arts, education, and more.

The Health Insurance Resource Center

www.healthinsurance.org

A site with information on health insurance designed for the self-employed, individuals, or small businesses.

Kiplinger

www.kiplinger.com

The site of this financial organization has financial news and investment tips and advice.

The Motley Fool

www.fool.com

A site with advice on many elements of financial planning, including investing, insurance, IRAs, and other retirement plans.

The National Association for the Self-Employed

www.nase.org

A resource for owners of small businesses; membership benefits include discounted health and dental care, financial advice, and more.

The National Financial Planning Support Center

www.fpanet.org

This site has an advanced search feature to help find a financial planner in your area.

Nolo

✐ *www.nolo.com*

The site of this legal publisher has much free legal information, including resources for independent contractors and entrepreneurs.

Personal Budgeting and Money-Saving Tips

✐ *www.personal-budget-planning-saving-money.com*

A site with advice on planning a budget, record keeping, and saving money.

The Quicken Financial Network

✐ *www.qfn.com*

A site with online tools like a savings calculator and debt-reduction planner.

The Small Business Administration

www.sba.gov

This site has information on obtaining a grant or a loan from this government agency.

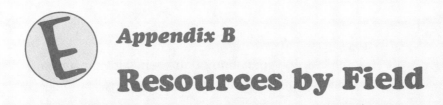

Appendix B

Resources by Field

The following resources (many of which also appear in various chapters of this book) are divided into the following career categories: arts and media; circus; home-based; law enforcement; outdoors; personal coaching; service, volunteer, and political; and travel and international.

Arts and Media Careers

Actor's Equity
✎ *www.actorsequity.org*
The union for stage actors and stage managers.

Agent Research
✎ *www.agentresearch.com*
A site that offers free verification of an agent's legitimacy and credentials, with fees for more extensive searches.

Backstage
✎ *www.backstage.com*
The Internet edition of the theater trade journal *Backstage*.

Danceusa.org
✎ *www.danceusa.org*
A great general resource on the dancing world.

FreelanceWriting.com
✎ *www.freelancewriting.com*
A site for freelance writers with resources and job listings.

JournalismJobs.com
✎ *www.journalismjobs.com*
A valuable resource for aspiring and working print, television, and radio journalists, with news, resources, and job listings.

Literary Market Place (LMP)
✎ *www.literarymarketplace.com*
A costly ($399 per year), but very valuable, subscription site associated with the massive directory of publishing companies and resources.

Models.com

✍ *www.models.com*

An excellent resource on the modeling business with listings of top agencies, photographers, make-up artists, and more.

Novelists, Inc.

✍ *www.ninc.com*

A membership site for fiction writers, with a free trial period available.

PlusModels

✍ *www.plusmodels.com*

A site with advice for large and lovely women on how to get started in the modeling business, plus health and beauty tips, and a discussion board.

The Screen Actor's Guild (SAG)

✍ *www.sag.org*

The union for actors who work in movies and television.

TriggerStreet.com

✍ *www.triggerstreet.com*

Actor Kevin Spacey's Web site where the work of aspiring screenwriters can be seen and critiqued by industry professionals and fellow writers.

Variety

✍ *www.variety.com*

The newspaper known as the show-business Bible has a very helpful Web site, with many elements available to subscribers only.

WritersMarket.com

✍ *www.writersmarket.com*

The online presence of the popular publishing resource.

Circus Careers

CircusWeb
✍ *www.circusweb.com*
Information on the history of circuses and circus life, with links to current circuses.

The Clown Resource Directory
✍ *www.clownville.org*
Links to clown classes, camps, events, workshops, and more.

Ludwig's Flying Trapeze Resource Page
✍ *www.damnhot.com*
A Web site with links to trapeze schools in the United States and around the world, job listings, and more.

Mooseburger Camp
✍ *www.mooseburger.com*
The Web site of a leading clown school.

Ringling Brothers Barnum & Bailey Circus
✍ *www.ringling.com*
Background on this most famous circus and information on upcoming tours.

3 Ring News
Clowning Around
Clown Alley
Tops and Calliope
Four leading trade publications for clowns and circus performers.

Trapeze School of New York
✍ *www.trapezeschool.com*

Trapeze Arts (San Francisco)
✍ *www.trapezearts.com*
The Web sites of two leading trapeze schools.

Home-Based Careers

Busy Kids
www.busy-kids.com
A site with the individual state regulations for opening a day-care center.

Council for Professional Recognition
www.cdacouncil.org
Information on the eligibility requirements and a description of the Child Development Associate credential.

The Humane Society of the United States
www.hsus.org
Resources and job information on animal care and control, and the animal shelter and control personnel training program.

International Nanny Association
www.nanny.org
Information on becoming a nanny.

National Animal Control Association
www.nacanet.org
Career information for animal control officers at all levels.

National Childcare Association
www.nccanet.org
Information on the eligibility requirements for the Certified Childcare Professional designation.

National Dog Groomers Association of America
P.O. Box 101
Clark, PA 16113
www.nationaldoggroomers.com
You can get a list of state-licensed grooming schools by sending them a stamped, self-addressed, business-size envelope.

PayPal

✍ *www.paypal.com*

A common method of payment for Internet transactions such as buying and selling on eBay.

Pet Sitting.biz

✍ *www.dog-walking.com/dog_walkers.html*

Information on how to start a pet sitting or walking business.

Telecommuting Jobs

✍ *www.tjobs.com*

An Internet service that connects telecommuters with employers, including a resume-posting feature.

TutorNation

✍ *www.tutornation.com*

A site that helps parents find tutors for their children and helps tutors find work; it charges a $45 lifetime membership fee for tutors and it is free for those looking for tutors.

Yard Sale Search

✍ *www.yardsalesearch.com*

A site with numerous tips for holding your own yard sale and finding bargains at other people's.

Law Enforcement Careers

All Criminal Justice Schools

✍ *www.allcriminaljusticeschools.com*

A list of schools across the country that offer courses and degrees in subjects like private investigations, forensic science, criminal psychology, and others.

Outdoors Careers

The All-Outdoors Whitewater Rafting Company

www.aorafting.com

A rafting-school Web site that tells what a typical school will teach you.

Backdoor Jobs

www.backdoorjobs.com

Information on job opportunities in camps, rafting, and even overseas.

CoolWorks

www.coolworks.com

A resource for jobs in camps, national parks, ranches, ski resorts, and amusement parks.

Destination Wilderness

www.wildernesstrips.com

A company that runs rafting trips, whale watches, and other outdoor adventures.

National Ski Patrol

www.nsp.org

The Colorado-based headquarters of the national organization for ski patrol members.

The Outdoor Network

www.outdoornetwork.com

Job listings and news for many outdoor industries, and an opportunity to post your resume for employers.

Sail Training

www.sailtraining.org

The "Billet Bank" link of this Web site has sailing job opportunities.

U.S. Office of Personnel Management (OPM)

✑*www.usajobs.opm.gov*

A comprehensive listing of available government positions in hundreds of fields, including park ranger postings.

Personal Coaching Careers

The Coach Training Alliance

✑*www.coachtrainingalliance.com*

An organization with general information on personal coaching and on the programs available and training you need to become a certified coach.

Coach U

✑*www.coachinc.com*

A leading provider of training for personal coaches.

FindYourCoach.com

✑*www.findyourcoach.com*

A service that helps individuals find the right personal coach.

Service, Volunteer, and Political Careers

AmeriCorps

✑*www.americorps.org*

Information on how to join this national service organization.

Amnesty International

✑*www.amnestyusa.org*

The American site of the British-founded human rights organization provides information on how to get involved.

Ask A Missionary

✑*www.askamissionary.com*

Answers for frequently asked questions about aspects of the missionary life.

The Center for Intercultural Training

✍ *www.cit-online.org*

A site with information for new missionaries to help them adjust to working abroad.

The Corporation for National and Community Service

✍ *www.nationalservice.org*

Listings of community-service job postings that include both paying positions and internships.

Cross Cultural Solutions

✍ *www.crossculturalsolutions.org*

An organization that operates volunteer programs in Brazil, China, Costa Rica, Ghana, Guatemala, India, Peru, Russia, Tanzania, and Thailand.

Harvard University's Office of Career Services

✍ *www.ocs.fas.harvard.edu/resources/government/govtweb.htm*

A list of resources for politics and political careers.

"I-to-I"

✍ *www.i-to-i.com*

An organization that sends volunteers abroad on I-Ventures, Mini-Ventures, and Earning-Ventures last of these are paying jobs working overseas.

Girl's Pipeline to Power

✍ *www.girlspipeline.org*

A site for young women to learn about politics and become involved themselves.

Greenpeace

✍ *www.greenpeace.org*

The main site for the international environmental organization.

Habitat for Humanity

✍ *www.habitat.org*

The site for this house-building organization, with listings of local offices.

MisLinks

✍ *www.mislinks.org*

A basic resource for all elements of missionary work.

Peace Corps

✍ *www.peacecorps.gov*

The main site for the U.S.-government–sponsored volunteer program.

Peace Corps Writers

✍ *www.peacecorpswriters.org*

A site with the writings of returned Peace Corps volunteers describing their experiences and the countries they lived in.

The Politix Group

✍ *www.politixgroup.com*

Job resources for careers in politics.

Save the Children

✍ *www.savethechildren.org*

Information about the history of the organization, how to sponsor a child for only $28 a month, and volunteer and employment opportunities.

Sending Experienced Retired Volunteers Everywhere (SERVE)

✍ *www.serve-intl.org*

An organization for those who would like to use their experiences in life and work helping others.

United States Congress

✍ *www.congress.org*

This official Web site of the United States Congress will provide information on your elected representatives.

Travel and International Careers

American Passport

✍ *www.americanpassport.com*

A business not affiliated with the government that claims it can get you a passport within twenty-four hours.

An American Abroad

✍ *www.anamericanabroad.com*

Extensive travel information on topics such as currency exchange and travel insurance.

Au Pair in Europe

✍ *www.princeent.com*

General information and a placement service for finding positions as an au pair in Europe.

Au Pair Search

✍ *www.aupairsearch.com*

The International Au Pair Association

✍ *www.iapa.org*

This site provides placement information for au pairs in Europe.

The Bombard Society

✍ *www.bombardsociety.com/jobs*

Information on ground crew and other positions with this European balloon tour operator.

Carnival Cruise Lines

✍ *www.carnival.com*

Information on available jobs with this popular cruise line.

Club Med

✍ *www.clubmedjobs.com*

Job listings for this worldwide resort operator.

Council on International Education

✍ *www.cie.uci.edu/iop/teaching.html*

Resources for finding teaching opportunities in many countries, such as Japan and Thailand.

EFLWEB

✍ *www.u-net.com/eflWeb*

Information on job opportunities for English language teachers, with a TravelZone for information on the culture of many countries.

The Japanese Exchange and Teaching (JET)

✍ *www.jetprogramme.org*

A program for Westerners to help Japanese teachers with English instruction at the junior high and high school levels.

Linguistic Funland

✍ *www.linguistic-funland.com*

Links to job postings for ESL teaching positions worldwide, offering the opportunity to post your resume to be viewed by interested schools.

The Norwegian Cruise Lines

✍ *www.ncl.com*

Job listings in a variety of fields for this major cruise line.

Overseas Jobs

www.overseasjobs.com

Valuable information on overseas employment, including job postings and a free e-mail newsletter you can sign up for.

Princess Cruise Lines

www.princess.com

Job listings from a major cruise-ship company.

Projects Abroad

www.projects-abroad.org

Information on opportunities for teaching abroad, journalism, veterinary work, conservation, archeology, and more in countries around the world.

Roadie.net

www.roadie.net

A fun resource for all roadies, including a list of American and British roadie slang.

TeachAbroad.com

www.teachabroad.com

Information on teaching and studying abroad, internships, language schools, and more.

Tramp News

www.payaway.co.uk/trampnews.shtml

An online journal on the Working Traveler Web site that is an excellent source for information and personal accounts of seasonal and temporary workers across Europe.

University of Michigan International Center

www.umich.edu/~icenter

Information and links about working and teaching abroad.

U.S. State Department Passport Services

✍ *www.travel.state.gov*

Information on how and where to obtain a passport. You can find forms for passports at this site, or you can call the National Passport Information Center at ☎ 1-900-225-5674. This site also provides information on expedited services.

The World Health Organization

✍ *www.who.int*

Centers for Disease Control and Prevention

✍ *www.cdc.gov*

Two sources for information on vaccinations you need to visit various countries abroad.

Index

D

da Vinci, Leonardo, 102
Daily Variety, 73
Dance Vision, 63
DanceUSA.org, 268
dancing
  auditions, 60–61
  ballet, 59, 61, 62, 79
  dance companies, 61, 79
  instructors, 61–63
  in movies, 58–59
  resources for, 268
  schools for, 60, 61, 62, 63
  on stage, 58–62
  styles of, 62, 63
  on television, 61
  workouts, 59–62
day-care center, 152–56, 271
De Niro, Robert, 68
dealer pickups (DPUs), 148
dental insurance coverage, 234–35
Destination Wilderness, 273
detectives. *See* private detectives
dinner theaters, 61, 80
diseases abroad, 31–35
dissatisfaction, *xi*, 3
diversity, 12–13
Do What You Love and the Money Will Follow, 8
dog-walking services, 158–60
dot-coms, 3–5
drama school, 68–69
drivers, 147–49
Drop Dead Gorgeous, 118
DuBois, Blanche, 75

E

e-commerce, 4, 165–66
e-mail spams, 179–80
Earning-Ventures, 207, 275
eBay, 172–76

economy, 3–5
ECO.org, 222
EFLWEB.com, 21, 278
Elements of Style, The, 83
Elite Model Agency, 122
employee benefits, 5
employee loyalty, 5
employers, 5, 6
English, teaching, 19–22
environmental causes
  community service, 225–27
  Greenpeace, 220–22
  internships, 222–23
Environmental Protection Agency (EPA), 222, 254
exchange programs, 23
expendability, 6
expenses, 242–43. *See also* budgets

F

Farley, Chris, 66
fashion models, 112–17
FBI Academy, 203
fears, conquering, 6–8
Federal Bureau of Investigation (FBI), 200, 202–3
federal law enforcement jobs, 200–204
Feel the Fear and Do It Anyway, 8
Feld, Irvin, 131
fiction writing, 87–89. *See also* writing
film schools, 77
films, 70, 71, 77. *See also* movies
Final Draft, 89
FinanCenter.com, 246, 264
financial assistance. *See* financial planning; grants
financial investigators, 196
financial planning
  budgets, 241–45
  credit cards, 247–49

hard times, 250
importance of, 239–41
retirement plans, 164, 240
tips for, 243, 244, 245
working with planners, 245–47
Financial Planning Association, 244
FindYourCoach.com, 186, 274
fitness models, 115
Flashdance, 62
food service management, 13
Ford, Harrison, 79
Ford Model Agency, 122
foreign language skills, 15–16, 19–20, 37–38
Fosse, Bob, 59
Foundation Center Online, 253
franchised agents, 72, 76
Fred Astaire, 63
freelance writing, 90–92. *See also* writing
FreelanceWriting.com, 268
fruit picking, 16–17
fulfillment, *xii*, 8, 9
full-service agents, 72
Fuller, Millard, 215
funding
  from foundations, 254–55, 259
  grant writing, 255–60
  need for, 253
  RFPs, 255
  sources for, 251–53
Fundsnet Services, 264
future plans, *xii*, 6

G

G-Men, 200–204
garage sales, 176
Getty Foundation, 259
ghostwriters, 95–96. *See also* writing
Girls Club, 226
Girl's Pipeline to Power, 275
global community, 12–13

The EVERYTHING Series!

BUSINESS

Everything® **Business Planning Book**
Everything® **Coaching and Mentoring Book**
Everything® **Fundraising Book**
Everything® **Home-Based Business Book**
Everything® **Leadership Book**
Everything® **Managing People Book**
Everything® **Network Marketing Book**
Everything® **Online Business Book**
Everything® **Project Management Book**
Everything® **Selling Book**
Everything® **Start Your Own Business Book**
Everything® **Time Management Book**

COMPUTERS

Everything® **Build Your Own Home Page Book**
Everything® **Computer Book**
Everything® **Internet Book**
Everything® **Microsoft® Word 2000 Book**

COOKBOOKS

Everything® **Barbecue Cookbook**
Everything® **Bartender's Book, $9.95**
Everything® **Chinese Cookbook**
Everything® **Chocolate Cookbook**
Everything® **Cookbook**
Everything® **Dessert Cookbook**
Everything® **Diabetes Cookbook**
Everything® **Indian Cookbook**
Everything® **Low-Carb Cookbook**
Everything® **Low-Fat High-Flavor Cookbook**

Everything® **Low-Salt Cookbook**
Everything® **Mediterranean Cookbook**
Everything® **Mexican Cookbook**
Everything® **One-Pot Cookbook**
Everything® **Pasta Book**
Everything® **Quick Meals Cookbook**
Everything® **Slow Cooker Cookbook**
Everything® **Soup Cookbook**
Everything® **Thai Cookbook**
Everything® **Vegetarian Cookbook**
Everything® **Wine Book**

HEALTH

Everything® **Alzheimer's Book**
Everything® **Anti-Aging Book**
Everything® **Diabetes Book**
Everything® **Dieting Book**
Everything® **Herbal Remedies Book**
Everything® **Hypnosis Book**
Everything® **Massage Book**
Everything® **Menopause Book**
Everything® **Nutrition Book**
Everything® **Reflexology Book**
Everything® **Reiki Book**
Everything® **Stress Management Book**
Everything® **Vitamins, Minerals, and Nutritional Supplements Book**

HISTORY

Everything® **American Government Book**
Everything® **American History Book**
Everything® **Civil War Book**
Everything® **Irish History & Heritage Book**

Everything® **Mafia Book**
Everything® **Middle East Book**
Everything® **World War II Book**

HOBBIES & GAMES

Everything® **Bridge Book**
Everything® **Candlemaking Book**
Everything® **Casino Gambling Book**
Everything® **Chess Basics Book**
Everything® **Collectibles Book**
Everything® **Crossword and Puzzle Book**
Everything® **Digital Photography Book**
Everything® **Easy Crosswords Book**
Everything® **Family Tree Book**
Everything® **Games Book**
Everything® **Knitting Book**
Everything® **Magic Book**
Everything® **Motorcycle Book**
Everything® **Online Genealogy Book**
Everything® **Photography Book**
Everything® **Pool & Billiards Book**
Everything® **Quilting Book**
Everything® **Scrapbooking Book**
Everything® **Sewing Book**
Everything® **Soapmaking Book**

HOME IMPROVEMENT

Everything® **Feng Shui Book**
Everything® **Feng Shui Decluttering Book, $9.95 ($15.95 CAN)**
Everything® **Fix-It Book**
Everything® **Gardening Book**
Everything® **Homebuilding Book**

All Everything® books are priced at $12.95 or $14.95, unless otherwise stated. Prices subject to change without notice.
Canadian prices range from $11.95–$31.95, and are subject to change without notice.

Everything® **Home Decorating Book**
Everything® **Landscaping Book**
Everything® **Lawn Care Book**
Everything® **Organize Your Home Book**

EVERYTHING® *KIDS'* BOOKS

All titles are $6.95

Everything® **Kids' Baseball Book, 3rd Ed.** ($10.95 CAN)
Everything® **Kids' Bible Trivia Book** ($10.95 CAN)
Everything® **Kids' Bugs Book** ($10.95 CAN)
Everything® **Kids' Christmas Puzzle & Activity Book** ($10.95 CAN)
Everything® **Kids' Cookbook** ($10.95 CAN)
Everything® **Kids' Halloween Puzzle & Activity Book** ($10.95 CAN)
Everything® **Kids' Joke Book** ($10.95 CAN)
Everything® **Kids' Math Puzzles Book** ($10.95 CAN)
Everything® **Kids' Mazes Book** ($10.95 CAN)
Everything® **Kids' Money Book** ($11.95 CAN)
Everything® **Kids' Monsters Book** ($10.95 CAN)
Everything® **Kids' Nature Book** ($11.95 CAN)
Everything® **Kids' Puzzle Book** ($10.95 CAN)
Everything® **Kids' Riddles & Brain Teasers Book** ($10.95 CAN)
Everything® **Kids' Science Experiments Book** ($10.95 CAN)
Everything® **Kids' Soccer Book** ($10.95 CAN)
Everything® **Kids' Travel Activity Book** ($10.95 CAN)

KIDS' STORY BOOKS

Everything® **Bedtime Story Book**
Everything® **Bible Stories Book**
Everything® **Fairy Tales Book**
Everything® **Mother Goose Book**

LANGUAGE

Everything® **Inglés Book**
Everything® **Learning French Book**
Everything® **Learning German Book**
Everything® **Learning Italian Book**
Everything® **Learning Latin Book**
Everything® **Learning Spanish Book**
Everything® **Sign Language Book**
Everything® **Spanish Phrase Book,** $9.95 ($15.95 CAN)

MUSIC

Everything® **Drums Book (with CD),** $19.95 ($31.95 CAN)
Everything® **Guitar Book**
Everything® **Playing Piano and Keyboards Book**
Everything® **Rock & Blues Guitar Book (with CD),** $19.95 ($31.95 CAN)
Everything® **Songwriting Book**

NEW AGE

Everything® **Astrology Book**
Everything® **Divining the Future Book**
Everything® **Dreams Book**
Everything® **Ghost Book**
Everything® **Love Signs Book,** $9.95 ($15.95 CAN)
Everything® **Meditation Book**
Everything® **Numerology Book**
Everything® **Palmistry Book**
Everything® **Psychic Book**
Everything® **Spells & Charms Book**
Everything® **Tarot Book**
Everything® **Wicca and Witchcraft Book**

PARENTING

Everything® **Baby Names Book**
Everything® **Baby Shower Book**
Everything® **Baby's First Food Book**
Everything® **Baby's First Year Book**
Everything® **Breastfeeding Book**

Everything® **Father-to-Be Book**
Everything® **Get Ready for Baby Book**
Everything® **Getting Pregnant Book**
Everything® **Homeschooling Book**
Everything® **Parent's Guide to Children with Autism**
Everything® **Parent's Guide to Positive Discipline**
Everything® **Parent's Guide to Raising a Successful Child**
Everything® **Parenting a Teenager Book**
Everything® **Potty Training Book,** $9.95 ($15.95 CAN)
Everything® **Pregnancy Book, 2nd Ed.**
Everything® **Pregnancy Fitness Book**
Everything® **Pregnancy Organizer,** $15.00 ($22.95 CAN)
Everything® **Toddler Book**
Everything® **Tween Book**

PERSONAL FINANCE

Everything® **Budgeting Book**
Everything® **Get Out of Debt Book**
Everything® **Get Rich Book**
Everything® **Homebuying Book, 2nd Ed.**
Everything® **Homeselling Book**
Everything® **Investing Book**
Everything® **Money Book**
Everything® **Mutual Funds Book**
Everything® **Online Investing Book**
Everything® **Personal Finance Book**
Everything® **Personal Finance in Your 20s & 30s Book**
Everything® **Wills & Estate Planning Book**

PETS

Everything® **Cat Book**
Everything® **Dog Book**
Everything® **Dog Training and Tricks Book**
Everything® **Golden Retriever Book**
Everything® **Horse Book**
Everything® **Labrador Retriever Book**
Everything® **Puppy Book**
Everything® **Tropical Fish Book**

All Everything® books are priced at $12.95 or $14.95, unless otherwise stated. Prices subject to change without notice. Canadian prices range from $11.95–$31.95, and are subject to change without notice.

REFERENCE

Everything® **Astronomy Book**
Everything® **Car Care Book**
Everything® **Christmas Book, $15.00**
　　　　($21.95 CAN)
Everything® **Classical Mythology Book**
Everything® **Einstein Book**
Everything® **Etiquette Book**
Everything® **Great Thinkers Book**
Everything® **Philosophy Book**
Everything® **Psychology Book**
Everything® **Shakespeare Book**
Everything® **Tall Tales, Legends, &**
　　　　Other Outrageous
　　　　Lies Book
Everything® **Toasts Book**
Everything® **Trivia Book**
Everything® **Weather Book**

RELIGION

Everything® **Angels Book**
Everything® **Bible Book**
Everything® **Buddhism Book**
Everything® **Catholicism Book**
Everything® **Christianity Book**
Everything® **Jewish History &**
　　　　Heritage Book
Everything® **Judaism Book**
Everything® **Prayer Book**
Everything® **Saints Book**
Everything® **Understanding Islam**
　　　　Book
Everything® **World's Religions Book**
Everything® **Zen Book**

SCHOOL & CAREERS

Everything® **After College Book**
Everything® **Alternative Careers Book**
Everything® **College Survival Book**
Everything® **Cover Letter Book**
Everything® **Get-a-Job Book**
Everything® **Hot Careers Book**

Everything® **Job Interview Book**
Everything® **New Teacher Book**
Everything® **Online Job Search Book**
Everything® **Resume Book, 2nd Ed.**
Everything® **Study Book**

SELF-HELP/ RELATIONSHIPS

Everything® **Dating Book**
Everything® **Divorce Book**
Everything® **Great Marriage Book**
Everything® **Great Sex Book**
Everything® **Kama Sutra Book**
Everything® **Romance Book**
Everything® **Self-Esteem Book**
Everything® **Success Book**

SPORTS & FITNESS

Everything® **Body Shaping Book**
Everything® **Fishing Book**
Everything® **Fly-Fishing Book**
Everything® **Golf Book**
Everything® **Golf Instruction Book**
Everything® **Knots Book**
Everything® **Pilates Book**
Everything® **Running Book**
Everything® **Sailing Book, 2nd Ed.**
Everything® **T'ai Chi and QiGong Book**
Everything® **Total Fitness Book**
Everything® **Weight Training Book**
Everything® **Yoga Book**

TRAVEL

Everything® **Family Guide to Hawaii**
Everything® **Guide to Las Vegas**
Everything® **Guide to New England**
Everything® **Guide to New York City**
Everything® **Guide to Washington D.C.**
Everything® **Travel Guide to The Dis-**
　　　　neyland Resort®, Cali-
　　　　fornia Adventure®,

Universal Studios®, and
the Anaheim Area
Everything® **Travel Guide to the Walt**
　　　　Disney World Resort®, Uni-
　　　　versal Studios®, and
　　　　Greater Orlando, 3rd Ed.

WEDDINGS

Everything® **Bachelorette Party Book,**
　　　　$9.95 ($15.95 CAN)
Everything® **Bridesmaid Book, $9.95**
　　　　($15.95 CAN)
Everything® **Creative Wedding Ideas**
　　　　Book
Everything® **Elopement Book, $9.95**
　　　　($15.95 CAN)
Everything® **Groom Book**
Everything® **Jewish Wedding Book**
Everything® **Wedding Book, 2nd Ed.**
Everything® **Wedding Checklist,**
　　　　$7.95 ($11.95 CAN)
Everything® **Wedding Etiquette Book,**
　　　　$7.95 ($11.95 CAN)
Everything® **Wedding Organizer,**
　　　　$15.00 ($22.95 CAN)
Everything® **Wedding Shower Book,**
　　　　$7.95 ($12.95 CAN)
Everything® **Wedding Vows Book,**
　　　　$7.95 ($11.95 CAN)
Everything® **Weddings on a Budget**
　　　　Book, $9.95 ($15.95 CAN)

WRITING

Everything® **Creative Writing Book**
Everything® **Get Published Book**
Everything® **Grammar and Style Book**
Everything® **Grant Writing Book**
Everything® **Guide to Writing Chil-**
　　　　dren's Books
Everything® **Screenwriting Book**
Everything® **Writing Well Book**

Available wherever books are sold!
To order, call 800-872-5627, or visit us at everything.com

Everything® and everything.com® are registered trademarks of F+W Publications, Inc.